EARLY TUDOR GOVERNMENT, 1485–1558

S. J. GUNN

St. Martin's Press   New York

First published in the United States of America in 1995

Printed in Malaysia

ISBN 0–312–12493–7

Library of Congress Cataloging-in-Publication Data
Gunn, S. J. (Steven J.)
Early Tudor government, 1485–1558 / S. J. Gunn.
p.   cm. — (British history in perspective)
Includes bibliographical references and index.
ISBN 0–312–12493–7
1. Great Britain—Politics and government, 1485–1558.   I. Title.
II. Series.
DA325.G86   1995
320.942—dc20   94–34078
                                                       CIP

For My Wife

CONTENTS

PREFACE

More colleagues, friends and students than I can name here have helped in the making of this book. Cliff Davies and John Watts read drafts of all of it, and I owe a great deal to their comments and to discussions of its themes with each of them over a number of years. Steven Ellis, Gerald Harriss, Eric Ives and Simon Payling read and commented upon individual chapters, and I have many others to thank for stimulating conversation about aspects of the subject at various times, most notably George Bernard and Richard Hoyle. My students at the universities of Newcastle and Oxford, especially those from Merton and St Peter's Colleges, have contributed by the ideas in their essays, their arguments in tutorial, and their preparedness to look profoundly unconvinced when I have tried out some wayward notion on them. My historical colleagues at Merton, Robert Gildea, Roger Highfield, Richard John, Matthew Kempshall, John Roberts, Philip Waller and the late Ralph Davis, have encouraged and inspired me even when their research interests were far from my own. Jeremy Black as series editor and Vanessa Graham at Macmillan have been helpful and understanding. So have the staffs of the libraries and archives in which I have worked, and those who have allowed me to cite their unpublished theses or forthcoming work, Peter Cunich, Ronald Fritze, Dominic Luckett, and Susan Vokes. My parents, to whom my first book was dedicated, have been as encouraging in this venture as they were in that; so, in her own way, has my daughter, whose turn for a dedication will, I trust, come in time. But this book is dedicated to my wife, in gratitude for all her cheerful encouragement and loving support.

Merton College, Oxford
S. J. G.

INTRODUCTION

The subject of this book has provoked sharp controversy amongst historians. Within the early Tudor period, different generations of scholars have tried to identify different passages of decisive change in the practices or institutions of government. From the late nineteenth century, it was argued that the reign of Henry VII was a new beginning for the monarchy, introducing stronger and more effective rule. Historians agreed that this marked, in effect, the end of the middle ages, though they disagreed over whether the result was an unpleasant 'Tudor despotism' or a progressive regime kept in step with national opinion by its use of parliament. More recently, the battle of Bosworth has gone out of fashion as the threshold of a new age. Henry, VII's style of government has been seen as largely imitative of his Yorkist predecessors, drawing in turn on Lancastrian and earlier practice. Meanwhile attention has shifted to a different part of the period. It has been contended that Thomas Cromwell's ministry in the 1530s formed the watershed between characteristically medieval and characteristically modern forms of government in England. Many have disagreed. I shall try to avoid reviewing the resultant debates in undue detail, but the first part of this introduction will necessarily contain an exploration of the light they shed on the difficulties of understanding early Tudor government and the means we might adopt to overcome those difficulties.

The heat of these arguments over Henry VII's 'new monarchy' and Thomas Cromwell's 'revolution in government' should not surprise us: the conduct of government in early Tudor England was, after all, hotly debated at the time. The virtues and vices of Henry VII's kingship were topics for argument – and for political show-trials – no sooner than he was dead. More comprehensive still was the questioning of Henry VIII's regime by the rebels of 1536. They challenged not only the royal assault on the church's wealth, interference with local religious life, and tolerance of heresy, but also the levels of taxation on the laity, the king's choice of councillors and

bishops, his use of parliament, his determination of the succession to
the throne, his alterations to the law of treason, his profitable
revision of the feudal land law, the workings of the legal system
(including the habit of punishing jurors who reached inconvenient verdicts) and the lack of governmental intervention in
landlord–tenant relations. Such wide-ranging and serious debates
suggest that both Henry VII's reign and the 1530s brought changes
in the practice of government sufficiently drastic to alarm contemporaries. What remains to be determined is what historians have
debated all along: the causes, effects, timing, interrelationship, per-
manence and significance of such developments.[1]

The Historiographical Problem

The best way to penetrate beyond the stormclouds of debate
amongst experts on the early Tudor period is to seek to set its developments in the context of the preceding centuries, and that will be
one of the primary aims of this book. But this raises a profound
problem. By and large, historians of the later middle ages and of
early Tudor England do not speak the same language. We might usefully date the divergence back to 1953, though that is of course to
oversimplify. In that year two of the most influential English historians of the later twentieth century produced classic statements of
their views. At Oxford K. B. McFarlane gave his Ford Lectures on *The
Nobility of Later Medieval England*, while at Cambridge G. R. Elton published *The Tudor Revolution in Government*. Each sought to break free
from the received, essentially Victorian, framework for the analysis of
English constitutional and political development, in which the long
struggles of kings, nobles and parliament eventuated in the wonders
of the nineteenth-century constitution. In this scheme, the fifteenth
and sixteenth centuries saw a swing from Lancastrian constitutionalism through the self-seeking noble anarchy of the Wars of the Roses
to the innovative 'new monarchy' and the Tudor despotism. Yet
McFarlane and Elton headed in opposite directions.

  McFarlane determined to analyse later medieval political society
in its own terms, and in particular to divest himself of the assumption
that the ruler is usually right, the tendency to be 'deeply and often
blindly attached to the kingly office', which he detected in most of

his colleagues. He turned away from the constitutional history of the Victorians (an approach, he felt, 'more concerned to define the law of the constitution than to prove the realities of political power'). But he also reacted against the detailed analysis of the development of the institutions of government, which had partly superseded the constitutional approach in the work of T. F. Tout and his pupils earlier in the century. 'Institutions sometimes seem to have a life of their own,' wrote McFarlane, 'but this is only an appearance ... Their life is the life of the men who make them.'[2]

The result was a series of judgements on the workings of later medieval government which have lit the way for most of its students ever since. The interests of king and nobles were not fundamentally opposed: 'It is only under-mighty kings who have over-mighty subjects.' Thus the art of kingship consisted in giving the same lordship and measured reward to the great men of the realm that they gave to those below them in the social system of the day. This system had been tagged bastard feudalism by the Victorians, who saw it as a degeneration from the purer feudal loyalties of the past, but was rescued from the pejorative overtones of the phrase by McFarlane. 'The king', he concluded, 'was in fact the good lord of all good lords ... only an ill-advised ruler confined his patronage to the few.' Such kingship could be made to work with remarkable effect, as Henry V, and in McFarlane's view the early Tudors, showed. Indeed, 'the baronage favoured a strong monarchy rather than a weak'. Thus 'The only New Monarchy that England ever had came in with William the Conqueror', and it was misguided to see the machinery of later medieval government as fatally defective and in need of drastic repair or replacement. McFarlane would admit that 'there is no harm in asserting that English justice in the fourteenth and fifteenth centuries was capable of improvement', but all in all he would not 'subscribe to the recent tendency to regard the royal administration and in particular the exchequer as hopelessly inadequate to its tasks'.[3]

Elton's perspective was radically different. His route away from traditional constitutional history was precisely that institutional administrative history practised by Tout and repudiated by McFarlane. The first five footnotes of chapter 1 of *The Tudor Revolution in Government* are to Tout's *Chapters in Medieval Administrative History*, and one early reviewer hailed the book with the words 'in Mr Elton the early Tudor period at last has its Tout'. Like McFarlane, Elton was happy to dispense with the 'new monarchy', seeing Henry VII as a reinvigorator of medieval rule rather than the protagonist of anything more novel. In this he was encouraged by the work of J. R. Lander (and subsequently of B. P. Wolffe), who stressed the strengths of Edward IV's kingship and the similarity of much Yorkist administration to that of the first Tudor. Yet Elton replaced the Victorian narrative with a new kind of teleology, one which abandoned the swings from constitutionalism to despotism with a dramatic transition from medieval to modern government, situated in the 1530s and driven by the 'deliberate and profound reforming activity' of Henry VIII's chief minister Thomas Cromwell. This was a matter of administrative change, in which 'in every sphere of the central government, "household" methods and instruments were replaced by national bureaucratic methods and instruments', but it was also much more. Such changes 'accompanied, resulted from, and in a manner assisted in the creation of the monarchic nation state', 'the self-contained sovereign state in which no power on earth could challenge the supremacy of statute made by the crown in parliament'.[4]

Elton's primary aim was thus to identify and account for change over time, where McFarlane's was to analyse the workings of society in depth across the fourteenth and fifteenth centuries. Elton's focus was centralist, concentrating on the activity of central government rather than its impact on local society, while McFarlane worked upwards from his examination of bastard feudalism in the localities. The two approaches were never likely to mesh easily. McFarlane might also have suspected Elton of being a 'king's friend', for Elton defended the Tudors against the charge of despotism by stressing the constitutional and legal propriety of the Tudor regime, while still seeing it as part of a tradition of 'strong rule preventing anarchy and preserving order'.[5]

The differences in approach between Elton and McFarlane have fundamentally shaped the subsequent historiography of the periods on either side of 1500, but to make sense of early Tudor government one has somehow to draw these two worlds together. Where they have met in the past there has generally been friction, for many of the most thoroughgoing criticisms of Elton's thesis were anticipated by McFarlane, and many have indeed been written by McFarlane's pupils. One early line of attack echoed McFarlane's views on the tendency of historians to take the side of assertive rulers rather than their subjects, noble or otherwise. This was most evident in J. P. Cooper's debate with Elton about Henry VII, the monarch whose reign fell most obviously on the boundary between the spheres of influence of the two great interpretations. Elton thought Henry's reputation for rapacity verging on the tyrannous unjustified: he might have been harsh on occasion, but was essentially doing what was 'most conducive to strong and good government in England', 'trying to restore solvency and power to the Crown, but ... also trying to bring peace, justice and order to the realm'. Cooper thought this view 'too narrowly restricted to the interests of the Crown'. Here presumably, as in a subsequent debate, Elton felt himself to have been unfairly characterised as a 'brutal worshipper of power and success'.[6]

Elton's views on the nature of medieval and early modern government were at odds with McFarlane's stress on the viability of later medieval governmental machinery. G. L. Harriss elaborated the arguments against Elton implicit in this side of McFarlane's work. He questioned the novelty of many of the attributes of Elton's newly forged sovereign state of the sixteenth century, finding both the establishment of a national church and the supremacy of statute strongly prefigured in the fourteenth- and fifteenth-century English polity. More tellingly still, he argued that the fluid and improvisatory household government of Henry VII and the Yorkists was merely a temporary aberration. Elton treated it as quintessentially medieval and ripe for replacement by a new system of regulated, efficient and interlocking institutions typified by the privy council, the secretaryship of state, the court of augmentations and its successor the reformed Elizabethan exchequer. But Harriss argued that the exchequer of the fourteenth and earlier fifteenth centuries was more truly representative of medieval methods. As a single body supreme in national finance, working to clear and undeniably bureaucratic procedures but capable of considerable speed and sophistication when required, it seemed to fulfil Elton's criteria for Cromwellian modernity. The Elizabethan outcome of the Yorkist and Tudor experiments was not the supremacy of a new bureaucratised institution going under the old name of the exchequer, but the restoration of the old bureaucratic exchequer after two generations of turmoil. Harriss found similar patterns in the history of the secretariat and the royal council. For him it was not the outmoded inefficiency of medieval institutions that prompted the expedients of Edward IV and his successors, but a political failure, the disaster of Henry VI's reign. In Harriss's view the fifteenth and sixteenth centuries fitted into a much longer era of 'mixed monarchy', bracketed between constitutional and governmental changes, in the thirteenth and fourteenth centuries and in the later seventeenth century, much more fundamental than any occurring in the early Tudor period.[7]

A third line of disagreement with Elton's thesis has been taken up most strongly by David Starkey. He stresses the role of politics, fluctuating personal rivalries and transient royal personalities in the processes of governmental change, to the exclusion of Elton's rational, long-term, state planning. This approach is typified by Starkey's depiction of the privy chamber, the most intimate department of the royal household, as the nerve-centre of politics and government throughout the crucial period of Elton's administrative revolution. In the early Tudor context this analysis is in tune with the revisionist historians of the Reformation, who stress short-term political factors in England's move towards protestantism, rather than any deeper compulsion to reform or overthrow the medieval church. But it also fits very well with the world of later medieval politics recreated by some of those who have developed McFarlane's insights. They depict a polity in which ruthless competition for royal bounty and local dominance were the driving forces at court and in the localities, and royal personality almost the sole key to effective governance. Like the balance between ruler and subjects and the legacies of the later medieval state, the impact of politics is a theme this book will have to consider. It is a theme with particular dangers, as some later medievalists have begun to point out. There is a temptation, especially because of the relatively unforthcoming nature of most later medieval sources, to assume that political life was based on calculations of more or less crude material self-interest. But this runs the risk of neglecting entirely the influence of ideas – religious, constitutional, even moral – on the political actors. It threatens to write off all initiatives in policy as short-term tools in the political struggle, rather than the serious and statesmanlike attempts to solve real problems which some of them certainly were.[8]

Other frustrations face the historian in the borderlands between the later middle ages and the early modern period. Some historians, notably Lawrence Stone and M. E. James, have written at length on the development of Tudor government and politics in a very different mode from Elton. They set governmental change in a rich framework of economic, social, cultural and ideological change. Here they come closer than Elton or his critics to the analysis of state formation pursued by historians of continental Europe, with their debates about the relationship between local elites and state power, the local significance of administrative intensification, the spread of notions of obedience and civility, the relationship between religious, social, and political change, and so on. Yet the focus of Stone's and James's work is less helpful than one might hope in investigating the processes of state formation in early Tudor England, those Elton essentially wished to tie to Thomas Cromwell and his administrative reforms and other measures, since Stone's interest concentrated on the Elizabethan and early Stuart period, as to a lesser degree did James's.

This in itself is instructive, for it posits an alternative chronology and an alternative set of criteria for the change from medieval to modern centred by Elton on the 1530s. Stone called the years 1580–1620 'the real watershed between medieval and modern England', while James placed the sharpest changes in what he termed the shift from lineage society to civil society in the period 1570–1640. Unfortunately, this periodisation feeds so many new factors into their equation – steep population growth, sustained price inflation, literacy for the middling sort and university education for the gentry, the spread of popular protestantism and so on – that it is hard to project their analysis backwards with confidence into our period. James has written at greater length than Stone on the early Tudors, but has not engaged in much detail either with the later medieval roots of the changes he describes, or usually with regions outside the extreme north, which was probably exceptional in many respects. Moreover, much of his detailed interpretation of early Tudor developments has been called into question. Nonetheless, the work of such historians should provide us with an inspiring model, and with a number of useful analytical themes. What it cannot do is provide a ready bridge to the fifteenth century, where few if any scholars have pursued similar lines of enquiry.[9]

Much the same is true of the explosion of writing by social historians which has marked both the later medieval and early modern periods since the 1960s. We know vastly more about ordinary people and the impact of government, central and local, upon their lives than any previous generation of historians might have thought possible. It is therefore feasible to write a history of government which sees it as a process of negotiation between ruler and ruled, not only at the level of king and nobility or crown and parliament, but also at that of manor, village, and borough. At least until very recently, however, much of the best work along these lines has been done in the periods before and after that which interests us. The later fifteenth and earlier sixteenth centuries again fall into the gap between later medieval and early modern history, and bridging the gap may have at times to be a ramshackle affair. It is symptomatic that the treatment of the period in a history of English state formation written in the early 1980s by two historical sociologists was heavily reliant on Elton's work.[10]

The Comparative Approach

Lastly we should consider two other ways of assessing early Tudor developments which do not depend so obviously on an interpretation of their later medieval foundations. These are, in essence, to compare early Tudor England with later Tudor England, and to compare it with contemporary states on the continent. Each approach has featured in the debate between Elton and his critics. The examination of mid-Tudor and Elizabethan England in search of the impact of early Tudor changes has been undertaken most notably by Penry Williams. In his most extended study, Williams – citing McFarlane in his first four footnotes – concluded that while the Tudor period as a whole did see important changes in the machinery of state, especially in the 'style of government', and in the success of law enforcement, in some ways bureaucratic efficiency even declined over the Tudor century. The dynasty had not 'created a new and powerful state', and many early Tudor developments proved ephemeral. This did not make Tudor government unsuccessful: for Williams there was achievement enough in surviving the economic and social strains of the period, establishing protestantism, and generally 'securing compliance' by a judicious mixture of propaganda and patronage, coercion and consultation. In outline it is a plausible and satisfyingly wide-ranging case, but its breadth and its perspective from 1603 necessarily deprive it of some of the sharpness of focus on the early Tudors which should be our concern here. Nonetheless, its example is another to follow. In particular, we shall have to look with care at the reigns of Edward and Mary. In specific terms this is because the administrative restructuring of 1547–54 is so central to the debate over Cromwell's administrative reforms: did it consolidate, reverse, or just obscure the programmatic change attributed to him by Elton? In general terms it is because the mid-Tudor reigns constitute not merely a judgement on the changes begun by Henry VII and Henry VIII, but also an essential working-out of those changes.[11]

Most of the scholars we have mentioned have compared England with other countries in one way or another. On the broadest plane, continental states may be used as general parallels, to suggest what sort of developments were taking place in fifteenth- and sixteenth-century Europe, and therefore what one might expect in England. The tendency for rulers, whether catholic or protestant, to take an ever tighter grip on the affairs of their national churches would be a good example. More specifically, such comparisons can be used to measure Tudor government by a more realistic standard than modern abstractions, for instance by comparing the efficiency of the English fiscal system with those in France and Spain. Thirdly and most intriguingly, one can ask how developments elsewhere directly affected England. They seem to have done so in two ways. As rulers competed for diplomatic prestige and strained their state machinery in the search for military victory, international relations served as a motor for state growth. Moreover, the ideas put into execution in that growth may well have derived from observation of other rulers.[12]

Most Tudor councillors had travelled abroad as diplomats or soldiers, and many of them had close links to the London merchant community. This brought familiarity only with a narrow range of England's neighbours, primarily France, the Netherlands and Scotland; contact with Spain, Germany or Italy was rarer, though not uncommon. But even within this sphere there was much in the statecraft of Louis XI or James IV, Charles the Bold of Burgundy or Ferdinand of Aragon to prompt reflection in English observers. Quite what they made of it we can usually only guess, though we might find some guidance in the comments of some of their continental contemporaries who have left us their impressions, notably Commynes and Machiavelli. In particular we have to guess at the lessons learned by the future Henry VII in his long exile in Brittany and France, but it is hard to doubt that they lent his kingship some of its more unusual qualities. His calculated suspiciousness, preference for handpicked subordinates, preparedness to confront noblemen, ecclesiastics and urban elites, elevation of personal dignity and sheer hard work resemble the traits of Louis XI or Charles the Bold or both, and the political style of these rulers must surely have been the subject of instructive discussion at the court of the dukes of Brittany, threatened by Louis and often allied with Charles.

Influence on specific policies is harder to demonstrate, though the foundation of a royal guard in 1485 was attributed by contemporaries to imitation of the French court.[13]

Signs of general interest in what might be learnt from other countries are easier to find. English writers from Sir John Fortescue in the mid-fifteenth century to Sir Thomas Smith in the mid-sixteenth made detailed comparisons with French government and society (usually unflattering to the French). More fleetingly, Fortescue discussed events as far away as Bohemia, and Smith touched on Italian, German, Spanish and Swiss affairs. Henry VII's minister Edmund Dudley even compared England (sketchily) with Ottoman Turkey. Thomas Cromwell commissioned translations of German chronicles and read books on Italian history in the 1530s. An explicit statement of the utility of such study was made in 1549 by William Thomas, the clerk of Edward VI's privy council. In the preface to his *Historie of Italie* he wrote that he wanted it to acquaint Englishmen with the good and bad examples shown by Italian governments. There and in the material he produced for the political education of Edward VI, Thomas made considerable use of both Machiavelli and Commynes.[14]

The comparative approach, then, has some contemporary warrant, as well as some utility for the historian. But it also has dangers beyond those of speculation about the analytical skills of the adolescent Henry Tudor or the likelihood of his young grandson's acquiring a taste for Machiavelli. Because historians of England can rarely study other countries in the same depth as their own field of research, they are heavily dependent on the conclusions of other historians to provide comparative material. There is thus an inherent risk of circularity of argument, as one historian expects to find what the other has found because he too expected to find it. This is most true for those who seek universal trends such as proto-bourgeois revolution in the history of the early modern state, but it may also manifest itself in subtler ways. There is also the problem of balancing general trends against national peculiarities. Thus it is now widely agreed that the parallel drawn by previous generations of historians between the threat from Roman law to customary law in Germany and that from Roman law to the common law in England was misconceived, since the common law was far too well entrenched to be overwhelmed as German legal systems were, and there was no real drive for such a change in England. Finally there is the problem that many fascinating parallels actually tell us very little. Ivan the Terrible of Russia was as keen as Henry VII to ensure the good behaviour of his subordinates by tying them up in an intricate network of financial bonds. We can conclude that neither was a pleasant man to work for, but Henry's different circumstances and his failure to match the massacres, deportations and random terror inflicted on his people by Ivan make the comparison of little real use.[15]

The historiography of early Tudor government determines in part the questions we shall have to ask about it, and also the material available to answer those questions, but I have tried not to let it determine the structure of this book. For one thing, tracing the debates about Elton's thesis, or indeed about the 'new monarchy', beyond a certain point is an increasingly sterile exercise. As Elton himself wrote in 1964, arguments about how revolutionary a revolution has to be to deserve the name of revolution risk degenerating into 'a pointless quibble over words', while judgement on such questions as the relative stature of parliament in the polity at different points between 1300 and 1700 is so dependent on the perspective one adopts that it is 'possibly the sort of question that each man may decide for himself.'[16] It is also virtually impossible to engage in, or to analyse, such debate without caricaturing or at least over-schematising the views expressed by other scholars. No doubt I have already done so here. Moreover, as I have tried to suggest above, the most serious problems thrown up by any survey of the historiography of the period are those which have not yet been properly confronted: how the fifteenth-century England illuminated by countless studies building on McFarlane's insights could recognisably have been the base for the kind of developments argued over by Elton and his critics; and how far the wider context applied to later developments by Stone and James can be read back into the early Tudor period. In attempting to tackle these issues I have arranged the book using four themes in the activity of government which seemed, taken together, to cover all the essential aspects of the relationship between government and society. Each chapter tries to expound a term central to fifteenth- and sixteenth-century thought about the nature of government: lordship, justice, livelihood and empire. Chapter 1 considers the crown's ability to manage local society and its politics, and the king's relations with his leading subjects in the court and council, in warfare and otherwise. Chapter 2 focuses on the crown's ability to meet its subjects' demands for justice, and chapter 3 on its ability to fund its activities in politically acceptable ways. Chapter 4 examines the development of the crown's grip on the lives and loyalties of its subjects, and the changing nature of the state.

The Legacy of Medieval Government

In the second part of this introduction, two fundamental – though perhaps largely unanswerable – questions must be posed. How did later medieval government really work, and what notions were available in the later fifteenth and early sixteenth centuries to those who might go about changing it? The first thing to stress is that England in 1485 was a very old, intensively and uniformly governed monarchy by any contemporary European standards. Those who fought at Bosworth stood as far removed in time from the Anglo-Saxon kings who had unified the realm and established some of the basic lineaments of its governmental structure – counties, boroughs, sheriffs, writs – as we do from those who fought at Bosworth. Magna Carta, the conquest of Wales and the origins of parliament were more distant from them than the French Revolution is from us. This means, for example, that the state-building mechanisms most evident in the continental monarchies' absorption of newly conquered territories may be harder to isolate in England. But medieval government was far from static, witnessing successive waves of administrative intensification, primarily fiscal and judicial, from the Conquest to the fourteenth century. By the time of the Wars of the Roses there was thus a highly developed governmental machine, as one historian of later medieval administration described it, 'an ordered, formalized, professional, parchment-bound thing of proper forms and channels'. Anyone who doubts that it was bureaucratic in at least one sense of the word should remember that by the 1330s several thousand writs a year arrived at the office of the sheriff of each county, were enrolled and were copied for forwarding to the appropriate hundred bailiff, while the originals were retained to be endorsed with a reply and returned to the various central government offices that had issued them.[17]

This is a peculiarly apposite example with which to illustrate one of the basic problems in assessing later medieval government. For the answer that went on the writ frequently had more to do with what suited the sheriff or his friends than with any objective reality.

Official, institutionalised power was inextricably mixed in later medieval government with the unofficial power – landed wealth, social status and control over manorial tenants – of the men who ran the government, the gentry who served as sheriffs, justices of the peace, and all manner of commissioners, and the lords who oversaw the affairs of whole regions and, with the king, of the realm itself. Problems were often better solved, indeed justice better done, by the informal power of a great man than by recourse to formal, institutional means, and the institutions only worked because the great men – led and inspired to this end by the king, who in turn heard the voice of local society in the counsel of the lords – saw to it that they did so.[18]

The hybrid nature of this system helps to explain the nature of the crisis brought on by Henry VI's utter incapacity to rule. Deprived of royal coordination, the informal side of the system degenerated into political infighting, woefully distorting the institutions of government in the process. It was thus political breakdown that brought about governmental breakdown, and not vice versa. But it was no surprise that some contemporaries felt that a strengthening of the formal, institutional side of government was the proper response to such a breakdown; nor that a reassertion of the informal aspects of royal activity – Elton's household system, and indeed Starkey's stress on personality – should have been necessary under the Yorkists and early Tudors to create the conditions for such a strengthening. Correspondingly, if the results of such action were to be evident in changes in the balance between official and unofficial resources in the government of the localities, such changes might be quite subtle but in the modification of a hybrid system none the less significant for that. Landed wealth was important in the exercise of local power in England in the nineteenth century as it had been in the ninth, but that did not mean that no change of note had taken place in the system of government in the intervening years.

The experience of Henry VI's reign, the only one about which Shakespeare managed to write three plays, loomed over his successors. History, after all, was regarded as the prime source of political wisdom, and was fundamental to the education of rulers and their advisers. The esquires of Edward IV's household were expected to spend their time constructively in 'talkyng of cronycles of kinges and of other polycyez', while the hapless Henry VI himself found the knotty problem of the duke of York's claim to his crown thrown back to him by his lords in 1460 'in so much as his said Highness had seen and understanden many divers writings and chronicles'. Studying 'many Cronicles olde', argued George Ashby in his *Active Policy of a Prince* of *c.*1470, enabled a ruler 'so to guyde hym in siche cases lyke/ As other men dudde that were polletike'. The next century's humanists felt exactly the same, though they put it very differently: 'what incomparable delectation, utility and commodity shall happen to emperors, kings, princes and all other gentlemen by reading of histories' wrote Sir Thomas Elyot in his *Boke Named the Governour* of 1531. The overall lesson of the mid-fifteenth century, and certainly one the Tudors wanted their subjects to draw from it, was that almost anything was better than another civil war. But Henry's failure also highlighted more specific problems in royal judicial and financial policy and the management of patronage.[19]

Attitudes to Government

The way such issues were viewed depended on the preconceptions of the viewer. Among those who counselled Henry VI's successors, we might identify different ways of looking at the world of politics and government which influenced the counsel they gave and the policy it helped to form. Four stand out, three of them shaped by different varieties of professional training, and the fourth and vaguest by intellectual inclination or general education. Oldest was the code of chivalry, shared by at least the upper reaches of the nobility and gentry, and perpetuated by military service under the king, participation in tournaments at court, and its status as the cultural badge of a military ruling class. In the right circumstances this could be turned very effectively into a cult of loyalty to the royal war-leader and fount of honour, and a means to reinforce the pyramidal systems of patronage that tied together any later medieval or early modern state. It also taught, though in a minor key, a duty of public service, especially in the enforcement of justice. Many of the leading councillors and courtiers of Henry VII and Henry VIII, from the thirteenth earl of Oxford and Sir Edward Poynings to Charles Brandon, duke of Suffolk, and Sir Nicholas Carew, were models of chivalrous service to their prince. But some features of chivalry made its more disruptive devotees – above all the late Elizabethan earl of Essex – awkward presences in the governing elite of Tudor England. It

tended to stimulate warmongering and individualism, and a dangerous touchiness over slights to noble self-esteem and contempt for
social inferiors, even when they were vested with authority by the
crown.[20]

More dynamic than chivalry in shaping governmental change were
the views of the common lawyers. The common law was an old discipline, but there are many signs that it was attaining a new self-
confidence and intellectual power in the later fifteenth and early
sixteenth centuries. Competition for entry to the profession was
intensifying. Legal education was becoming more formalised and
thorough, and the wider intellectual culture of leading lawyers was
becoming more impressive. A string of brilliant textbooks codified
and disseminated legal learning, from the technicalities of
Littleton's *Tenures* (printed more than twenty times between 1482
and 1547) to the more general masterpiece of Christopher St
German, *Doctor and Student* (first published in sections in 1528–31).[21]

Meanwhile, common lawyers were entering royal counsels in
greater numbers as the later fifteenth century progressed, accounting for nearly two in five of all lay councillors under Henry VII. They
included some of the most notable ministers of the decades from
the 1480s to the 1560s: William Catesby, Sir Thomas Lovell, Sir
Richard Empson, Edmund Dudley, Sir Thomas More, Sir Thomas
Audley, Sir Richard Rich and Sir Nicholas Bacon. Even when such
men were not dominant in government, the judges and legal officers
of the crown were a constant influence on royal policy and legislation. The lawyers' common education and social life at the inns of
court, and their common professional experience in the courts at
Westminster, tended to breed a common outlook. This was roughly
in favour of expanding the crown's power along lines congruent
with the English legal and constitutional traditions best understood
and administered by themselves, and centring on statute law, parliament and the common law courts. Inherent in this, as we shall see,
was an instinct for curbing both the political role and privileges of
the church and the local dominance of the nobility, evident in
varying degrees in the writings of Fortescue, Dudley and St German,
as in the judges' campaigns against sanctuary, ecclesiastical jurisdictions, retaining, the evasion of feudal dues, and so on.[22]

The greater and lesser churchmen who constituted a powerful
presence among the crown's senior ministers to the fall of Wolsey,
and retained substantial influence to the death of Mary, understandably disagreed with the more rabid common lawyers about the

relationship of church and state, even before protestantism complicated the issue. In one row Bishop Nykke of Norwich denounced
Henry VII's attorney-general Sir James Hobart as 'the enemy of God
and his churche'. However, most of the clerics who counselled the
Tudors were not just churchmen, they were highly trained civil
lawyers. Episcopal statesmen who were theologians, like John Fisher
or Thomas Cranmer, were the exception amongst a procession of
men such as John Alcock, John Morton, Richard Fox, William
Warham, Cuthbert Tunstall and Stephen Gardiner who were experts
in Roman jurisprudence. Of the 40 Englishmen promoted to bishoprics between 1485 and 1529, 36 were graduates; 24 of them were
lawyers, mostly civil lawyers, and these civilians' prominence on the
bench of bishops was greater than it had ever been before. Such
growing importance was equally evident among the wider body of
graduate clergy, amongst whom the proportion trained in the civil
law had risen steadily over the previous three centuries.[23]

This discipline was of relevance to the church, for it was closely
allied to the canon law administered in the church courts, but it was
also of use in government, in the expanding equity courts and in
international law and diplomacy. Like the common law, it had both
practical and theoretical effects on its practitioners. They had mostly
studied abroad and travelled widely as diplomats, and this tended to
give them not only advanced cultural tastes and a notable interest in
political theory, but also a certain detachment from English affairs.
Thus Peter Courtenay, bishop of Exeter and Henry VII's first keeper
of the privy seal, had studied law at Padua in the early 1460s while
Antonio de' Roselli was teaching in the faculty. Roselli was one of
the highest theoretical exponents of the power of rulers in fifteenth-
century Europe. Courtenay was also a friend of John Tiptoft, earl of
Worcester, the highly educated and Italophile lord high constable
infamous for his ruthless pursuit of Edward IV's interests and his use
of 'the law of Padua' in treason trials. Doctors' Commons, a dining
club formed in the 1490s, was the civil lawyers' approximate equivalent to the inns of court as a social centre. There they were able to
share and develop their ideas in the company of other members of
London's intelligentsia such as the theologian John Colet, the
English humanists Thomas More and William Grocyn, and the
Italian humanist historian Polydore Vergil. If this facilitated a cooler
and more comparative appraisal of the country's state, the trend was
reinforced by civilians' familiarity with the very different social and
political system in which Roman law had originated, a familiarity

made more self-conscious by the early penetration of humanist thought into legal studies in such works as Guillaume Budé's *Annotations on the Pandects* of 1508. Budé, a correspondent of More, Tunstall and Henry VIII's humanist secretary Richard Pace, was much given to comparisons between classical and French institutions; Tunstall's copy of the *Annotations* still survives in Durham Cathedral Library.[24]

To modern eyes some of the most sophisticated and detached appraisals of the problems of early Tudor England, and the possible remedies for them, seem to come from men with interests in the civil law, notably Thomas Starkey and Sir Thomas Smith. Starkey told Cromwell that he had studied the civil law 'that I myght therby make a more stabyl and sure jugement of the polytyke ordur & custumys usyd amonge us here'; Smith was a self-proclaimed enthusiast for the comparative and historically critical jurisprudence of Budé, Alciati and Zasius. Smith, moreover, was representative of a trend that kept the civil law mind in the corridors of power even after the demise of the great civilian bishop-statesmen, as one of a string of laymen educated in the civil law – Sir Thomas Wriothesley, Sir William Paget, Sir William Petre, Sir Thomas Wilson – to occupy the increasingly central office of secretary of state. Earlier examples of civilian political analysis are harder to find, but the anonymous continuator of the Crowland chronicle may provide one. He seems to have been a legally trained cleric with an interest in chancery procedure and diplomacy, perhaps Dr Henry Sharp, who studied civil law at Padua and Oxford. His account of the period from 1459 to 1486 shows a sharp analysis of government and politics, and as frank an admiration for Edward IV's foresight and preparedness when necessary to ignore 'foolish propriety', as for Louis XI's 'remarkable cunning'. He clearly felt that the monarchy as an institution had been weakened by dynastic strife, and that the marriage of Henry VII and Elizabeth of York was the best means to restore peace and begin to settle public affairs once more. His work may well give an insight into the views brought to the service of the Tudors by men like Morton and Fox.[25]

Three important attitudes to the development of the state might have come to such men from a training in Roman law. One was a general predisposition to elevate the power of the prince by analogy with that of the Roman emperor. This was evident among the French civil lawyers, who produced increasingly absolutist analyses of royal power from the 1530s to the publication of Jean Bodin's *Les six livres de la république* in 1576, the foundation of the modern theory

of sovereignty. Thomas Cromwell, displaying the eclecticism of interests and flexibility of argument that made him such an effective
statesman, tried to prompt Gardiner in this direction in a political
debate of 1539, claiming that the civil law allowed the king 'to have
his will and pleasure regarded for a law ... *quod principi placuit*, and
so forth ... I have somewhat forgotten it now'. Gardiner would not
be drawn on that occasion, telling Henry VIII that 'the form of his
reign, to make the laws his will, was more sure and quiet'. Gardiner
was considerably more forthcoming in another context, that of the
royal supremacy over the church, where his assimilation of Henry to
the Christian emperors of Rome underpinned both his personal
acceptance and his published defence of the royal case.[26]

A third area, into which Gardiner's theological conservatism
would not let him stray far, was exemplified by Paget's attitude to
religion as a matter for moderation in the interests of social and
political stability. As Gardiner reminded him, 'ye told me once ye
love no extremities and the mean is best', a view consonant with the
principle Paget laid out for Protector Somerset, that 'Society in a
realm doth consist and is maintained by mean of religion and law'.
Petre's ability to serve as a privy councillor from Henry's reign to
Elizabeth's, as Paget would have done too if not rebuffed in 1558,
was fair testimony to their regard to interest of state in matters of
religion. Smith was attacked from both ends of the doctrinal spec-
trum for his neutrality in religious matters.[27]

In such questions it is admittedly hard to disentangle the
influence of university studies in Roman law from those of the wider
humanist culture spreading through English education in the first
decades of the sixteenth century. Starkey and Smith were each as
much a humanist as a civilian, if not more. Paget, like several of his
colleagues in government in the 1540s – Lord Chancellor
Wriothesley, chancellor of the augmentations Sir Edward North,
and chief gentleman of the privy chamber Sir Anthony Denny – was
a product of Colet's new London foundation St Paul's School, an
institution so fashionably humanist that Erasmus himself had specially written some of the Latin textbooks and devotional texts used
by the boys. The effects of the reception of humanism in England
are clearly of great significance but are hard to pin down. Humanist
educational fashions, works and ideas arrived in waves, the legacies
of which are hard to separate. Individual patrons and scholars were
active throughout the fifteenth century, and the mainstream of
English thought was probably as much influenced by the dilute

Ciceronianism of Magdalen College School and a number of later fifteenth-century Oxford colleges as by the brilliance of More and Erasmus some decades later. Humanist influences are also hard to separate from others, not least because their reception in England was more eclectic and utilitarian and rather less confrontational than in some other countries. By the 1530s and 1540s, the influence of humanist and protestant ideas is particularly hard to separate in what Elton memorably called 'a splendid porridge of reformist yearning'. And while Erasmus' impact on England is undeniable – in Oxford in 1520 his works, which were not on the university syllabus, were selling better than those of Aristotle, which were – among Elizabethan undergraduates he was read for his moral and pious as much as his social or political content, and alongside protestant authors and large helpings of Cicero and other classics; the whole mixture appealed to puritan divines whose views on the church were a long way from what one might think of as Erasmian moderation.[28]

Critical study of classical texts and ancient history probably did cultivate a more analytical and distanced way of considering the issues of the day and prescribing policies to deal with them, though in this it blended with an English tradition of analytical writing – first on economic and social matters, then on political – which ran back into the fourteenth and fifteenth centuries. Training in effective style and rhetoric, a major element in humanist education, could sharpen the expression of the resulting conclusions, and classically inspired confidence in human abilities might even encourage attempts to improve society by positive action. Certainly enthusiasts for classical education hoped for such good effects. Edmund Harvel urged Starkey to use his learning to 'bring the realme to an antike form of good living', and Elyot thought the study of ancient constitutions would enable the construction in England of 'a publike weale equivalent to the grekes or Romanes'. A Ciceronian ideal of individual service to the common weal ran from William Worcester in the 1450s to Richard Morison, Thomas Starkey and Sir Thomas Elyot in the 1530s and beyond. An allegiance to some form of meritocracy generally accompanied it. As Morison put it, 'give the government of commonwealths into their hands that cannot skill thereof, how many must needs go to wrack?' But the comforting neo-Platonic belief in natural hierarchies which accompanied much later fifteenth-century humanism, admiration for the citizen aristocracies of the ancient world and contemporary Venice, and the practical fact that humanist education rapidly became just another badge of a gentleman's social superiority, made this aspect of humanism less than revolutionary. Learned virtue of the humanist sort did propel some men of comparatively humble origins to power in Tudor England, but no more so than expertise in the common law or university education and a clerical career had done for some generations.[29]

When it came to more specific issues, humanists agreed about remarkably little save the virtues of humanism, and there was as little a concerted humanist policy for the state as for the church. More's *Utopia* or Erasmus's *Praise of Folly* were devastating satires on all manner of contemporary abuses, but offered no practical remedy save perhaps the cultivation of individual virtue through education. Italian humanist political discussion was so hard to adapt to the English situation that Starkey had a constant struggle to invent or adapt English words with which to express his meaning; More never tried to translate *Utopia* and gave up on his *Richard III*. More's humanism sharpened his fears of royal tyranny; Morison's humanism equipped him to write in elegant Latin verse to Prince Edward in 1539 'only equal the acts of your parent, the wishes of men cannot go beyond this. Surpass him, and you have surpassed all the kings the world ever worshipped'. Admiration for the golden mean in religion may have been the result of the humanist learning Sir Nicholas Bacon picked up at university, but we should remember that both Edward VI and Mary were given first-rate classical educations, with diametrically opposed results.[30]

We shall have to return to these various strands of thought, especially in chapter 4. But we must always bear in mind how complex was their interaction, even at the level of the individual. This is particularly the case with humanism, where we might light on More and Bacon as humanist common lawyers, Tunstall and Smith as humanist civil lawyers and John Tiptoft, earl of Worcester, and Henry Howard, earl of Surrey, as protagonists of humanist chivalry. Chivalry could be almost as protean, as the Order of the Garter drew in churchmen as its chancellors and low-born statesmen like Audley as enthusiastic knights. There were real tensions between these outlooks, some of which we have already examined. Some common lawyers at least feared a civilian coup against the English legal system, while their own profession was generally criticised, as in any age, for exploiting its gift for obfuscating technicalities to make money out of other people's troubles. Many humanists were scathing about chivalry – Smith thought jousting a particular waste of time – and their distaste was doubtless repaid in kind, though the pen has proved mightier than the sword in leaving evidence of its point of view. Certainly Paget's learning won him no plaudits from Surrey, who responded to the humbly born secretary's intervention in his trial by telling him that 'the kingdom has never been well since the King put mean creatures like thee into the government'.[31]

Such polarities might have been perpetuated, for each of these casts of mind had its own educational institutions: the great noble households for chivalry, the inns of chancery and inns of court for the common law, the universities for civil law and the new grammar schools – of which there were as many set up in south-west England between 1499 and 1524 as over the entire preceding century – for humanism. Yet by the mid-sixteenth century it was far from unusual for a young man with good prospects to have studied in at least three of these contexts. Each discipline had its own language: law French for the common lawyers, a version of Anglo-Norman replete with technical terms; an equally technical form of medieval Latin for the civilians; a self-consciously purified classical Latin for the humanists, with Greek for the seriously inclined; and an English full of high medieval French words – prowess, hardiness, service, loyalty, honour, sovereign – for chivalry. Yet experts in each communicated readily with one another in an English vernacular rapidly arming itself to tackle any issue with words from all these sources and more. Moreover, they did so not only face to face at court but also in print before the public, for classical and humanist works were appearing in English translation in large numbers by the 1530s, as were lawbooks like *Doctor and Student* and classics of chivalry like Froissart's *Chronicles*. Each of these modes of thought was in its own way conducive to the growth of royal power, but the particular lines of development of the Tudor state would be shaped by their dazzlingly complicated interplay. Visual reminder of the fact was provided for contemporaries by a woodcut used in many editions of Littleton's *Tenures* and other lawbooks by the printer Richard Pynson: it showed an enthroned and imperially crowned king surrounded by judges, clerics and aristocratic courtiers, all apparently offering their counsel.[32]

Hardest of all to classify are the monarchs and their chief ministers, men who had to blend others' ideas into policies and their justifications. Superficially the most versatile was Henry VIII. He was able to argue fine points of chivalrous honour in wartime and fine points of theology and canon law in the Reformation. He quoted common lawyers at recalcitrant bishops and browbeat recalcitrant common lawyers as though his will really did have the force of law. He was even willing to make a (brief) attempt at learning Greek. But more hard work went into the eclecticism of his two greatest ministers. Wolsey himself was well able to organise a war, judge a lawsuit, reform a monastery and instigate a major artistic project (though, as he found to his cost, not all at the same time). But his grander achievements rested more on a catholicity of personnel. He tied together noble councillors rendering honourable service, clerical civil lawyers and lay common lawyers into some of the greatest judicial, fiscal and social enterprises ever seen in England, partly under the inspiration of humanist ideas. His successor Thomas Cromwell was both the more personal and the more surprising version of a man for all seasons. This apparently untrained but widely travelled Putney boy picked up enough common law to practise in London and eventually to draft statutes, enough more recondite learning to read with profit such political thinkers as the fourteenth-century Marsilius of Padua and the humanist Machiavelli as well as Erasmus' new Latin translation of the New Testament, and enough evangelical religion to give consistent support to its preachers once in power. Situating such remarkable men properly in their context is a daunting task, but it is one we must now attempt.[33]

1

LORDSHIP

Effective kingship in later medieval England depended on successful management of local and central politics. This demanded a judicious combination of two varieties of lordship. The king had to offer what contemporaries called good lordship to the noblemen and gentry who dominated local society and helped him rule by their counsel; he had to impose what contemporaries called heavy lordship on the recalcitrant, to enforce their obedience to his will. The lessons of history suggested that the best qualification for such management was extensive experience as an independent politician before one's accession. Edward I and Henry V, highly successful kings at home and abroad, had each passed long and varied apprenticeships in war and politics before taking up the reins of kingship. Within the limitations of his nineteen years, Edward IV had done the same. Henry VI, on the other hand, king from the age of less than nine months, had allowed disputes among noblemen and gentlemen at the local level and partisan domination of his court to interact, with devastating effects. By this measure neither Henry VII nor Henry VIII looked good prospects for kingship. One was a powerless exile for the fourteen years before his accession. The other was a younger son whom his father would not send away to the Welsh Marches to learn the business of government, as he had sent his elder brother Arthur to his death at Ludlow Castle in 1502. Some of these deficiencies, of course, could be remedied by listening to experienced counsellors. Each king made sure that such men were available: at least 35 councillors of Edward IV served on Henry VII's council, and the continuity on either side of 1509 was greater still. But in himself all Henry VII had to call on was his observation of French and Breton politics;

all Henry VIII could choose between was an instinctive reaction against some of his father's policies and a natural assumption that they should be continued.[1]

The result was that both kings broke the rules of later medieval English kingship, at times to a breathtaking extent. But they survived, even through such alarming crises as the revolts of 1497 and 1536, and in the process they laid the foundations for a new kind of government. In almost every sphere the late Henrician regime was more interventionist, more ambitious and more powerful than even that of Henry V, the paradigm of effective late medieval kingship. The growth of the power to govern sprang from the interaction of the Tudors' determination to be obeyed on their own terms – probably an ill-conceived and certainly a hazardous ambition by late medieval standards – with a series of underlying changes in England's social and political structure. These significantly modified the relationship between king, noblemen and gentry, and the wider relations between central government and those exercising local control of towns and outlying regions. They centred on the expansion of the crown lands, the court, and the royal administration, and the changing nature of the king's council, regional institutions and the nation's military resources.

The Royal Demesne

Edward IV's regime represented both the apogee of late medieval kingship and the beginnings of something different. Royal government of the localities in the fourteenth and fifteenth centuries rested on the interplay of crown, peers and gentry. The exact terms of that interplay varied from county to county and from time to time, and historians – who have mostly studied one county at one time – disagree over the extent to which the gentry were usually subservient to noble leadership. What does seem clear is that where a nobleman's landed wealth, personal abilities and cultivation of a bastard feudal following among the gentry made him a natural leader in local society, most kings were prepared to recognise and utilise that leadership, and allow a fair degree of freedom in its exercise. Edward IV was certainly quite prepared to rule through locally dominant noblemen and did so with skill, arbitrating their quarrels and using his patronage and his direct interventions in local affairs to confirm the supremacy of those prepared to serve him loyally.

However, especially after 1471, he became increasingly assertive in delineating the areas in which individual peers might expect to exercise authority. He set up half-a-dozen regional hegemonies for his relatives – including his Woodville relations by marriage – and for his closest intimates. He redistributed lands and offices in the royal gift to reinforce the power of these magnates, using parliamentary acts of resumption. And when the landed power of other noblemen made them potential rivals for local leadership, Edward dealt with them decisively. Thus the earl of Northumberland was persuaded to play second fiddle to the king's brother Richard, duke of Gloucester, in the north. The duke of Buckingham and the earl of Pembroke were excluded – one tacitly, one by formal exchanges of lands and titles – from influence in the areas where they would naturally have aspired to it. Even the king's brother Clarence found himself deprived of one block of estates in 1474 to extend the control of William, Lord Hastings, in the North Midlands. The combination of landed power and visible royal backing made Edward's magnates at their best highly effective managers of local politics. Gloucester, Hastings, and Prince Edward's councillors in Wales and the Marches, like the Stanleys in the north-west, were all active in arbitrating disputes, overseeing appointments to local office and securing good order – though by no means perfect peace – in the areas under their control: they acted like traditional magnates. But they were visibly the king's men. Their position represented a clear shift in the previous balance between royal power and that generated by noble status and landed wealth.[2]

Edward's use of such men was a refinement of previous kings' reliance on and reinforcement of the local power of trustworthy nobles, but it was not as novel as the other major theme of his policy in the 1470s. In the 1460s he had used the land forfeited by his political opponents to endow his noble supporters, many of them newly elevated to the peerage, just as Richard II, for example, had done in the 1390s. But in the 1470s he kept an increasing amount of land in his own hands, and this expansion of the royal demesne was to be imitated on an ever larger scale by Richard III, Henry VII, and Henry VIII. Its impact is hard to quantify except in terms of very rough global figures for the crown's landed income. By the time of Richard III, this was already three times larger than in Henry VI's reign; by the later years of Henry VII it was five times larger; by the 1540s and

1550s it was perhaps ten times larger. At first sight the proportion of the land in England this represented was not striking, but what mattered more than overall figures was the balance between royal and noble landholding.[3]

For the local leadership of the late medieval nobility rested on a surprisingly narrow landed base. In Lancastrian England as a whole, the gentry's landed wealth outweighed that of the peerage by more than two to one, and in many counties the proportion was four or five to one. Even in the North Riding of Yorkshire, dominated by the Nevilles, the Percies and several lesser noble houses to the virtual exclusion of the crown estate, the gentry held nearly twice as many manors as the peers in 1475. But before Edward IV began to expand the royal demesne, the peers' total landed income was more than twice that of the crown (even including the Duchy of Lancaster revenues which were not all available to Henry VI). By the 1520s the expansion of the demesne had significantly modified this balance. In a sample of counties studied using the taxation returns of 1522–5, the gentry and the church each held about a third of the land, the nobility's share ranged between 1 and 7 per cent, and the crown's equalled or exceeded it, at between 4 and 6 per cent. At least in the West Riding of Yorkshire, the Dissolution of the Monasteries and political forfeitures of 1535–46 produced a further dramatic change. While the nobility's share of income from land (including tithes) rose only from 8 to 9 per cent, and the gentry's rose from 40 to 48 per cent, the crown's tripled from 9 to 27 per cent.[4]

Figures such as these recall the spectre of the gentry controversy of the 1950s, when grand theories about the rise and fall of whole classes rested on questionable calculations about long-term transfers of landed wealth. But detailed local studies bear out the view that the expansion of the royal demesne brought major changes in the crown's management of local affairs. The primary reason was that land was much more than a source of revenue. It brought lordship over men, tenants who could be called upon for military service abroad, at home or in local disputes, who sat on juries, and sometimes even voted in parliamentary elections. Thus the royal demesne provided men to do the king's bidding, or more immediately the bidding of the knights, esquires and gentlemen who acted as the king's stewards, bailiffs and receivers. Such county gentry were in turn bound into the king's service rather than that of some locally predominant magnate. But they probably enjoyed a freer hand than as members of a peer's affinity, because the king was unable to give the detailed attention to local affairs exercised by the most effective noble 'good lords'. For this reason – rather than because of the alliance between the Tudors and the middle classes beloved of some Victorian historians – the power of the crown and the local dominance of the gentry went hand in hand.

In Lancastrian England it was the counties in which the crown enjoyed a significant landed interest, above all those where the Duchy of Lancaster estates were concentrated, that saw developments presaging those to come under the early Tudors. Here there was frequent direct contact between the king and the county gentry, the peerage was largely excluded from dominance in local politics, and more confident and independent gentry elites emerged than those in counties under the sway of magnates. As the crown lands spread, so did this style of political management. It arrived in Warwickshire after 1478, when Edward IV decided to keep in his own hands the estates of the earldom of Warwick on the basis of which the Beauchamps and Nevilles had directed local affairs. It reached into the north-east after 1483, when Richard III kept under his control as king the estates which had enabled him to govern the north as duke of Gloucester. And as a number of the greatest noble houses of early Tudor England found their lands under royal confiscation, whether permanently (like the Stafford dukes of Buckingham and the de la Pole dukes and earls of Suffolk), or temporarily (like the Howard dukes of Norfolk, the Percy earls of Northumberland and the Courtenay earls of Devon), it gained a foothold in most parts of the country.[5]

Even when such developments produced comparatively small alterations in landholding, local power structures were susceptible to considerable change under their impact, because the location of noble estates in the later middle ages was scarcely ever such as to facilitate the domination of an entire county, the unit on which most administration and thus most local political life was based. The West Riding of Yorkshire alone has been analysed as falling into seven separate zones of influence in the early sixteenth century, presided over by four peers and three leading knights. Extensive hegemonies like that of Richard Beauchamp, earl of Warwick in the 1430s, demanded the negotiated engrossment of a range of smaller local power blocs. Many peers exploited the Dissolution to concentrate their landholdings, and this could reinforce their political position, as it did the Howards' in Norfolk. But even the Stanleys, one of the most consistently powerful noble houses of the sixteenth century, found themselves hampered in their rule of north and east Lancashire by the fact that the centre of gravity of their patrimony lay in the south-west of the county. As the crown estate grew, the negotiation required to extend noble influence beyond the base provided by such a landed patrimony was one in which the king's voice suddenly carried more weight.[6]

One sign of the political impact of the growth of the demesne was the rise of a new kind of regional magnate, whose power rested not so much on his own landholdings as on his responsibility for the crown lands in the area where he held sway. Hastings was the prototype, for his rule of the Midlands relied largely on his stewardships of the Honours of Leicester and Tutbury and of many other crown estates. Others followed under Henry VII, notably Giles, Lord Daubeney, in Somerset and Dorset, and Charles Somerset, Lord Herbert, in the Welsh Marches. The balance between land and office in the construction of Herbert's power is clearly reflected in the fact that nearly 40 per cent of his son's total income came from his local offices (in most of which he had succeeded his father), rather than from his own estates. In the Duchy of Lancaster counties in the past, similar leading office-holders and aspiring brokers of royal power had sometimes emerged from amongst the leading gentry, as the Vernons did in Derbyshire. But they had not operated on a par with the great landed magnates as Hastings or Daubeney did.[7]

The Crown and the Gentry

In general the expansion of the royal demesne encouraged the diffusion of power at county level, as office on the crown lands and the status, wealth and military leadership of the crown's tenants it brought was shared out among the gentry. Moreover, it can be argued that this happened just when the gentry's mood was right for the assumption of a more independent role in local affairs as the best way to assure their own interests, dissatisfied as they may well have been with the destructively partisan leadership displayed by the peerage in the Wars of the Roses. Even amongst the gentry the long-term trend was to greater diffusion of authority, as the commissions of the peace steadily expanded. In the West Riding there were 7 local knights, esquires and gentlemen JPs in 1439, 14 in 1456, 25 in 1513 and 45 in 1545. In Kent the number of resident gentry JPs doubled between 1517 and 1528 alone. Many factors interacted to produce this effect. By the late fifteenth century the leading families in each county were no longer prepared to leave the office of JP to the lawyers and minor gentry who had sustained most of the work of the bench (often as the nominees of dominant noblemen) earlier in the century. This was a reflection of the increasing centrality of the commission in county administration, a trend further amplified through the sixteenth century, and of the increasing powers accorded to the individual JP. The greater gentry pressed for places, and almost without exception obtained them. Yet ambitious lawyers could not be left off as their expertise was, if anything, more important to the bench's operation than it had been in the past. Meanwhile, noblemen still aimed to protect their interests by lobbying for the appointment of their estate administrators and other followers, and the opening of a wider variety of routes to the court increased the options for gentlemen eager to have themselves recommended.[8]

These demand factors were supplemented by those of royal supply. It was in the crown's interest to secure places on the county bench for royal household men, serjeants-at-law, trusted clerics, and others who might pursue the king's interests with special vigour. At times of crisis they were injected into the commissions in huge numbers, as in 1472–3 and even more widely in 1492–5. Otherwise they were inserted in small handfuls, especially by Henry VII and Wolsey. More generally, the expansion of the commissions probably aimed to avoid their dominance by tiny, self-interested cliques of the sort that had run some counties under the Lancastrians. The inflation of the West Riding bench after 1536 seems deliberately to have aimed to draw in lesser gentlemen who might act as a collective brake on the knot of knightly families whose feuds had disrupted local society over the previous four decades. Meanwhile, as the JPs' powers of arrest, criminal investigation and social supervision increased, so the utility of a denser network of resident justices to secure good order across the countryside became ever more evident. In addition the gentry, even those below the rank of the JPs, were coopted into government by their appointment to a host of other commissions. These ranged from those already traditional – to deal with drainage problems, to muster troops, to collect taxes and so on – to the newer initiatives of taking evidence for the equity courts, finding victims for Henry VII's fiscal feudalism, and dissolving the monasteries. As government by commission developed more intensively from the middle of Henry VII's reign, even peers became noticeably more assiduous in their attendance at quarter sessions and their use of the powers that the office of JP – to which they were named almost without exception – gave them.[9]

Earlier kings had not neglected the possibility of enhancing their direct power over the localities by the construction of a royal affinity amongst the gentry like that maintained by a great nobleman. The county elites' landed wealth and military potential, combined with the central role in local administration and parliamentary politics they had gained by the late fourteenth century, were too obvious for such an opportunity to be overlooked. Richard II and Henry IV, however, had had to construct such a following by retaining knights and esquires with substantial fees. Such a procedure was ruinously costly, and produced an analogue only of the brittle and incoherent noble affinities bred by large-scale indentured retaining, not of the more durable followings based on estate and household service which sustained the most impressive examples of local hegemony among their noble subjects. A larger royal demesne made for a more effective royal affinity (just as the sections of Henry IV's affinity based on the Duchy of Lancaster were those most useful in gaining and keeping the throne for him). In his insecure early years, Henry VII retained knights and esquires by annuities on a large scale, especially in Lancashire, Cheshire and the North Midlands. But thereafter such expedients were reserved for very unusual situations, notably the establishment of Prince Arthur in the Welsh borders, when 18 leading Herefordshire and Shropshire gentry were retained in his service, and the interludes between the wardenships of powerful local noblemen on the northern borders, when local gentlemen who might otherwise have been feed by the warden became royal pensioners.[10]

Various factors intensified the difference between the old royal affinities and the new. From Henry V's reign on, but with ever increasing force under Richard III, Henry VII and Henry VIII, kings insisted on the exclusivity of royal service. The king's office-holders and even his tenants were to be retained only by the king; the king's servants were to wear no other lord's livery. As Henry VIII fumed at Sir William Bulmer, who had appeared at court wearing the duke of Buckingham's badge, 'He would none of his servauntes should hang on another mannes sleeve'. Such exclusivity was viable because the king's service, provided he were an effective and interventionist king, was intrinsically more attractive than that of any other lord. It became all the more so as the royal administration began to expand to cope with the growing demesne, providing ever larger numbers of posts for the ambitious lesser gentry. These were men, often with legal training, keen to carve their way into securely landed society and the role in county politics that went with it. They had been one of the most dynamic, and the most disruptive, elements in the local politics of noble good lordship; and from the 1530s, the availability of monastic lands to lease and purchase enhanced yet further the attractions to them of service to the crown which might provide the right contacts necessary to benefit from the Dissolution. Not all of them lost the dangerous edge of their fifteenth-century predecessors: Holbein's portrait of Sir Richard Southwell, the augmentations receiver and later general surveyor of crown lands, shows scars on his cheek and neck which may date back to his involvement in a nasty murder in the Westminster sanctuary in 1532. Their recruitment ran in parallel, as we shall see, with that of other gentlemen of similar standing and ambitions, but presumably different temperament and gifts, to the royal service at court.[11]

Meanwhile, the culmination of a process of laicisation of the crown's administrators which had begun in the fourteenth century set almost every royal officer on the same path to landed gentility. By the 1530s even men whose equivalents twenty years earlier would have been clerics, collecting their rewards in benefices, were buying up monastic lands and settling into county society. Two of the leading figures in the Dissolution, both highly trained civil lawyers, the master in chancery Sir William Petre and the admiralty court judge Sir John Tregonwell, did so in Essex and Cornwall respectively. Clerics in royal service had their uses in the management of local society, serving on the regional councils and, as bishops, at times using their landed power to control a county as effectively as any loyal peer. Outside the peculiarity of the palatinate of Durham, Richard Fox's dominance of Hampshire during his 27 years as bishop of Winchester is the best example. But most clerics seem to have found it harder than gentlemen or peers to combine activity in central government with local influence, not least because of the transience of their position in local society. Even those like Archbishop Warham who sought to entrench their relations amongst the gentry of their see did not make the long-term impact of the greatest lay administrators.[12]

For those gentlemen most successful in central administration made spectacular fortunes even under the ungenerous Henry VII. The lands accumulated by Sir Reynold Bray, who passed from the service of the king's mother to that of the king and became an influential chancellor of the Duchy of Lancaster, were probably worth well over £1000 a year by his death, and extended to 18 counties at their peak. Edmund Dudley's lands lay in 13 counties, and his goods were valued at £5000 at his fall. In Henry VII's reign such fortunes were made more by the exercise of influence than by direct royal reward. Under Henry VIII and the mid-Tudors, when royal bounty flowed more freely, such men reached the peerage as Lords Audley, Rich, Paget, North, Williams and so on, and built landed inheritances to match. For each of these there were many who rode the tide to more local prominence, like Leonard Beckwith, a Lincoln's Inn lawyer from the East Riding. He used the court of augmentations receivership in Yorkshire (and a talent for peculation) to gather a landed estate worth £181 a year, a knighthood and a seat on the council of the north. The more such men served the king, the more his power to intervene in local society increased, and the more such interventions were induced by them in pursuit of their own interests, the more local society became accustomed to them. The more local society became accustomed to direct interventions by royal power, the more even those who were not royal servants looked to such interventions to solve their problems. This was one among many instances of what one might call positive feedback which combined to increase the power to govern.[13]

A particular example of this trend was the rise of the ministerial household. The king's ministers had always numbered among their personal servants clerks who helped in their governmental work, as was probably inevitable when all documents had to be written and copied by hand. But the steady expansion in governmental business after 1500, and the engrossment of control over much of that business by individual ministers, bred huge establishments which looked to contemporaries like alternative centres of politics and administration to those around the king's person. As John Skelton jibed at Wolsey,

> The kynges courte
> Shulde have the excellence;
> But Hampton Court
> Hath the preemynence!

Ministerial servants were central to the execution of important policies such as Wolsey's enclosure commissions, and service in ministerial households provided one of the great strands of continuity in
Tudor government. Thomas Cromwell and Stephen Gardiner served
Wolsey, Thomas Wriothesley and Ralph Sadler served Cromwell,
William Cecil and Thomas Smith served Protector Somerset. For
many men less able than these it provided a fast track to royal favour
and local influence. Both Wolsey and Cromwell promoted their
trusted servants to enhance governmental control over the localities,
and took the sons of locally influential peers and gentry into their
households. Cromwell found room for more than a dozen of the
latter from Devon and Cornwall alone. As with royal service, the
effectiveness of the ministers' support for their servants drew others
to petition them for assistance. This in turn enabled them to deploy
the royal patronage to which they had privileged access to manage
the county elites ever more closely. Once again monastic land was a
key element.[14]

The Role of the Court

However, even after the creation of such institutions as the general
surveyors, the court of augmentations and the court of wards had
multiplied the crown's servants among the administrative gentry,
another magnet was still more important: the court. Attachment to
the royal household had been a central element in the creation of
Richard II's and Henry IV's royal affinities, but it became even more
fundamental under the Yorkists and early Tudors. It was no coincidence that the demesne-based magnates Hastings, Daubeney and
Herbert each served as lord chamberlain of the household, while
other locally dominant noblemen after 1471 were also often senior
officers at court. Thomas, Lord Stanley, was lord steward under
Edward IV, Robert, Lord Willoughby de Broke, under Henry VII,
George Talbot, earl of Shrewsbury, under Henry VII and Henry VIII,
Charles Brandon, duke of Suffolk (with the grander title of lord
great master), in the 1540s. John, Lord Russell, like his predecessor
as the dominant south-western magnate Henry Courtenay, marquess
of Exeter, held a place among the king's most intimate servants in
the privy chamber. Even those locally powerful peers who held no
household office were often prominent in court ceremonial, and

recognised as influential about the king when they did happen to be at court, as the duke of Bedford, and the earls of Derby and Oxford, were in Henry VII's reign. To some extent this was a continuation of the later medieval assumption that the court was where the nobility counselled the king. But it was also a reflection of change. As royal power increased, so access to that power became ever more important; as royal patronage expanded, not least through the expansion of the demesne, so access to that patronage became more desirable.[15]

In Henry VI's reign the king's servants had exploited his feckless generosity to turn the household into a predatory but bloated and incoherent self-help organisation. In the 1450s Queen Margaret and her partisans tried to shape it into something more efficiently partisan. Under the Yorkists, household men again enjoyed an effective monopoly of major crown patronage. But this time there was more sense that their multifarious services to the king, not least in the household-based administration of the expanding demesne, should earn them such reward. In Edward IV's territorial reordering of the 1470s, his servants of knightly rank played a double role. They linked the more distant regional authorities to the court by their participation in, for example, Gloucester's affinity or the prince's council. They also acted as the king's lieutenants in his personal management of the politics of the south-east, where many of them were prominent members of the county elites, and leaders of the risings of 1483 against Richard III. Meanwhile the household was becoming effectively conterminous with the wider royal affinity as supernumerary posts – with no regular duties in the king's domestic life – were created to attract county gentry into the king's service. Thus there were at least 48 esquires for the king's body in Richard III's reign, 93 in 1509, and 148 in the 1520s. That this was a deliberate policy as well as a response to demand is evident at least in Wolsey's time, when the gentry recruited into nominal royal service were those already prominent in the governance of their counties.[16]

The benefits of involvement with the court for such men were significant even at their least tangible. Service to the king, however occasional, conferred social status, and precedence lists clearly put esquires for the king's body, for instance, ahead of other esquires. Such ranking was visibly demonstrated to local society when one sat ahead of the other on the JPs' bench, and mattered enough to provoke Tudor gentlemen to heated argument and even fisticuffs when called into dispute. There was also a vague but powerful sense that the king's influence stood behind his servants, a sense readily exploited by the ambitious. There were other rewards far easier to measure. These were available even to an occasional courtier such as Sir Robert Plumpton, an established member of the Yorkshire elite and a retainer of the Percy earls of Northumberland. His estates suffered from the unwelcome attentions of Henry VII's councillor Sir Richard Empson, who claimed some of them and then tried to exploit his legal victory over Plumpton to take more. Plumpton found the best response was to seek appointment as a knight for the king's body, and then approach the king for support. The rewards of the court were all the more evident in the lives of the men who made careers there. Service gentry – men outside the county establishment, of the sort who had filled the households and retinues of the great lords in the past in the hope of favour and social advance – now clamoured to serve the king, just as did their administrative counterparts (and the distinction between the two groups was often a fuzzy one) who had staffed the lords' councils and estate organisations. In one spectacular instance, Henry VIII's groom of the stool – who looked after his close stool (commode) and attended him while he used it – Sir William Compton, raised his landed income from about £10 to nearly £1700 a year, built up a vast assemblage of offices on the crown estates, and laid the foundations for his grandson's elevation to the peerage.[17]

In general terms such careers, like those of a Bray or a Dudley, increased the king's power, in that men he chose to favour were making a dramatic impact on local society. In moments of crisis household men might be appointed to county office wholesale, as they were to the shrievalties in 1485 and 1497. Moreover, for those known to be close to the king, and powerful at the local level because of it, success bred success. Other landowners tended to buy their friendship with fees, or appoint them stewards of their estates. Hastings received at least 27 such grants, reinforcing his power and, at one remove, the king's. And in theory, any who abused royal favour might be removed from office at court and on the crown estates, and thus from local supremacy, more readily than those reliant largely on the power given by their own landholding. Yet removals from office were few, except among those who failed to render military support to Henry VII, and in some ways the centrality of the court ran against the king's interests. Those who claimed a special relationship with him might abuse the influence it brought them to oppress others without his knowledge, just as those who wore the livery of great lords in the preceding centuries had done.

The inflation of patronage as the demesne expanded made its distribution harder to control. Those adept at seeking out and combining
numerous small grants from the king could construct a local dominance for themselves, reinforced by their ability to act as brokers for
those outside the court, which it is not always clear the king
intended them to have. Thus Henry VIII and Wolsey evidently had
no idea at Compton's death exactly what offices he had managed to
collect.[18]

Some of Henry VIII's early grants of office to his courtiers were so
plainly silly as to invite rapid revision: the appointment of Compton
as chancellor of Ireland, for instance. But others about the king
indulged in more insidious empire-building. From the early 1520s
William Brereton, a groom of the privy chamber, collected a series of
leases and offices on the crown lands in Cheshire and North Wales
to make himself both rich and powerful. His gross income in
1534–5, of £1236, would not have disgraced an earl (though over
£1000 of it came from crown fees, farms and annuities), and a contemporary called him 'a man wiche in the sayd countye of Chester
hadd all the holle rewle and governaunce under owre sovereigne
lord the kynges grace'. His use of the power he had gained was
unsavoury, extending to the protection of murderers and the elimination of a local rival by rigged trial and immediate execution. Soon
enough Thomas Cromwell and Rowland Lee, president of the
council in the Marches, had to work to restrain or remove him.
When he was executed as one of Anne Boleyn's supposed lovers his
offices and leases were, probably with some deliberation, distributed
very widely.[19]

One might perhaps expect such mishaps more in the reign of
Henry VIII, impetuously generous and often inattentive to minor
detail, than in that of his father. But Henry VII too was keen to
advance his courtiers, by advantageous marriages with the widows of
his feudal tenants-in-chief as well as through local office and small
grants of land, and their irruption into local society could be almost
as disruptive. Most of Henry's household men inserted into
Warwickshire caused trouble of one kind or another, while in
Oxfordshire Edmund Hampden and his servants managed to fall out
violently not only with two leading gentry families, but also with the
students of Oxford University. As the power to govern directly
increased, so the difficulty increased of wielding that power without
disturbing the localities to a counter-productive degree. Meanwhile
the pressure increased on the monarch to do just that, by promoting

the interests of the ever larger and ever more insistent swarm of suitors that surrounded him.[20]

Kings sought privacy to avoid such pressure, Henry VII and Henry VIII most obviously in the creation of the privy chamber, a private set of rooms with its own select staff, insulated from the hurly-burly of the court. The move worked to some extent, and perhaps more for Henry VII than for his son, but even the father found that the quest for royal favour pursued him wherever he hid. By the end of his reign his groom of the stool, Hugh Denis, was spending freely on land, probably from the profits raised by his ability to mention suitors to the king at appropriate moments. The man who used to bring Henry his clothes in the morning, William Smith, was married to Warwick the Kingmaker's niece and was piling up offices and leases in Staffordshire, Lancashire and elsewhere. Wolsey, concerned to regulate the distribution of royal patronage for the sake of good governance and his own reputation amongst suitors, tried to restrict the ability of Henry VIII's privy chamber staff to petition and influence the king, but without much success. And with patronage went politics, all the more so as religious polarisation took hold from the 1530s and adherents of the new and the old faiths competed for the king's support even in his most private moments. The precise balance between the exercise of Henry VIII's will and the exercise of influence upon it in any individual decision is as hard to judge as the precise balance between leading ministers and personal servants amongst those seeking to influence the king. But it is clear that those around Henry – like those around his father or his children – thought it worthwhile to try to persuade him, and to enlist the support of his most intimate servants in doing so. Here the second spectre of Henry VI's reign began to loom as the first was laid to rest. Central politics became harder to control as the crown's increasing ability to control local politics intensified the pressures on the king from those keen to have that power deployed on their behalf.[21]

In turn there was a danger that the rivalries of central politics might be all the more effectively and destructively exported to the counties. How far this happened generally, even in the late Elizabethan contest between Essex and the Cecils, is a moot point. In some counties nearer London, notably Hampshire and Kent, it does seem clear that local politics divided along religious lines from the 1530s as reformists sought and found the backing of Thomas Cromwell, Protector Somerset and like-minded patrons, and their rivals looked to any available succour at court. In most areas,

however, allegiances were far more complex, not least because magnates eager to spread their good lordship as widely as possible could
not afford to select their friends on the basis of religion. One index
of the effect of larger political issues on local affairs was the practice
of purging the commissions of the peace. This began in the Wars of
the Roses with the exclusion of the most extreme partisans of either
side. Thereafter it continued on an occasional basis, probably as a
reflection of central politics. The Devon bench was purged when
Lord William Courtenay fell in 1502, those for Kent and
Gloucestershire when Buckingham fell in 1521, and several followers
of Empson and Dudley lost their seats in 1509. Wholesale purging
became standard practice as successive regimes found themselves
increasingly at odds with preceding religious policy. One in three resident Suffolk JPs lost his seat in 1553, one in three again in 1558.
Despite all the readjustments under way, the crown still had to
respect the realities of local power. Henry VII's response to the
involvement of two dozen Somerset gentry in the revolt of 1497, frus-
trated as they were by Daubeney's near-monopoly of crown favour in
the shire, was to broaden the base of his control there, even drawing
in some of those compromised over the revolt. The majority of those
implicated in the rebellions of 1536 could not be removed from
authority lest the entire governing class of the northern counties
vanish at a stroke. Even a number of reformist JPs purged in Surrey
on Mary's accession or after Wyatt's rebellion had soon to be
restored. Government remained a dialogue between ruler and ruled,
but now between crown and gentry as much as between king and
noblemen.[22]

Retaining and Military Organisation

A further effect of the expansion of the demesne was to offer a
redistribution of military resources, beneficial not least because
kings who could raise troops could defeat or outface rebellions, as
Henry VII and Henry VIII showed they could in 1487, 1489, 1497
and 1536. The crown in the later middle ages was largely dependent
for armed force on the recruitment by the nobility and gentry of
their own tenants and servants. This could scarcely be changed
overnight, not least because the threat of armed violence by noble-

men's and gentlemen's household servants and tenants was one of the ultimate sanctions of the social order. There was no money for a standing army like that in France, Spain, or the Netherlands, as Northumberland proved when he tried to maintain a small one in the second half of Edward's reign and had to disband it for financial reasons. What the Tudors wanted was not to eliminate the existing systems of military recruitment, but to control them. As a first step, the deployment of stewardships on the crown's estates could be used to elevate the king's servants to the leadership of substantial forces, raised by mustering the king's tenants with their own. Thus Lord Darcy and Charles Brandon, Viscount Lisle, led two of the largest contingents in the invasion of France in 1513, despite possessing only modest estates compared with other peers. By 1544 the same was true of the gentlemen of the privy chamber. For the campaign of that year they raised thousands of men, sometimes in individual retinues the size of those commanded by the richest noblemen. Yet retaining raised more complex problems than could be solved merely by the exploitation of the demesne.[23]

The precise relationship between the construction of bastard feudal affinities and the recruitment of armies for royal service has been the subject of a longstanding chicken-and-egg debate. But whichever came first chronologically, or predominated among the motives of those leading or joining affinities, by the fourteenth and fifteenth centuries the process of raising troops for war was closely related to the textbook evils of bastard feudalism. Gentlemen and yeomen retained by a lord to raise troops for the king's service when called upon to do so might equally raise a force for the violent conduct of disputes. Those retained to serve in war might earn their fee in peacetime by abusing their influence within local administration in the interests of their lord. Perhaps worst of all, any lord or gentleman might assemble an armed force on a short-term basis, without the expense of retaining fees, by handing out liveries – clothing in his personal colours or bearing his heraldic badge – thus generating a capacity to exercise violence unrelated to the natural balance of power determined by the local distribution of landed wealth. Kings were not blind to the problems presented by liveries and retaining, and neither were the parliamentary commons, who complained about them from the 1370s. Henry IV and Edward IV in particular passed increasingly stringent legislation to restrict the distribution of livery and the retaining of followers, arming it with procedural short-cuts to facilitate prosecutions. But enforcement remained intermittent, as political concerns overrode any momentum from the judges for a more consistent attack, even after Edward's statute of 1468.[24]

Henry VII and his councillors approached the issue with a characteristic combination of breadth of sweep and attention to detail. In 1485 Henry put the entire peerage on oath not to break the statutes, as Edward had done. But he followed this up by securing an opinion from the judges in 1486 that all retaining bar that for household service or legal counsel broke Edward's act, thus effectively eliminating the act's hamstringing clause permitting 'lawfull service'. Prosecutions were regularly mounted from the first years of Henry's reign, and where retaining formed part of a wider tangle of law-and-order problems special fast prosecutions were coordinated by king and council from the late 1480s. Finally, in 1504, a statute even more restrictive than that of 1468 was passed, though it was limited to Henry's lifetime. This was probably a sign of resistance in parliament like that met by Edward in 1468; nevertheless a fresh wave of prosecutions followed.[25]

Henry's aim, like Edward's or Richard III's, was not to abolish retaining, but to harness it. Like Richard, he met prolonged military crisis by securing undertakings from those he trusted to hold a specific number of men ready to serve. Eventually Henry systematised licensing to a remarkable degree, prescribing the number of men each licensee was allowed to retain, ordering regular musters, and requiring that the names of all those retained should be submitted to his secretary. The combination of prosecution and licensing gave the king very flexible control over the distribution and use of effective armed force. Even the distribution of the king's livery by his estate officers was investigated to prevent their using the resulting retinues for their own purposes.

Henry's system made him more militarily secure as the reign went on. In 1487 and 1489 he had had to rely heavily on the resources of a few loyal peers – Bedford, Oxford and Derby – and a range of North Midlands gentry and household men. But as the licensing scheme was consolidated he could count on ever wider circles of royal officers, gentry and townsmen, often grouped under the leadership of his closest associates. Thus Sir Thomas Lovell led a licensed retinue of 1365, and even the king's mother Lady Margaret Beaufort retained on a large scale. The result impressed foreign observers. One claimed that by 1507 Henry had prepared 'as many as 40,000 men of war, the finest and strongest men seen for a long while, and made them hold themselves ready in their homes'. Another noted that Henry did not depend on the military strength of his nobles, because he had appointed men in receipt of his fees to perform military services, men 'who he knows can be trusted on any urgent occasion'. Similar principles were applied even in Ireland. There parliament legislated against retaining in 1494–5 with a specific exemption for lords in the Marches of the Pale, where constant warfare with the Irish necessitated its continuance. They, however, were to enter certificates of those they had retained, and answer for their behaviour.[26]

Henry's theme of flexible control persisted throughout the Tudor period. Wolsey made an example in star chamber of several peers who had failed to disband their retinues when the licences issued for Henry's first war with France were revoked at its end in 1514, and in Lancashire prosecutions were still being mounted in the 1530s and 1540s. Such was the shadow of the statutes that several peers hesitated to raise troops to suppress the Pilgrimage of Grace until explicitly licensed to do so, and the marquess of Exeter was banned from court and lost his place in the privy chamber in 1531 in response to false allegations that he had been retaining illegally in Cornwall. Licences to retain were still being issued to councillors and others in the 1560s, and proclamations commanding the enforcement of the 1468 act were issued as late as 1572 and 1583. The retinue was a long time dying, and with the return of war in the 1580s it revived as the best means to raise effective cavalry for expeditions overseas. However, in the long term the political unacceptability of its misuse – repeatedly punished in the council courts and elsewhere, as we shall see in chapter 2 – was increasingly matched by military irrelevance.[27]

It was the strain placed on the system of raising a national army composed of retinues by Henry VIII's ever larger campaigns that exposed its deficiencies. In 1522 Wolsey tried to refurbish the recruitment mechanism by the 'General Proscription'. This was an ambitiously comprehensive survey of the landlord–tenant (and steward–tenant) relationships that underlay the recruitment of retinues, and of the wealth that determined the arms individuals were meant to possess. The effects were positive in the short term, in the raising of armies in 1523. But the effort was soon wasted, as the accelerating speed of turnover in landownership and the associated weakening of bonds between landlord and tenant broke the back of the retinue system. By the 1540s the government found itself writing to the wrong people – at times to people who had been some while dead – to ask them to raise troops, and landlords found their tenants refusing to serve unless military duties were specified in the terms of their leases. Henry took refuge in the older obligation of all able-bodied men to serve in the militia, the basis of defensive arrangements even in the fourteenth and fifteenth centuries when retinues were used for campaigns abroad. But when troops mustered by county commissioners were drafted abroad from 1544, their preparedness and equipment were found even more wanting than those of the retinues. Henry tended to plug the gaps in his armies with foreign mercenaries, but the Marian regime grasped the nettle as the fall of Calais loomed. They gave the militia system clear priority over the retinue system, and laid the basis – albeit in rather confused fashion – for the future organisation and equipment of the militia in the statute of 1558.[28]

Noble Power

The effect of all the changes we have reviewed so far was not to destroy the power of the nobility, but to modify it. Noblemen, even those without major offices or influence at court, remained powerful in early Tudor England. Individually they were richer than almost everyone else, their rank alone still earned enormous respect, and their influence over their tenants was still considerable. Yet they did not enjoy the sort of independent jurisdiction or other powers of their French or Spanish equivalents; the exercise of their power was heavily dependent on their relationship with the king above them and the gentry, with their collective preponderance in landed wealth and their dominance of the local administrative system, immediately below. Wise kings would seek to harness noble power rather than confront it, and this was done the more readily because the peers generally looked for royal leadership as their fathers and grandfathers had done. However, kings might – and Henry VII and Henry VIII did – seek to alter in various ways the terms on which the nobility served.[29]

Service in war was one activity traditionally central to the self-image of the nobility. The desire to serve the king conspicuously well in battle in order to gain honour was one any wise king would cultivate. Thus the Tudors intensified the later medieval development towards the identification of honour with service to king and commonwealth, thereby coopting noble service to their own projects. The courts and campaigns of Henry VII and Henry VIII became the centre of a national chivalrous cult. These kings, and perhaps even Mary, were as aware as Edward IV of the historical truth presented to his parliament in 1472 that 'it is not well possible ... that justice, peace, and prosperity hath continued any while in this land in any king's days but in such as have made war outward'. A slow but steady demilitarisation of the governing classes was perhaps rendering this dictum less relevant by the mid-sixteenth century. Elis Gruffydd of the Calais garrison complained that the new captains sent out from England in 1545 were 'a lot of feckless boys who were sent to school to learn to count money and become auditors rather than soldiers'. But such change had been occurring over a very long period, perhaps ever since the Norman Conquest, and within landed society it worked from the bottom upwards. It was still as true for Henry VIII in 1513 and 1544 as it had been for Edward IV in 1475 that a muster of the peerage on the scale of that for the Agincourt campaign had the potential to unite the king and his greatest subjects in a mutually gratifying enterprise.[30]

Early Tudor noblemen also continued to serve the king in the oversight of regional government, using their own resources of landed power as much as any offices they might hold on the crown's estates. The earls of Shrewsbury, Oxford and Derby did so conspicuously under Henry VII: Shrewsbury, for instance, was consulted over the appointments of sheriffs for five Midland counties in 1500, and regularly arbitrated disputes among the local gentry. The second and third dukes of Norfolk played a similar role under Henry VIII, and below the level of such leading magnates many peers took a more modest part in local government. At times Henry VII and Henry VIII even used hereditary grants of land to equip noblemen to control a particularly sensitive area, much as any earlier king might have done. The Stanleys in Lancashire in the 1480s might be one example, though this may have been as much a reward for services rendered at Bosworth and Stoke as a strategy for political control. Henry VIII's endowment of Lord Russell in the south-west in the 1530s, or Charles Brandon, duke of Suffolk, in East Anglia in the 1510s and Lincolnshire after 1536, provides clearer instances.[31]

Even these examples give pause for thought. Brandon submitted to a wholesale transfer from one region to another at the king's behest:

Henry was treating one of his intimates not so differently from the dismissive way Edward IV had converted the second earl of Pembroke into the first earl of Huntingdon. In general Henry VII was cautious over committing the rule of any area to one man, probably too cautious when dealing with those regions where the crown estate was not large, and the initial result was confusion and conflict of the sort that troubled north Warwickshire in the first two decades of his reign. His son too was generally allergic to the natural assumption of the previous century, that when a great lord with a strong landed base and a gentry following to match was available to oversee an area, he should more or less automatically be allowed to do so. In 1528 he reacted with annoyance when he suspected that the earl of Kildare, the greatest magnate in the English Pale in Ireland, 'goeth fraudelently about to colour, that the Kinge shuld thinke, that His Grace couthe not be served there, but oonly by hym'. He gave the duke of Norfolk similarly short shrift in 1537, when Norfolk argued that the crown had no option but to appoint noblemen as wardens of the northern Marches. Here Henry was thinking along the same lines as his father's councillor Edmund Dudley. He wrote of noble aspirations to 'the fruite of honorable dignitie': 'in all cases lett them not presume to take it of ther owne auctoritie for then it will suerly choke them'. This seems to be a common lawyer's viewpoint, similar to that of Sir John Fortescue in the previous generation, with his concern about noblemen 'myghty in thair contraes to do what them liste'.[32]

It became common wisdom in the governing circles of Tudor England that the king's role was not merely to regulate the relations between noblemen, but to limit their power over their social inferiors. William Thomas, clerk of Edward VI's privy council, told the king that 'if the Prince be good, like as he keepeth his Commons void of power, even so he preserveth them from the Tyranny of the Nobility. For he is the same bridle in Power over his Nobility, that the Nobility is over the Commons.' More bluntly, Elizabeth's councillor Lord Buckhurst told the earl of Shrewsbury in 1592, 'Your Lordshipp must remember that in the policy of this Common Wealth, we are not over ready to add encrease of power & countenance to such great personages as you are.' There is a distinct change of tone here, even allowing for political circumstances, from Bishop Russell's draft speech for the opening of Edward V's parliament in 1483. Assuming that 'the polityk rule of every region wele ordeigned stondithe in the nobles', Russell could only exhort them to accord with one another, since it was 'the lordes and nobille men ... in whoos sure and concord

demenynge restithe the wele of alle the commen'. With this went a
growing sense that the nobility should be entrusted with power only
so long as they used it well. As Henry VII himself told the earl of
Northumberland and the archbishop of York when they appeared
before his council accused of riots, 'it should rather have been to
both their honours to have given good example to other men than to
have been of such demeanour', especially because they were 'such
persons as the King's grace had chiefly committed to governing and
authority in the parts of the north'.[33]

Actions reinforced such words. The indictment of the earl of
Suffolk in king's bench for murder in 1498, and far more so the executions for murder of Lord Dacre of the South in 1541 and Lord
Stourton in 1557, were quite unprecedented. The executions were
all the more shocking because carried out by hanging, as though
these errant peers were common criminals. In Stourton's case the
impact was both demonstrated and intensified by the printing of his
confession as a piece of sensationalist journalism. Meanwhile the
newer and more dynamic principles were ingrained in the operation
of the equity courts of star chamber and requests, where the allega-
tion that one's opponent was a great man abusing his position was a
sure way to gain a hearing. Some peers at least found their social
inferiors, even their tenants, all too ready to exploit the opportunities this presented.[34]

If the attitudes of kings and ministers challenged noble power from
one direction, other factors threatened their leadership of the gentry.
The widening spread of court office, and hence of access to the king,
made it harder for even a nobleman with large and concentrated
landholdings and a strong relationship with the monarch to exercise
the sort of hegemony that his equivalent might have done a hundred
years earlier. When Henry VIII ordered the duke of Suffolk to move
to Lincolnshire in the later 1530s, he was freed from the competition
with the duke of Norfolk and other peers which had dogged his
attempts to construct a power-base in East Anglia. He still found,
however, that he was faced by an alternative axis in local politics,
linked to the court by Sir Thomas Heneage as chief gentleman of the
privy chamber. Early in Elizabeth's reign, the fourth duke of Norfolk
found it hard to reconstruct his father's and grandfather's dominance in Norfolk and Suffolk for similar reasons. Even in the days of
the second and third dukes, the more distinguished gentry of their
circle, such as the Townshends of Raynham, seem to have placed as
much value on their links at court and their relations with their

fellow-gentry as on the dukes' patronage. For those noblemen resident in the counties nearest London, where courtiers and leading administrators settled thick and fast, the hope of any kind of exclusive leadership of local society was even more forlorn. Conversely, the fifteenth-century noble house which probably did preserve its regional dominance most effectively into the later sixteenth century was that of Stanley. The Stanley earls of Derby presided over a Lancashire where the gentry very rarely sought or obtained office at court.[35]

The core of the classic bastard feudal affinity was the great household: a centre for educating the sons and daughters of the gentry, brokering marriages and other alliances between them, arbitrating their disputes, and exercising hospitality to the wider political community of the county or region. Amongst the greatest peers such households still flourished in the first decades of the sixteenth century. The earl of Oxford's household numbered over 100 in wages and perhaps 300 all told, the duke of Buckingham's and the earl of Northumberland's nearer 200 and 500. Indeed, the tendency was if anything for households to grow larger, just as estate stewardships were multiplied, to legitimate the payment of fees and granting of livery to gentlemen which would otherwise contravene the retaining statutes. In 1517 Buckingham managed to distribute livery quite legally to 199 people. Buckingham's hospitality was equally prodigious, and one feast at his new residence of Thornbury Castle in Gloucestershire in 1508 attracted 459 guests, including 6 knights from Gloucestershire and Somerset. This was not eccentric atavism. The Howard dukes of Norfolk, though more at ease with the Tudors, were similarly lavish hosts. They entertained a dozen East Anglian knights at Framlingham Castle in the course of 1526–7, and 235 guests in total on 30 December 1526. Even smaller households, numbering 70 or 80 servants like Lord Clifford's or Lord Darcy's, were clearly important in the maintenance of their local influence, their personnel often drawn from the lord's tenantry and forming the nucleus of his retinue for war.[36]

Hospitality on the Howard scale demanded a level of expenditure beyond all but the richest peers: the average nobleman's taxable income in the 1520s was £801, a third or less than that of the half-dozen richest families. Even Buckingham, the wealthiest of all, ran into financial ruin in the attempt to keep house in such style and cut a magnificent figure at court. His attempts to remedy the situation by exploitative landlordship only served to undercut his power further by alienating the loyalty of his tenants, while his personal abrasiveness may well have undermined any friendship he won by his hospitality. He reportedly told his neighbour Lord Berkeley 'that hee shall be faine to feed piggs ... which is more meet for him than any other person', and made a habit of falling out with those who worked for him. Buckingham is a reminder that the courtly skills learned in the great households had to be exercised to make and maintain friendships if noble power were to be articulated effectively in local society: it was not easy to be an early Tudor magnate, even if, like Buckingham, one checked and signed one's account books diligently.[37]

Meanwhile it was already becoming harder for the households of the great peers to compete with the king's court or even with the households of the great ministers as centres of personal advancement and political influence. In one way it was a success for a nobleman to secure promotion into the king's service for his servants and followers. They could be expected to retain some loyalty to their old master, and any proven ability as a broker of royal patronage was liable to attract other ambitious men to his service. Yet even the greatest early Tudor peers seem to have found that any administrative and political talent they found amongst the gentry leached too rapidly for comfort out into royal service and an independent role in county politics. At the same time the universities and inns of court seem to have been already set on the course of providing a suitable education for public life to an ever-growing number of the sons of the gentry, drawing them away from the service in great households which had been the norm. By the end of the sixteenth century, inflation, the competing demands of keeping up fashionable appearances in London, and ideals of hospitality changing under the impact of humanism had combined to make further serious inroads on the great household as a social and political centre.[38]

These changes did not of course make all the significant gentry break their links with any peer. But they made such links ever more a matter of deferential cooperation than of dedicated service, even for gentry below the ranks of the very rich and locally influential – ersatz peers like the Vernons of Haddon – among whom this had been the case earlier. Moreover, for those gentlemen who did wish to pursue a career in service the market in patronage appears to have been ever more fluid. Although the Howards, Talbots, Stanleys and others did command the service of successive generations of some families, Yorkshire gentlemen seem to have chosen fairly freely between the Percies, the Cliffords and even more distant lords such as the duke of Suffolk. For a more instinctual and durable loyalty, rooted in the areas of their estates, peers had increasingly to look to the yeomanry and lesser gentry. As Thomas, Lord Seymour of Sudeley, advised his noble friends in Edward VI's reign, to build a secure following they must cultivate 'the head yeomen and frankelyns of the cuntreye', because the gentlemen 'have sumwhat to loose'. Such men were not negligible forces in the politics of manor and village, especially at a time when between a half and three-quarters of all communities lacked a resident gentleman; their role in leading revolts is sufficient testimony to that. They were well able to organise the tenantry for land disputes, as they did for the Talbots as late as the 1590s. But they had no stake of their own in county politics, and those ambitious to develop one usually had to move beyond exclusive loyalty to one peer. Moreover, their independent-mindedness probably grew with their wealth and literacy from the mid-sixteenth century. They were not the stuff of the great affinities of the past.[39]

One institutional development did produce by Elizabeth's reign an artificial replacement for the oversight of local government that would have been expected of a locally dominant landed magnate in the previous century. This was the rise of the lord lieutenant, an officer born of the public order crisis of Edward VI's reign, and one who wielded wide powers of administrative supervision in addition to his military role as commander of the county militia. When suitable noblemen were available and trusted, they were regularly appointed, as the Stanleys were in Lancashire and the Talbots in Derbyshire. However, the Elizabethan government felt itself quite able to insert a court peer with no landed base in a county when necessary, as Lord Hunsdon was appointed in Norfolk in 1585, and for most Elizabethan lords lieutenant the crucial qualification was not their nobility but a seat on the privy council. By the last decades of the reign, those most comfortably dominant in the politics of their counties were the peers able to bolster their landed position with strong influence on the council and at court, notably the Cecils and Sackvilles.[40]

Council, Councillors and Secretaries of State

The natural authority of noblemen was also called into question by developments in the king's council. The privy council, an omnicompetent body of clearly defined membership which by 1601 contained only five peers, was the central institution of later Tudor government. But the route by which it attained that position is far from clear. What seems to have happened is that under the Yorkists and early Tudors the small administrative council of the later middle ages, a body led by the chancellor and treasurer and staffed by a handful of bishops, lesser clerics and household knights, took on more and more exclusively the political role of counselling the king. Formerly this had been shared with the wider peerage, who acted as the king's 'natural counsellors' either informally at court, or more formally in great councils. In Henry VII's reign formal great councils were still held, resembling sessions of the parliamentary lords, sometimes reinforced by town representatives. They were useful for sounding out the political nation about difficult issues, usually involving foreign affairs, in a more flexible setting than that of parliament. But they did not last into the next reign in any recognisable form. Large council meetings of a less comprehensive kind did, and nearly half the peers attended one or more between 1509 and 1529, just as two-thirds of the peers had done in Henry VII's reign.[41]

The daily reality of Henry VII's council was very different. Most meetings were attended by perhaps half-a-dozen men, clerical officers of state like Morton and Fox, household peers and knights like Daubeney and Lovell, and common lawyers and administrators like Dudley and Bray. The lawyers in particular grew in prominence as the reign went on, just as they had been doing since 1471. This reflected in part the ever growing judicial workload of the council as the king and his councillors intervened more frequently in local politics, which we shall examine in more detail in chapter 2. But it also fitted the varieties of administrative business coming before the council, first as the demesne and the land revenue organisation expanded, then as the security scares and intensive fiscal exploitation of Henry VII's reign brought closer and closer supervision of individuals. Under Henry specialised offshoots of the council developed to meet these tasks, the general surveyors for the crown lands and the council learned in the law. But they were never clearly institutionally separated from the council as a whole, and there was considerable overlap in function, just as no attempt was made to separate the judicial and administrative activities of the council whether sitting at Westminster or at court on progress. In its fluidity and omnicompetence, Henry VII's council resembled the council of a great magnate; no surprise for two reasons. Many of its most influential personnel, notably Bray and Empson, were drawn from the Duchy of Lancaster council which was the king's council as a landed magnate. And many of its functions, notably the coordination of estate management and the arbitration of disputes, were precisely those performed by magnate councils in the previous centuries. Just as the royal councils in the Marches of Wales and in the north had their origins in the oversight of the prince's estates under Edward IV and of the estates Richard III had held as duke of Gloucester, so the increasing prominence of the king's council in central government was partly tied to the growth of the crown estate.[42]

Henry VIII's accession sharpened the council's role, as his father's surviving councillors took on some of the characteristics of a regency council to direct government while the young king found his feet. Henry used Wolsey first to subvert, then to trump their control. But even under Wolsey's chairmanship the council remained the centre of administration and political counsel, as well as the bearer of an intensifying judicial workload. It was this judicial expansion that forced change, as it threatened to crowd out other business. Wolsey adumbrated a solution in the Eltham Ordinances of 1526, splitting a judicial council off from a political council of fixed membership, but never implemented the plan. Instead it was realised in the decade after his fall, as two council courts, star chamber and requests, achieved an institutional identity separate from a new privy council. The latter was based on the ring of political advisers active at court during the divorce crisis, and coordinated from 1533 or 1534 by Thomas Cromwell. Henry's takeover of Wolsey's palace at Westminster (which became Whitehall Palace) made it easier for a political council, performing the role naturally played by those around the king, to take on the functions of an administrative council coordinating the institutions based at Westminster. Yet the new privy council still split itself at times into a group with the king and a group at Westminster, as Edward IV's or Henry VII's council had done.[43]

Meanwhile the rise of an exclusive but omnicompetent council resurrected old debates about the nobility's status as natural counsellors and the king's duty to take counsel not from a narrow, self-interested circle, but from as wide a range of the great and the good as possible. These ideas surfaced in a number of contexts, notably in the demands of the rebels of 1536, and in the proposals of Thomas

Starkey. Starkey, who had studied in Italy, was inspired by his admiration for the Venetian constitution with its hierarchy of councils. In his *Dialogue between Pole and Lupset* of 1529–32 he argued for a standing council, headed by the noble holders of hereditary great offices such as the earl marshalcy, the great chamberlainship and the high stewardship, to keep a check on the king. However, as Henry pointed out in his reply to the Pilgrims, and as remained true later in the reign, in its composition his council was not very different from that he had inherited from his father: some hereditary peers, some newly created peers, some bishops, the leading knights of the royal household, and the most prominent financial administrators. Even the holders of three of the four hereditary great offices were leading councillors in the 1530s (and the fourth great office, the constableship, was being kept vacant). The situation was tidied up by the acts of precedence and proclamations of 1539, which integrated the great offices of state (chancellor, treasurer and so on), the hereditary great offices, the household offices held by peers or knights and the chief secretaryship into a single hierarchy of positions which both enhanced the status of the holders and qualified them for membership of the privy council. This gave Henry both an effective political and administrative body and a council that looked reassuringly weighted with noble gravitas. It probably also intensified the commitment to the council of those noblemen fortunate enough to be members.

The only real losers were the judges of king's bench, common pleas and the exchequer, frequently consulted by the privy council but edged out of membership by its shedding of the judicial load, and the bulk of the peerage, who could now exercise their role as natural counsellors only in parliament or in informal conversation with the king. For the dedicated and ambitious the parliamentary way became a route to a seat on the council, as some of the most active peers in the late Henrician house of lords went on to prominent conciliar careers under Edward and Mary. But the provision of informal counsel by those peers who were not privy councillors became ever harder as the privy council became entrenched in the court, where lodgings were provided for all its members by 1546, as they were not for other peers. Indeed, by Henry's death six of the sixteen privy councillors doubled up as members of his privy chamber, and at Whitehall and Hampton Court the privy council chambers were situated within the privy lodgings suites to which access was severely restricted.[44]

Cromwell's fall brought unequivocal institutional definition to the privy council in 1540, but its future was by no means assured. Protector Somerset largely abandoned it after the first year of his rule, preferring to govern through his household. Northumberland revived it as the central institution of government, albeit one dominated by his political allies as he purged those who would not cooperate with him. Then the circumstances of Mary's accession made her privy council an awkward blend of the Edwardian outsiders who first backed her claim to the throne and the Edwardian insiders whose defection ensured her success. The result by September 1553 was a privy council of 43, twice as large as those of Henry and Somerset, though Northumberland's had peaked at more than 30. While it was by no means as unwieldy in action as its size might suggest, not least because many of the councillors were inactive, it still saw an intensification of previous standing committee arrangements and a succession of partisan schemes for an inner 'council of state'. These aimed to guarantee the dominance of the Edwardian survivors, led by Paget, over the delivery of political counsel, especially to King Philip. This was at least a substantial distortion of the model evolved in the 1530s, and it was arguably only Elizabeth's accession and the return to influence of William Cecil, Northumberland's right-hand-man in conciliar management, that enshrined the omnicompetent privy council of twenty-odd members at the heart of the Tudor regime. What the developments of Henry VII's and Henry VIII's reigns do seem to have secured was greater public awareness of the council, as is suggested by the provisions made in Norwich in 1543 for the priests of chantries established by the craft guilds to pray not just for the king, queen and prince, but also for the king's council.[45]

One clear side-effect of the rise of the council, especially under Henry VII, was the rise in importance of individual councillors. Men such as Bray and the attorney-general Sir James Hobart coordinated the council's activities in their home areas, and thus became powerful locally even without collecting the offices and lands that gave a Daubeney or a Compton local weight (though in Bray's case those accompanied his success). They were achieving at the regional level what Cromwell and Cecil would achieve in national politics, a power driven largely by the management from the centre of conciliar administration in its impact on the localities. Bray's collection of fees and stewardships pales beside Cromwell's (much of it from quailing monastic communities), but the three earls, two barons and two noble dowagers who pensioned Bray must have felt they were buying an influence worth having: the earl of Northumberland thought so as early as 1487.[46]

Cromwell's position was all the more significant in that he was the first king's secretary to organise the council's work. The secretary had risen in political importance through the late fourteenth and fifteenth centuries. The secretaries of Richard III and Henry VII wielded substantial influence, all the more so as the signet office they ran played a growing role in coordinating the financial system. But they were often absent on embassy, as Henry VIII's earlier secretaries were, and it was Cromwell's tenure that made the post, in G. R. Elton's words, 'the centre and driving force of the administration'. In England as all over Europe – in Spain, France, and various German and Italian principalities – it was natural that secretaries of state should rise to prominence in an age of bureaucratic intensification. Cromwell's position, however, was as much a matter of political fortune as of administrative destiny – even his control of the king's paperwork rested partly on his ability to place trusted intermediaries in the privy chamber – and the volume of his correspondence and minuteness of his attention to local affairs owed much to the circumstances of the Henrician Reformation. None of his successors in the secretaryship before Cecil operated as a chief minister in the same way, corresponding with the leading gentry throughout the country and many other contacts, and overseeing appointments to local offices to secure the effective implementation of crown policy. Indeed, after Cromwell's fall the privy council as a body took over much of this correspondence and the political management it facilitated.[47]

Within the council Cromwell's successors (appointed in pairs since his devolution of the office onto his private clerks Sadler and Wriothesley months before his fall) did play a role unmatched by those who went before. They prepared agendas, linked the council to the monarch, and corresponded with ambassadors, military commanders and others in their own right as well as drafting letters from king and council. At least in Henry's later years, they also retained some influence over the distribution of crown patronage. And a succession of them profited mightily from their position. Sir Ralph Sadler and Sir William Petre, for instance, invested some £10,000 and £22,000 in land respectively during their careers. Paget and Wriothesley, who progressed to higher offices and peerages, did better still: their families were amongst the top third of the peerage by income in 1559.[48]

Personal Monarchy, Coercion and Reward

However dramatic the rise of ministers, privy council and secretaries, Tudor government remained focused on the monarch. He or she took the final decisions in great matters of state: war and peace, dynastic alliances, religious policy. Whether or not susceptible to influence, he or she also took all the significant decisions in matters of patronage. The elaborate arrangements formulated by Paget in 1550 for the discussion of petitions for royal grants in Edward VI's privy council show the difficulties of handling such questions without an adult king at the helm. A pot marked with the suitor's name was to be passed round the council board, and to vote for or against the grant each councillor was to drop either a white or a black ball into it. Presumably this was to be done surreptitiously to prevent rancorous post-mortems. Thus the Dudley regime might defuse the sort of ill-will caused by Somerset's arrogation to himself of the royal power to reward, and his inevitable failure to meet all aspirations.

An adult ruler could generate such frustration if his patronage was concentrated in an outrageously partisan way – Edward II, Richard II and Henry VI had done so – but most of the time Henry VII and Henry VIII avoided the problem. Amongst the peers, for instance, Henry VIII concentrated his rewards on the smallish circle who were active councillors, courtiers and military leaders, but found titbits in land and office for many others. Either indifference or the hope of reward seems to have kept the bulk of the peerage from the sort of grumbling indulged in by the duke of Buckingham, whose sense of his own natural importance was exceeded only by his incompetence and tactlessness. Wolsey and Cromwell also served a useful function as 'lightning conductors' in the king's relations with noblemen, as in other ways. Buckingham was convinced that the cardinal 'would undo all noble men if he could', while the conservative aristocrats around the marquess of Exeter thought that Cromwell did not care 'what becam of the nobyltye off the hole realme'. Henry was able to indulge in a reassuring reconciliation with his natural counsellors at the fall of each minister, though Buckingham and Exeter had preceded their bugbears to the block. Even Henry VII, less generous than his son, found rewards for a number of the peers prominent at his court even if not among the inner ring of his council, and by a policy of steady though slow reward for consistent service managed to win and retain the loyalty of former Ricardians like Thomas Howard, earl of Surrey.[49]

The quest for patronage was one aspect of the reality that political life at the highest level was a matter of personal relationships between the king and the leading members of the political nation. Those who won his friendship or inspired his confidence did better than those who did not, and even those chosen by the king to carry out his commands without any more tangible reward benefited by the authority and standing it brought them locally. On the larger scale this also made the political system a reflection of the royal character, in particular in the balance between persuasion, reward and coercion in the king's dealings with noblemen, prelates and gentry. Most of the time carrot and stick were inextricably linked, as in the flexible statutory procedures of attainder and resumption developed by Edward IV and refined by Henry VII. Acts of attainder were used to confiscate the estates of those convicted of treason, but could then be reversed. Some 84 per cent of those involving peers over the period 1453–1504 were undone sooner or later; often, it is true, after the advent of a new dynasty, but in the case of a quarter of Edward IV's and half of Henry VII's, within the reign in which they were passed. By this means the victims or their heirs were politically rehabilitated, though often, under Henry VII, at a substantial price. Meanwhile, acts of resumption were used to call in forfeited lands and other estates and offices from royal grantees, placing them almost as much on probation as those under attainder. Royal rhetoric frequently displayed a similar blend of exhortation and threat, as in the letters sent out to JPs and sheriffs in 1535, asking them to check on the bishops' implementation of the royal supremacy over the church. Recipients were informed that Henry had 'especially elected and chosen you among so many for this purpose' because of the 'special love and zeal which we suppose and think you bear towards us and the public and common weal, unity and tranquillity of this our realm'. But they were also warned that if they failed to comply with the king's instructions then 'we like a prince of justice will so extremely correct and punish you for the same that all the world besides shall take by you example'.[50]

There were times, however, when coercion or reward visibly predominated. The most obviously coercive phase of early Tudor government was the later part of Henry VII's reign. The dangerously aggressive attitude towards his leading subjects adopted by Henry at this time was the product of a number of factors. The constants were the king's concern to maintain close personal oversight of government, and to maximise his income. But these were focused towards the end of his reign by political and dynastic insecurity; 1497 saw a major revolt, 1501 brought the flight abroad of the Yorkist claimant Edmund, earl of Suffolk, and in 1500–3 Henry lost his wife, two of his three sons and several of his closest ministers. The king's reaction was to tighten his grip on the political nation to an uncomfortable degree. Many peers, bishops and leading gentry were heavily fined, often for technical offences, or required to enter into financial bonds guaranteeing their loyalty. Even those closest to the king were not immune. The fiscal aspects of this policy will be examined further in chapter 3, but it clearly also had a strong political side. As Edmund Dudley, one of its chief executants, wrote after Henry's death, 'the kinges grace whose soul god pardon was much sett to haue many persons in his danger at his pleasure'. Thus most of the bonds were to be paid off in small instalments, if at all, while the king was pleased with the person in question; if he became displeased, the sword of Damocles might drop.[51]

Such bonds had been used in the past to secure political loyalty, most widely perhaps by Richard III after the risings of 1483, but never so systematically. Henry had taken to them from the earliest years of his reign, and in part his reliance on them sprang from his determination to control his greater subjects rather than remove them by execution and start again with newly promoted peers, as Edward IV and Henry VIII tended to do. Thus the obverse of his policy was the decrease in numbers of the peerage during his reign, largely by natural wastage, from 55 to 42. Henry seems to have been particularly anxious about the loyalty of young members of the higher nobility whom he had not seen tested in the political furnace of the 1480s. His dealings with the duke of Buckingham and the earl of Northumberland, who both came of age in 1499 after lengthy minorities, and with the second earl of Derby, who succeeded his grandfather in 1504, seemed deliberately contrived to limit their power until they convinced him of their trustworthiness. Conversely, some of those he trusted most, such as his uncle Jasper, duke of Bedford, were notable for their lack of any heir to whom they might aspire to pass on their influence. Henry's was not an anti-noble policy *per se*; he just took comfort, and perhaps by the end a paranoid delight, from having a hold over people, whether noblemen, churchmen, or his own closest servants. It was a deeply symbolic moment when Henry took Sir Richard Empson's petition for the grant of a stewardship on the crown estates, and altered it from a grant for life to a grant during the king's pleasure.[52]

The young Henry VIII took a more relaxed attitude in matters of patronage, at times perhaps too relaxed, though given the public reaction against his father's policies he probably erred on the right side. It would have been impossibly hard for an inexperienced seventeen-year-old to conduct the sort of policy that even his grizzled survivor of a father found stirred deep resentments. The new king also cancelled many of the bonds taken by his father, and suspended payment on others, despite which those colleagues of Empson and Dudley who survived their fall made sure that bonds which represented genuine debts to the crown for defensible causes remained to be revived under Wolsey. Indebtedness to the crown soon revived as a political weapon, moreover. Henry and Wolsey used it as a leash on the dangerous francophilia of the duke of Suffolk in the 1510s. It was still an element in the crown's armoury under Mary, when those under suspicion of disloyalty were bound in large sums, offenders were squeezed hard to repay their debts, and those who served well were pardoned theirs. When Henry VIII took England through a crisis parallel to that of his father's later years in the 1530s, however, he resorted to blunter tactics. Monastic wealth and political forfeitures made the equation of loyalty with reward more blatant than ever, but at the same time the degree of coercion, organised by Cromwell but backed by the increasingly intimidating figure of the king, intensified. Traitors were attainted without previous trial from 1534, and one act in 1539, headed by Henry's cousins the marquess of Exeter and Lord Montagu, condemned more than a third of the sixteenth century's total of victims of attainder at one go. Only three of Henry's attainders were reversed in his lifetime.[53]

Henry's combination of largesse and wrath had predictable effects on the peerage. Its numbers revived until there were 51 peers at his death. Even so, he was then talking of the need for further elevations to replenish a 'greatly decayed' nobility, a wish his successors fulfilled to raise the rollcall to 57 peers by 1558. But the rate of political turnover also increased. Of the peers of 1558, 23 per cent were first-generation noblemen and a further 23 per cent second-generation. These newcomers replaced not only the victims of biological extinction – 16 per cent of the old peerage families in Henry's reign and 26 per cent of his own creations – but also those who fell under attainder, 17 per cent of the old houses and 15 per cent of the new. By previous standards these total extinction rates for the 38 years of Henry's reign – 33 per cent of the old peers and 41 per cent of those newly created – were by no means unprecedented. The average over the period 1300–1500 was for about one in four peerage families to die out in the direct male line every 25 years, and in 1400–25 the rate peaked at 35 per cent. What was new was the role of the axe. Even in 1450–1500, twice as many noble families died out naturally as by political violence. Also new was the low origin of some of those called upon to replenish the ranks of the peerage. Under most later medieval monarchs, knightly household administrators such as John Russell and William Paulet might have become barons, and royal relatives by marriage such as Edward Seymour and William Parr might have expected earldoms. That was what Henry gave them, and it was only the special circumstances of Edward's reign that enabled them to advance themselves higher. The heirs of men like Bray and his successor at the Duchy, Sir John Mordaunt, might likewise have entered the peerage in the past, though not often in the first generation after the founder. But Cromwell and Paget were another matter, as bitter contemporary references to them as a shearman and a catchpole, and Paget's degradation from the Order of the Garter in 1552, well reflect. Like the courtiers and administrators making their way in county society, the men who helped to refashion English government were themselves part of that government's refashioning of England's ruling elite.[54]

Towns and Cities

Thus far we have considered England's political structure in terms of noblemen, gentlemen, and the institutions of county government. But a substantial proportion of the population – maybe one in five – lived in partial insulation from that world. They were the citizens of chartered boroughs, of which there were 609 in 1500. These all enjoyed some degree of self-government. The most privileged hundred or so were, or became by the mid-Tudor period, largely independent of county administration. Indeed by 1461 ten of them – London, Bristol, York, Newcastle, Norwich, Lincoln, Coventry, Hull, Nottingham and Southampton – were counties in their own right, while Chester and Exeter joined this select band in 1506 and 1537. The major aspect of this independence was jurisdictional, and was deployed in economic and social regulation; we shall examine it further in chapter 2. But towns also aspired to a measure of political

independence, and several had tried to manoeuvre between magnates competing for local dominance in the fifteenth century. Such
detachment was hard to sustain for a number of reasons. At the
national level, towns needed help from those about the king, to
secure confirmation of their privileges and financial assistance in an
era of queasiness for most urban economies. And at the local level,
their attractiveness as social centres and reservoirs of military man-
power made them targets for noblemen eager to bind together
affinities of gentry and assure themselves of armed strength.[55]

Towns thus walked a tightrope, and continued to do so under the
Tudors. They spent large sums each year on presents and entertain-
ment for noblemen, gentry, lawyers and friends at court. But they
resisted as best they could those same patrons' interference with
their internal affairs, from Sir Thomas Burgh's attempt to rig the
mayoral elections at Grimsby in 1491, to the duke of Suffolk's efforts
to make one of his estate stewards a JP for Lincoln in 1545. Many
towns had repeatedly to forbid the retaining of their citizens by local
peers and gentlemen, and Worcester and York were still doing so in
the 1550s and 1570s respectively. Only in the question of parliamentary representation was compromise with outsiders the norm, at least
outside a handful of leading cities. The election of a well-connected
local gentleman or lawyer promised more adept defence of the
town's interests than an ingenuous alderman might manage.
Outsiders also commonly offered to serve without expenses. And the
nomination of at least one MP was frequently part of a borough's
relationship with a noble patron at court, increasingly often
dignified by the grant of the town's high stewardship. For the greatest peers of the sixteenth as of the fifteenth century, the ability to
nominate a clutch of burgesses was an important means of attracting
and retaining the service of ambitious followers, though ironically a
successful parliamentary performance might be yet another route
for the career-minded gentleman into the service of the crown.[56]

Royal power was harder still to keep at arm's length, especially
when expressed with the bluntness of a Henry VII. 'I most and woll
put in other rewlers that woll rewle and govern the Citie accordyng
to my lawez', he told the unfortunate mayor of York after rioting in
1494. Yet royal intervention in civic affairs was often turned to their
advantage by the richer citizens, who were tending to consolidate
themselves into tightly knit oligarchies in this period. In the older
royal boroughs, where urban government was conducted by a hierarchy of councils linked at the lower end to the craft guilds, power

tended to shift to the uppermost council, and access to that council tended to become more limited. A riotous response from the humbler citizens to this decline in political participation, or the perceived misgovernment it brought, might produce temporary concessions. But in the longer run it confirmed the crown's preference for the orderliness of rule by oligarchy, and town charters issued by the early Tudors tended to institutionalise such arrangements. Bristol and Exeter, with their new 'close corporation' charters of 1499 and 1504, exemplified the trend. Such developments were also often underpinned by economic changes, as the distribution of wealth within towns polarised. In the extreme case of Coventry, one of the great provincial economic centres, the entire office-holding *cursus honorum* linking master-craftsmen to mayor crashed in Henry VIII's reign, as the city's manufactures declined and the population halved in fifty years.[57]

Meanwhile, in towns without complex constitutional arrangements, the leading citizens used their dominance of religious guilds or manorial courts to exercise a similar leadership. They, too, tended increasingly to seek incorporation by charter. They aimed thereby to define their powers more clearly to a number of ends. At a time of economic dislocation and change, it was useful to control as far as possible both the local economy and the local implementation of social policy. Some towns needed to equip themselves to establish legal possession of communal assets acquired at the Dissolution of the Monasteries or chantries. Most wished to defend themselves against county authorities, assertive landlords and rival urban centres. Thus a wave of incorporations of new boroughs began in the early 1540s, peaking at more than four a year in Mary's reign, and enshrining urban oligarchy far and wide.[58]

Like the gentry at county level, town oligarchs had thus ridden the back of royal interventionism to consolidate their own power. Yet town government still remained more participatory than that of the countryside, above all in London. There changes in the 1520s and 1530s drew perhaps three in four adult males by the mid-century into the responsive system of ward government and livery companies. This reflected both the social mobility available to townsmen lucky enough to survive urban death rates, and the checks and balances necessary to maintain social stability in England's only city of European stature, home to perhaps one in twenty of the national population by 1558 as its population nearly tripled over the sixteenth century. London was especially jealous of its autonomy. In

1527 the common council's committee on the commonweal asserted that the council's acts 'ar of noo lesse strength then actes of the high court of parliament having this high libertie and large prehemynence'. But the capital suffered the same sorts of external pressures as other towns. Its elite clashed with the crown over royal attempts to nominate courtiers to civic offices as early as the 1430s, and such tensions revived strongly in the 1520s. The most assertive regimes sought to dictate the identity of the mayor himself: Henry VII did so in the 1500s, and Cromwell three years running in the 1530s.[59]

London's economic importance as the country's leading port added a layer of complexity to its relationship with the crown. Loans from the corporation, from the livery companies and from individual merchants were invaluable at moments of crisis, and made the Londoners worth courting: they were a vital ingredient of Yorkist success in 1460–1. On the other hand, ambitious fiscal initiatives like those of Henry VII and Wolsey hit wealthy Londoners hard enough to generate bitter ill-will, expressed in the London chroniclers' denunciations of Empson and Dudley, and played upon by John Skelton's satires on Wolsey. Worst of all, Henry VII intervened disruptively in the city's internal politics, backing the tailors against other livery companies and confronting the entire corporation over the terms of its charter in a fashion reminiscent of his deposed predecessor Richard II. The result was detrimental to good order in the city, as the fears of disorder there on Henry's death and the rising frequency of prosecutions for lewd words spoken against the aldermen testify.[60]

One obvious route for London's elite to secure the city's interests in the face of such pressures was through parliament. Under Henry VII and Henry VIII, the court of aldermen prepared a legislative programme for every session and lobbied the great men of the realm with gifts of wine to secure their assistance in securing its passage; but remarkably little was achieved. As the century went on, London lobbying improved in effectiveness at least for certain interest groups within the city, but this was part of a much wider recognition of mutual interest by civic and royal government. The men who managed this more cooperative relationship were royal ministers with strong city contacts, Thomas Cromwell the Londoner first among them, and thereafter a run of mid-Tudor and Elizabethan privy councillors, from Paulet and Petre to Cecil, Bacon, Walsingham and Leicester. They worked by personal connection as much as institutional dialogue, and their efforts marked the increasing importance of the alliance between the London Merchant Adventurers and the crown in the management of civic government, crown finances, and the national economy. Between 1470 and 1550 the cloth export trade, over which the Merchant Adventurers held the monopoly among domestic merchants, boomed; London engrossed an ever larger share of the trade; and the Merchant Adventurers came to dominate London. Thus men like Thomas Gresham, the brilliant young son of a lord mayor who eased the financial agony of the mid-Tudor regimes by manipulating the London–Antwerp cloth trade and with it the pound's position on the foreign exchanges, gained an influence in government greater than that of any merchants since the great woolmongers and bankers of Edward III's day. The fact that Gresham and his ilk also ran the country's capital city, unlike Edward's merchants, ensured them a more lasting voice in the counsels of state.[61]

Ireland, Wales and the North

London, then, shared in its own way in many of the trends we have seen elsewhere in the impact of early Tudor government: sometimes disruptive royal interventionism, a renegotiation of relations between the crown and local elites, and a growing role for courtiers and councillors in the management of such relationships. How far can such developments be detected in the parts of the realm furthest from the centres of government and administration, Ireland, Wales, and the northernmost counties of England? Each of these presented rather different problems to effective governance from the centre. Unlike the others, Wales was not a military frontier zone and, partly for this reason, had no resident noble houses of established local weight. The Welsh gentry did not live in defensible tower-houses like those in Northumberland or in the English Pale in Ireland. The Welsh administrative and legal system was also far more complex and intractably divergent from the English norm than that in the Pale or the north. All, however, shared to some extent an isolation from the penetration of London merchants and court careerists which was tying together the rest of the realm, and a certain degree of divergence from metropolitan culture, acute of course among the Irish and Welsh speakers of Ireland and Wales.

Ireland never saw a Tudor monarch, Wales saw only Henry VII and that, after the march to Bosworth, just briefly and in the Marches. Even the northern capital York was graced by Henry VII only in his early years, to lay the spectre of its Ricardian loyalties, and by Henry VIII just once in 1541 in response to the Pilgrimage of Grace. By then he needed no reminding that Ireland and northern England led the way as centres of conspiracy and rebellion against the Tudor crown.[62]

Given all these special factors, the degree to which early Tudor monarchs tried to implement similar policies in these regions to those in play elsewhere is a tribute to their consistency of purpose, but also perhaps reflects their lack of sensitivity. In Ireland and on the northern borders, as elsewhere, Henry VII and Henry VIII were quite prepared to utilise noblemen equipped by their landed power to exercise oversight of local affairs. But they expected such men to act on the terms they dictated, and in the context of border societies their expectations were unrealistic. The salaries of the wardens of the Marches, which had enabled the Percy and Neville wardens of the past to retain large numbers of local gentry in their service, were cut by Henry VII to around a tenth of their traditional level, following on gentler reductions by Edward IV. This limited the choice of effective wardens to those with extensive landholdings, and hence political influence and military resources, in the border counties: the Dacres in the west, the Percies in the east. The difficulties it involved even for them were already evident in the early years of Henry's reign. The need to fund a suitable retinue from his own estates put an enormous strain on the finances of the fourth earl of Northumberland: by his death in 1489, 42 per cent of his income went on fees. Attempts to use other northern peers – such as Cumberland and Westmorland in 1525–7 – foundered on their lack of private means to control border society, including the troublesome followers of the Dacres and Percies. Yet it was precisely the links between the Dacres and Percies and the thieving clans and violent gentry of the border uplands that made them disreputable in Tudor eyes.[63]

Like some historians, but probably wrongly, Henry VII and Henry VIII seem to have thought that the power of the northern peers was so great that only wilfulness prevented them from dictating the standards of the star chamber to their clients. In fact the Percies had been a highly fluctuating force since their heyday in the late fourteenth century, and the Dacres had joined the ranks of the leading northern magnates only with their acquisition of the Greystoke inheritance between 1487 and 1508. Neither could give absolute orders on the basis of ancient loyalty to the gentlemen of their followings, whose disposition to violence proved a blessing rather than a curse whenever the Scots attacked. The upland clans of Tynedale and Redesdale, who lived by raiding on both sides of the border, presented the same problem in still more extreme form. Henry VIII was at his most unrealistically optimistic when he insisted in 1537 that 'We do rather desire their reformation than their utter destruction'.[64]

Thus the border peers were caught in a vice. The third Lord Dacre of the North was fined £1000 in star chamber in 1525 for his tolerance of disorder. The fifth earl of Northumberland, though he readily adopted the cultural pose of the loyal courtier, still found himself harried by Henry VII and Wolsey over infractions of the king's feudal rights, violence in private quarrels, and contempt for conciliar justice. His son, raised in Wolsey's household, was in better odour with Henry VIII and did win office on the borders, at more reasonable financial terms, including the chance to name 69 local men who should be feed by the king to support him. But he was handicapped by recurrent ill-health and steadily deteriorating relations with his brothers. These led him to delegate military leadership to the young gentlemen of his household and his Clifford relatives by marriage, to whom he alienated the lands and offices necessary for such responsibilities. Eventually, as his early death drew on, he despairingly bequeathed all his estates to the king. Meanwhile the Dacres nearly suffered an equally spectacular downfall, as the fourth lord was tried for treason in 1534 on the accusation that he had struck deals with Scottish borderers during the brief war of 1532–4. He was acquitted, but fined heavily and dismissed from office.[65]

Similar allegations of cross-border contacts were regularly made against the Fitzgerald earls of Kildare, whose effectiveness as governors of Ireland relied partly on their murky dabbling in Gaelic politics. Here too there was unwillingness at court to make much allowance for the realities of border life. In the years 1470–1534, the Fitzgeralds were repeatedly appointed as governors, removed for misgovernance or political disloyalty, and then reappointed, often when the local followers through whom they ruled refused to cooperate with any alternative regime. Only when they overstepped the mark totally in the revolt of 1534 did Henry VIII turn to direct rule by an English governor with a subsidised garrison. This expedient had been found wanting when tried before, in 1492–6, 1520–2 and

1530–2. By the end of Henry's reign it was turning Ireland into the financially burdensome realm of military government and private-enterprise colonialism all too familiar from the reigns of Elizabeth and the early Stuarts.[66]

In the north too, recurrent restorations of the great families to border office ended for good only with the outright rebellion of 1569. The Dacres guarded the west March again from 1549 to 1563; the Percies were restored to the earldom of Northumberland and to the eastern wardenship in 1557, as war with Scotland loomed. The earl of Westmorland, the predominant lay magnate in County Durham, enjoyed considerable authority in the north under successive mid-Tudor regimes. But the incessant reversals in the local balance of power generated by the cyclical rise and fall of Dacres, Percies, Cliffords and Nevilles made a self-fulfilling prophecy of the Tudor suspicion that the magnates promoted disorder. As in the fifteenth century, uncertainty over where local power was meant to reside tempted the peers and their followers to settle their quarrels by force. Feuding between the Dacre and Clifford affinities marked the 1520s and 1530s; in the 1530s the Cliffords fell out with the crown's steward of Kendal; and from the 1530s to the 1550s Dacres and Cliffords alike ruffled with the newly prominent Whartons and their rising gentry allies. For in the north, unlike Ireland, a viable local alternative to the rule of the great magnates was on offer. It was probably no better a solution to the problems of the border – only a steady peace with the Scots would ease those – but in the eyes of the Tudors it was certainly no worse.[67]

The new style of royal management was introduced steadily, though with many variations in detail, over the 80 years following the accession of Richard III. It operated in parallel with, rather than in direct opposition to, the continuing use of the great regional families; yet it could not help but alter their position. As elsewhere, the new royal estates in the region and the proliferation of court office were used to tie local gentry to the crown's service and equip them to serve the king in collusion with the increasingly interventionist royal council. Many had been Percy, Clifford or Dacre followers, or came from families with traditions of service to those houses. Their involvement with the king, at least in the case of the Percy retainers, sprang naturally from the crown's administration of the Percy estates in successive generations, while the fifth earl was a minor (1489–1500) and after the sixth earl's death (1537–57). It did not necessarily signal hostility to their old masters – although it did in the case of Sir John Forster, the bitter opponent of Percy influence who came to dominate early Elizabethan Northumberland – but a certain detachment was inevitable. Henry VII, perhaps overambitious here as elsewhere, even intruded a number of courtiers from outside the region into northern office, but at this level the future lay with local men.[68]

Sir Thomas Wharton was the archetype. Of modest Westmorland gentry stock, he started out in Percy service in the 1520s, becoming one of the sixth earl's trusted lieutenants and starting to serve the crown directly. By 1537 he was deputy warden of the west March and held many of the crown stewardships and farms usually granted to sustain the warden himself. By 1544 he was warden, and made Lord Wharton to match. At his peak he was in receipt of more than £600 in fees from the crown, and in the course of his career he raised his landed income from about £100 to more than £750 a year. His appointment to the wardenship, like that of the equally parvenu Lord Eure in the east, was in practice *faute de mieux*, echoing experiments of Henry VII's in 1500–6. The fact was that no nobleman whom Henry VIII was prepared to trust would accept the post on the terms offered. Wharton's promotion also raised predictable problems, protracted and disorderly quarrels with the Dacres and Cliffords, and a loss of military cohesion among the border gentry. They saw no more reason to obey Wharton or Eure, for all their proven toughness, than they had to obey Cumberland or Westmorland in the 1520s. The rise of men like Wharton, then, was no easy answer to the problems of northern government, and as we have seen, the result was a series of fluctuations in policy. But the Elizabethan north was placed firmly in the hands of the new elite.[69]

One reason for this was their ready collaboration in two other aspects of Tudor policy for the north. These were the use of militarily able noblemen without local interests as royal lieutenants in the region, and the elaboration of the king's council in the north. Both began under Richard III and the president of his northern council, John, earl of Lincoln. They recurred patchily under Henry VII, notably in the successful spell by Thomas Howard, earl of Surrey, as king's lieutenant and deputy warden of the east and middle Marches from 1489 to 1500, and in Archbishop Savage's presidency of the 'Council of the King at York' from 1502 to 1507. Richard Fox as bishop of Durham (1494–1501) played a similar role in injecting the priorities of the court directly into northern life. Under Henry VIII and his successors, southern peers came and went with military emergencies, though it is an interesting commentary on the remaining potential for noble power in northern government that several felt like staying. Norfolk angled for the Percy lands after the Pilgrimage of Grace, and John Dudley helped himself to them, to the Northumberland title, and to a range of offices on the crown lands stripped from the see of Durham. Even some of the more transient peers built up links with the new gentry elite that enabled them to cooperate effectively in the king's service.[70]

It was the council in the north that became a permanent fixture. Its title and precise remit, in particular its control over the Marches, were tinkered with repeatedly between its re-establishment by Wolsey in 1525 and its consolidation under Elizabeth. This was primarily a judicial body, as we shall see in chapter 2. But it soon ranged widely over more general problems of administration and local politics, from the control of the border reivers to relations between landlords and tenants. And its individual personnel were as important as its institutional activity. They were led by a bishop or a peer (almost always drawn from the Midlands or south), and they sometimes included trusted local noblemen. But overwhelmingly they consisted of local gentlemen, common lawyers and clerics trained in the civil law. Some of these gave royal government in the north an invaluable continuity: Thomas Magnus, archdeacon of the East Riding, served on Henry VII's northern council before and after Savage's death, and survived to sit on the reconstructed council from 1525 to 1550. Sir Thomas Gargrave, the Wakefield lawyer who ended as vice-president of the council, survived almost as long in the next generation, from 1545 to 1579. From 1525 the councillors were also added to the commissions of the peace in the northern counties, strengthening their role in the detailed work of local government. And many of them were the same gentlemen who were rising to wealth and power in the crown's military and political service on the borders. Wharton joined the council in 1545; four of his fellow-councillors, Gargrave among them, led the mourners at his funeral in 1568.[71]

Contemporaries explicitly likened the northern council to the older established body in Wales and the English border counties. This began life in 1473 as the council of Edward IV's son the prince of Wales. Its aim, besides overseeing the prince's (or the king's) estates in the region, was deceptively simple: as defined in 1525, to keep Wales and the borders in 'pristine and sound good estate and order'.[72] But the obstacles in its way were formidable. First was the sheer administrative complexity of the Marches, a legacy of the piecemeal conquest of Wales. Each of the 45 or so marcher lordships had its own judicial and financial structure and officers. Many had passed into the crown's hands by Edward IV's reign, but others were held by his greatest noble subjects, absentees more eager to profit from their jurisdictions than to see justice done. Royal and noble lordships alike were all too often run by tyrannous local officials bent on quick profit, while felons moved with ease across the patchwork of jurisdictions to escape what justice there was. Moreover, the Marches' disorder tended to spill across into the English border counties from Gloucestershire to Cheshire. The shires of the principality of Wales, in the south-west and north-west, were superficially arranged more like English counties. But they were dominated by a handful of office-holders appointed for life. When held by families with the local landed power and social influence to exploit them effectively – the Gruffudds of Penrhyn are a classic instance – these posts offered even more opportunities for corruption and empire-building than those in the marcher lordships.

Five options thus presented themselves to the crown. Marches and principality alike might be left as they were, but regulated by the council's oversight. Secondly, as in the north, that oversight might be intensified by the appointment of the councillors as JPs in the border counties and officers in the crown's marcher lordships and in the shires of the principality. Thirdly, great men trusted by the king, with or without any natural base in Welsh politics, with or without any role in the council, might be given assemblages of offices in the principality and Marches and trusted to rule well. Fourthly, the remaining proprietors of private lordships might be bound in indentures for the Marches, undertakings to punish malefactors, cooperate in extraditions, and discipline wayward officials. Or, fifthly and most radically, Wales might be shired, entrusting the Welsh gentry with office as annual sheriffs, JPs and commissioners, like their English counterparts.

For the first 60 years of the council's existence, the first four options were blended in varying degree. The council operated almost continuously, although its powers were repeatedly refurbished, notably by Wolsey in 1525. As early as 1476 these were extended to cover the four English border counties. Indentures for the Marches were negotiated by Edward IV and renewed by Henry VII and Henry VIII, but proved hard to enforce and liable to fade. Great men came and went. Some were fleeting or ineffectual like

Buckingham under Richard III, or Suffolk under Henry VIII. Others were rather more effective such as Jasper Tudor, duke of Bedford, Sir William Stanley, Sir Rhys ap Thomas, and Charles Somerset, Lord Herbert under Henry VII. But those without a landed base in the area tended to rely on, and thus entrench the power of, local families like the Gruffudds of Penrhyn; those with a landed base in the area tended in the second or third generation to become rather a hindrance than a help to the implementation of the royal will; and those with major responsibilities elsewhere tended to neglect Wales. The council intervened periodically to restrain the more outrageous activities of men like Sir William Gruffudd or the deputies of Henry Somerset, earl of Worcester, but it was hard to replace them satisfactorily. Attempts to do so could provoke dangerous feuding like that between the Cliffords and Dacres. Councillors were periodically injected into local administration, notably by Edward IV, Henry VII, and Wolsey, but often lacked the confidence of local society, perhaps because they were usually under instruction to increase the king's revenues from Wales. Meanwhile efforts to centralise power over Welsh appointments in the king's hands brought only the advent of unscrupulous courtiers such as William Brereton.[73]

By the early 1530s the 'estate and order' of Wales and the border counties seemed to be deteriorating rather than becoming more 'pristine and sound'. Thomas Cromwell's first response was to secure the advancement of his close friend from Wolsey's service, the civil lawyer from Northumberland Rowland Lee, as bishop of Coventry and Lichfield, and president of the council. Lee, who led the council from 1534 to 1543, soon earned a reputation as a tirelessly itinerant hanging judge. He was assisted by statutory modifications to the judicial system in the marcher lordships in the year of his appointment, but already the pressure for more radical institutional change was gaining ground. Cromwell showed his usual talent for turning other peoples' ideas into acts of parliament. By a rather ill-coordinated series of statutes from 1536 to 1543, Wales was divided into thirteen shires, administered more or less on the English model. Lee disapproved of shiring, because he thought the Welsh gentry were too poor to be effective and independent-minded JPs, but he was unduly pessimistic. He and his successors in the council found it easier to supervise JPs and sheriffs than they had done the old officers, and the reforms harnessed a wider range of Welsh landowners to the work of government, making them to some extent self-regulating. Although the council in the Marches continued to play a useful coordinating role under Elizabeth and the early Stuarts, the development of Welsh government was thus set firmly, albeit belatedly, in the English pattern.[74]

The System under Strain

The forging of early Tudor government was a product of lengthy political crisis, initiated by the breakdown of Henry VI's reign and prolonged by the insecurities of those that followed. The greatest tests of the system were two further crises, one general, one specific. The range of problems encountered by the mid-Tudor regimes – demographic, economic, dynastic, diplomatic, political, and religious – made the years from the 1540s to the 1560s a comprehensive and sustained challenge to the Tudor state, which by and large it survived remarkably well. English kings had been as much troubled as Spanish, German and French rulers by rebellion and civil war in the fifteenth century, but Elizabethan England stood alone among its immediate neighbours – Scotland, France and the Netherlands – in avoiding full-scale religious civil war in the sixteenth.

More susceptible to detailed analysis for our purposes, however, was the crisis of the 1530s, induced by Henry VIII's divorce and Reformation. The enormity of the undertaking becomes ever more startling as the vitality of the later medieval English church is revealed. Henry disposed of a popular queen, destroyed flourishing religious practices, dissolved hundreds of familiar, sometimes even respected, monasteries, and executed those who got in the way, including two intellectuals famous around Europe and a number of his own leading noblemen and courtiers. In the process he survived the largest rebellion since 1381 and the worst invasion scare since 1386, without meeting the fate of Richard II, whose reign saw those twin upheavals.

Henry's success rested upon the mechanisms we have examined. The Dissolution itself offered not just a further wave in the expansion and exploitation of the royal demesne, but also wider opportunities. New regional hegemonies in troublesome areas could be endowed for men like Suffolk and Russell, and the dispersal of the monastic windfalls offered sufficient benefits to peers, gentry and urban governors to overcome whatever scruples they may have entertained. Royal administrators were reinforced on the Dissolution commissions by local gentlemen, often those with legal training, and the same was true – with increasingly careful selection of the ideologically committed – for the commissions to implement royal injunctions, dissolve the chantries, and sequestrate church goods under Edward. Thus the prospect of advancement for the able and ambitious was tied to cooperation in the enforcement of ever more radical policy. On the broader plane, all those with a stake in government were expected to monitor the country's obedience to royal commands, as JPs, sheriffs, bishops and peers were regularly instructed by circular letters. They did so with some enthusiasm, and Cromwell was showered with reports of the progress of reform or the activities of its opponents. These he investigated with considerable care, reproducing and surpassing both the thoroughness of Henry VII's watch on dynastic conspiracy and the unsettling penetration of his fiscal investigations. At times in the 1530s JPs were assembled *en masse* at Westminster to be briefed on policy, an innovation of Wolsey's. The regional councils too were called into play: in 1538 the council in the north was specially charged with supervising religious change, and in 1539 a short-lived council in the west was created to oversee the south-western counties.

When more general danger threatened, older mechanisms came into their own. Noblemen from Henry's trusted inner ring – Norfolk, Suffolk, Shrewsbury, Exeter, Rutland – raised and led the troops that confronted the rebels of 1536, and were duly rewarded. Grand musters were held in 1539 to prepare the militia to face invasion, and once again these loyal peers were to the fore, with the exception of Exeter, who had been tried and executed in 1538 and subsequently attainted, a warning to those tempted to waver in their commitment to the king and his policies. Meanwhile they took their place alongside the bishops and the bureaucrats on the increasingly dominant and well-defined privy council, shaping the policies whose local outworking they themselves oversaw. Many other factors contributed to Henry's survival in this self-induced crisis, and we shall examine some of them in subsequent chapters. But the greatest key to the implementation of the royal will in the 1530s was the exploitation of the various means to direct local politics refined over the previous 70 years.[75]

2

JUSTICE

The proper execution of justice was one of the most fundamental duties of kingship, ranking with the defence of the realm and the protection of the church. Every monarch was warned when taking the coronation oath: 'You shall make to be done after your strength and power, equal and rightful justice in all your dooms and judgements and discretion, with mercy and truth.' The dictates of the king's conscience were reinforced by the example of great rulers of the past celebrated for their wisdom in doing justice and making good laws, from Moses, Solomon and Justinian to St Louis and Henry V. And the need for justice was urged yet more sharply by the demands of practical politics. In a lecture to the lawyers of Gray's Inn in 1519, John Spelman the future judge argued the point from ancient history. 'The body politic of this realm of England ... is only preserved by justice', he maintained, 'for wherever justice is not well administered, there is decay of princes. For it well appears in divers chronicles that the Romans, for so long as they did justice, had dominion over the whole world.' Spelman did not need to cite the complementary example which gave special inspiration to the Tudors' concern for effective justice. Less than 60 years before he spoke, Henry VI had been deposed after three decades of royal incompetence and favouritism had crippled the judicial system, left the law (as the chronicler John Hardyng put it) as elastic as 'a Walshmannes hose', broken public confidence in the king and spawned feuds which fed into open civil war.[1]

As justice was necessary to political control, so political control was necessary to justice. Tudor rulers could and did legislate to improve the law, and create or reform institutions to apply the law more effectively. But, as contemporaries realised, such efforts could achieve little without reliable agents to put the laws into effect, and a consensus among the political nation in favour of cooperation with the king's justice. 'What avaylethe it', asked one chief justice in 1521, 'to have dume and deade lawes wretin or printed in our bookes unlest there were lyvely ministers to execute the same?' 'The law will never be properly enforced', opined another in 1485, 'until all the peers, both spiritual and temporal are in agreement, for the love and dread that they have of God or the king, or both, to execute it effectively. Then ... everyone else will obey readily, and if they will not they will be punished, and then everyone will take warning from them.'[2]

Such statements, of course, contain certain assumptions about the nature of justice which might not have been shared by fifteenth-century noblemen or the communities in which they presided over a form of justice more determined by the realities of social power. Yet the judicial viewpoint fitted the history of the previous three and a half centuries, during which royal jurisdiction had steadily made inroads on successive areas of local society. On the other hand, we must beware of analysing the judicial functions of government in terms of simple polarities: good strong kings imposing justice on bad over-mighty subjects, or pure and efficient new courts sweeping aside the paralysis, chicanery and corruption of the old. The provision of justice had to be a cooperative enterprise between the king, the nobles, the gentry, the legal profession, and the villagers and townsmen who sat on juries, and one to which each of those groups made a distinctive contribution. All too often kings themselves did not promote disinterested justice, either for reasons of political convenience, or because they saw the law as a device to make money.

Further difficulties confront us in evaluating the success of the early Tudors in the provision of justice. The records of many minor, and some major, courts of law are completely lost, while those of a few survive in intractably vast bulk – four rolls a year for the court of common pleas, each two and a half feet long, nearly a foot wide and several hundred membranes thick. Usually the records give no indication which actions were legal fictions, which were settled out of court and which merely abandoned, and there is no way of knowing how many disputes and crimes were never brought to court at all. Clearly, successful perversion of the legal process leaves no trace in the records, and what evidence there is of such perversion normally survives only in the form of unverifiable complaints from those who had lost a lawsuit and wanted to reverse the result. From the point of view of the contemporary litigant, each court was merely one element in a complex system of alternative or complementary routes to redress, but it is now very difficult to reconstruct that system in its entirety and thus to place each court and each case in its proper context. But we must try.

The Judicial System

Five main types of courts constituted the early Tudor judicial system. Firstly church courts, administering their own English variant of the canon law of the catholic church, dealt with matters of ecclesiastical administration and clerical discipline, but also (and in greater volume) with the regulation of marriage and wills and the punishment of such varied moral offences as adultery, prostitution, slander, and breach of promise; the last enabled them to hear cases of debt produced by unfulfilled contracts. Secondly a wide range of local courts formulated and enforced by-laws about the use of common land, drainage arrangements and so on, implemented the medieval trading standards legislation concerning bakers and brewers, and heard many minor cases of assault or debt. Manor courts regulated landholding and exerted the lord's rights over his bondmen and other tenants, while borough courts were often given by the town's charter jurisdiction over cases which would otherwise have been heard in the king's courts. Many boroughs and other licensed markets also had special 'piepowder' courts to deal out rapid justice between merchants and their customers on market days. Other non-royal courts exercised a civil jurisdiction – that is, one in suits between parties as opposed to criminal prosecutions – wider than that of a single manor or borough, but the level of activity in these honour courts, soke courts and private hundred courts varied enormously and was often minimal.

Thirdly, the king's courts at county level combined older and newer systems. The sheriff's tourn and the county court survived from the days when the sheriff was the chief royal agent in the county, and in some places the county court still heard a fair number of civil suits. But the main focus of the county system was now the combination of assizes and quarter sessions. Twice a year the assizes, presided over by judges from the central courts and other senior Westminster lawyers, heard serious criminal cases and put civil cases from the central courts to the verdict of local juries. Four times a year the justices of the peace dealt with lesser criminal cases, and increasingly with local administration, at the quarter sessions. These royal courts sitting in the counties might be supplemented by special judicial commissions, such as those sent out to try traitors in the wake of a rebellion.

The fourth group of courts stood at the apex of the king's common law system and sat at Westminster, mostly jammed together in Westminster Hall. The king's bench exercised superior criminal jurisdiction, hearing cases on appeal from lesser courts or those sent up because they were unusually difficult or sensitive, and was able to hear a wide range of civil cases mostly based on the action of trespass, which implied some sort of personal damage done by the defendant to the plaintiff. The common pleas did more civil business, especially in debt and land conveyancing, though there were areas of competition between the two courts. The exchequer was still a fairly specialised court whose relatively small litigation grew out of the collection of the king's revenues. Parliament was still referred to as a court, but no longer functioned as one in the normal sense of the word. Fifthly, it is convenient but, as we shall see, rather misleading to separate off from these the other central courts, the chancery, the council and its offshoots (star chamber, requests and the council learned), the admiralty court for matters maritime, and the administrative courts of duchy chamber, general surveyors, augmentations, wards and liveries, and first fruits and tenths. These tribunals all applied in civil cases the same law as the common law courts, but proceeded according to equity, seeking a solution that was just in conscience even if the technical rules of the common law courts would not have allowed them to reach it. This approach freed the equity courts to recognise social realities, and they often sought a fair compromise between the interests of two parties, rather than one which fulfilled the rigid (and sometimes manifestly unfair and unrealistic) requirements of the common law. The regional councils in the Marches and the north exercised their jurisdiction over civil pleas in the same way, but also had, like star chamber, a criminal competence.

We might add to these five groups all manner of more specialised courts, from the court of chivalry which ruled on matters heraldic, and the court of claims which resolved the inherited claims of various individuals and corporations to perform particular ritual acts at each coronation service, to the private admiralty courts which dealt with rights of wreck and claims to the ownership of washed-up whales, dolphins and sturgeon along particular strips of the coast; but it is safe to assume that the vast majority of civil suits and criminal prosecutions in early Tudor England were shared between these five groups of jurisdictions. Regional variations, such as the jurisdiction of the palatine courts in Cheshire, Durham and Lancashire, were less significant than they might seem, since in practice their procedures imitated those of the system centred at Westminster.

Some idea of the volume of civil business in different courts can be gained from the figures in Table 2.1. These must be treated with care as they have been worked out by different historians using widely varying methods. None the less, three major shifts in the pattern of litigation between 1485 and 1558 are evident: decline and recovery in the king's bench and common pleas; a boom followed by a levelling-off in the chancery and the conciliar courts; and a collapse in the church courts. A fourth change, harder to document systematically but equally evident from the records, was a general movement of business from local manor or borough courts into the king's courts at the centre, part of a long-term process but moving with some acceleration in these years. Short-term fluctuations in the level of activity of any court were often attributable to specific factors such as the disruption caused by plague outbreaks or rebellions (and some such freak years have been ironed out of the figures in Table 2.1), or broader influences such as recession in the economy at large, but the long-term shifts need explaining. Unfortunately it is often hard to decide how far they resulted from government initiative, how far from the self-interested promotion of a court by the lawyers and administrators who ran it and whose fees depended on the level of business it could command, and how far from the tactical choices made by countless litigants and their legal counsel in search of the best way to win their lawsuits.

The Equity Courts: Chancery

The way these forces combined can be seen most clearly in the rise of the equity courts. Chancery led the way, as its business grew strongly under the Lancastrians, boomed under the Yorkists and Henry VII, and expanded further under Henry VIII. The chancellors themselves were partly responsible for this, as a run of bishops highly

Table 2.1 Trends in Civil Litigation
(Average number of cases per year in all or a significant part of each period except where specified otherwise)

	Henry VII	Wolsey	Later Henry VIII	Mary/early Elizabeth
King's bench (procedural steps, five-year running means)[a]	499 (1503–4)	393 (1526–7)	321 (1539–40)	778 (1556–7)
King's bench (fee index, 1448–9 = 100)[a]	64 (1503–4)	62 (1526–7)	36 (1539–40)	355 (1556–7)
Common pleas (cases in advanced stages)[b]	1600			3200
Common pleas (fee index, 1448–9 = 100)[a]	60 (1503–4)	21 (1526–7)	51 (1539–40)	108 (1557–8)
Chancery (petitions)[c]	571	770	1243	1300
Council attendant (registers)[d]	< 125			
Council in star chamber (proceedings)[e]	>12	120	150	147
Court of requests (registers)[f]		86	137	
London commissary court[g]	> 1000	< 400	93	
Canterbury consistory court[h]	693 (1486)	93 (1535)		

[a] E. W. Ives, *The Common Lawyers of Pre-Reformation England. Thomas Kebell: a case study* (Cambridge, 1983), pp. 202–5.
[b] C. W. Brooks, *Pettyfoggers and Vipers of the Commonwealth: the 'Lower Branch' of the Legal Profession in Early Modern England* (Cambridge, 1986), p. 51.
[c] N. Pronay, 'The chancellor, the chancery, and the council at the end of the fifteenth century', in *British Government and Administration: Studies presented to S. B. Chrimes*, ed. H. Hearder and H. R. Loyn (Cardiff, 1974), pp. 88–9; Brooks, *Pettyfoggers*, p. 54.
[d] *Select Cases in the Council of Henry VII*, ed. C. G. Bayne and W. H. Dunham (Selden Society 75, 1956), pp. lxxiii–iv.
[e] J. A. Guy, *The Court of Star Chamber and its Records to the Reign of Elizabeth I* (Public Record Office handbooks 21, 1985), p. 9.
[f] J. A. Guy, 'Privy Council: revolution or evolution', in *Revolution Reassessed: Revisions in the History of Tudor Government and Administration*, ed. C. Coleman and D. R. Starkey (Oxford, 1986), p. 83.
[g] R. M. Wunderli, *London Church Courts on the Eve of the Reformation* (Cambridge, Mass., 1981), p. 22.
[h] B. L. Woodcock, *Medieval Ecclesiastical Courts in the Diocese of Canterbury* (Oxford, 1952), p. 125.

trained in the civil law which inspired much of the practice of the equity courts, culminating in John Morton (1486–1500) and William Warham (1502–15), were followed by the less academic but vastly energetic Wolsey (1515–29), the hard-working common lawyers Thomas More (1529–32) and Thomas Audley (1532–44), and the gifted lay civil lawyer Thomas Wriothesley (1544–7). These men facilitated the growth of their court by personal attention to judicial work and reforms in organisation and procedure. The stagnation of chancery in the mid-Tudor years can be partly blamed on their successors, men such as the 'aimless and indecisive' Archbishop Heath (1556–8). Only when Sir Nicholas Bacon streamlined chancery's business in the 1560s did major growth recommence.[3]

Litigants were attracted to chancery for a number of reasons. The fact that the chancellor was one of the king's leading ministers in itself gave the court an aura of authority and full access to the power of central government in enforcing its decisions. One began a case not by fitting one's problem awkwardly to the most appropriate of a limited range of Latin formulae, as in the common law with its fixed forms of action, but by stating one's grievance to the chancellor in all its particularities in a bill in English. The mechanism used by the chancellor to make one's opponent appear to answer the case, the subpoena writ, which told him that he would owe the king £100 or a similar sum if he did not appear, was considerably more effective than the slow escalation of pressure – more bark than bite – which the sheriff was supposed to exert to ensure appearance in the common law courts. In chancery, expert judges led by the chancellor himself – More personally took part in nearly half the suits passing through the court – tried to reach a fair decision based on the evidence of witnesses and documents, often emerging with a compromise solution. In the common law courts, the justices refereed a verbal wrestling-match between the parties' lawyers over the form in which a question of fact could be put to a jury to produce a winner-take-all verdict. Chancery could enforce observance of contracts and of the use, the landholding arrangement devised to avoid feudal dues and to enable land to be bequeathed by will, neither of which was fully recognised by the common law. These two classes of business (though in what proportion remains controversial) helped to make its fortune. Lastly, chancery could revise the decisions of lesser courts, and this brought it an influx of business from litigants disappointed elsewhere. Thus 90 per cent of its commercial contract cases under Wolsey came on appeal from inferior jurisdictions, often from borough courts, though many of these appellants met only further disappointment in chancery, 85 per cent of appeals from London's courts, for example, being turned down by the cardinal.[4]

Its flexibility, speed and power made chancery popular: too popular for its own good. Technically it could not decide who owned land, as that was a matter for the common law. But it could decide if someone was unjustly holding on to the deeds which were the evidence of landownership, and thus preventing a trial of the rights to the property in the common law courts, which required the deeds to prove ownership. As early as the 1470s lawyers latched onto this action as one way to bring their clients' land disputes into chancery. Detinue of deeds was becoming a formula to fit the court's way of doing things as much as any form of action in king's bench or common pleas. Together with the use and other devices, it flooded chancery with litigation about landownership, until under Wolsey it constituted some 67 per cent of chancery's business, and under Edward VI some 87 per cent of enrolled decrees – chancery's most important judgments – concerned land. This clogged the court with business which should really have been settled elsewhere, and which frequently had to be sent back into the common law courts. In this it was only one symptom of the hardening of the arteries inevitable in a court gorged with litigants and exploited by legal counsel whose interests lay in evolving tactics to harness its powers to their clients' needs – or of course in devising tactics to obstruct the court if it seemed likely to find against their clients. Hence the need for constant reform by the chancellors, in what looks like a losing battle. By Elizabeth's reign the shock of the subpoena had faded and defendants frequently ignored it, and the average case took more than a year longer than the 20 months of Wolsey's chancellorship. Hence also broader changes in the court's approach: by the 1540s chancery was starting to administer a law based on precedents like that of the common law, a long way from the medieval vision maintained by Wolsey of a flexible tribunal correcting individual injustices according to the dictates of conscience.[5]

A force beyond the dynamism or otherwise of the chancellors and the state of the market in litigation contributed to these changes in chancery: the lobbying of the common lawyers. In the 1520s and 1530s some of them argued that the growth of equity – in particular as administered by Wolsey – was subverting the entire structure of English law. For that reason they were to some extent reassured by the choice of the common lawyers More and Audley as chancellors. One

can see why some feared a drastic shift in the balance of the legal
system when king's bench and common pleas were in recession
(though still handling far more suits in total than the equity courts),
lawsuits over land were flooding into the equity courts and Morton,
Warham and Wolsey were using chancery injunctions to interfere with
litigation in other courts and at times to reverse common law verdicts.

With hindsight it seems that there was never any danger of a complete replacement of English common law by Roman civil law, for a
number of reasons. Chancery equity was thought of by nearly all
those involved as a corrective to individual injustices in the common
law, not as a separate and alternative system. Thus, for instance, the
common law judges were often called in to advise the chancellor on
the land law when chancery considered cases over land, and
common lawyers were conspicuous among the commissioners
Wolsey appointed to deputise for him in chancery in 1529.
Moreover, there can have been no hard-and-fast enmity between
common lawyers and the equity courts when it was the leading
common law counsel who advised their clients to use the equity tribunals and pleaded their cases before them. When there were tensions in practice, chancellors and chief justices alike opted to calm
them down. Wolsey removed Dr John Stokesley, the future bishop of
London, from his post in the court of requests and had all his decisions reviewed following complaints that he was deploying his civil
law training to the detriment of the common law. Likewise king's
bench was reluctant to rule in many of the cases brought before it
between 1501 and 1533 in which plaintiffs alleged that their opponents were breaching Magna Carta or the statutes on due process by
suing them before the council courts.[6]

Chancery's role in remedying defects of justice in the common law
system was never likely to be entirely uncontroversial – no one likes
being told they are wrong – and there had been attempts to set limits
on the rise of chancery equity as long ago as the reigns of Richard II
and Henry IV. However, those who conjured the spectre of a
takeover by the civil lawyers often did so to political ends, as at
Wolsey's fall and in the coup against Wriothesley in 1547, when he
was charged with destabilising land titles, stealing other courts' business, overusing injunctions and subpoenas, and making decrees
'grounded upon the Lawe Civile'. The more genuine threat was that
the unchecked growth of parallel jurisdictions would enable litigation to go round in circles for ever, but More showed that careful
consultation with the common law judges, caution in interfering

with suits in other courts or reversing their decisions, sterner enforcement of chancery's decisions and strict control of vexatious litigation could allow an active chancery to coexist with the common law courts even at the height of the debate about the threat of equity. Despite niggling over individual injunctions, a modus vivendi between chancery and the common law courts was successfully established from the 1530s until trouble flared up again under James I, fuelled by personality clashes and the newly worrying constitutional overtones of prerogative justice.[7]

The Equity Courts: Star Chamber and Requests

In the rise of equity, the conciliar courts followed on chancery's heels. The royal council had since at least the fourteenth century exercised judicial functions as an extension of the king's personal role as the fount of justice. It specialised in dealing with politically sensitive cases where the full-blown assertion of royal power might be needed to impose a settlement: violent perversions of the legal system, feuds amongst great men, and their abuse of the social and delegated governmental power they exercised over the king's lesser subjects. Hence the Lancastrian council's interest in cases where there was 'to greet myght on that oo[n] syde and unmyght oo[n] that othir'. In Henry VI's minority it had fulfilled this role fairly successfully, but its failures during his adult years illustrated the extent to which conciliar jurisdiction was a manifestation of the king's personal commitment to justice and a test of his political control over his leading subjects. Both were sadly lacking in Henry's case. Edward IV and Richard III each took a strong personal lead in judicial matters, intervening by letter and personal appearance in local disputes, and the Yorkist council was hearing an increasing number of suits by the end of Edward's reign. But the real boom in conciliar justice came under Henry VII and Wolsey.[8]

Henry followed the Yorkists in his personal judicial dynamism, sending out blistering letters like those to Sir William Say and Sir John Fortescue informing them that he had heard of their intention of confronting one another with 'unliefull assembles and conventicles of our people' at the next sessions of the peace in Hertfordshire, warning them not to do anything 'repugnant to the equitie of our lawes or rupture of our said peas, at your uttermost perell', and summoning them to Westminster so he could deal with their dispute. From early in the reign, Henry used his council as a forum for this personal drive to impose good order, taking notes in his own hand of the witnesses' depositions when Lord Dacre of the North appeared before the council accused of riot in 1488–9. But the mass of petitions for royal justice which flooded in in response to such initiatives was far too large for the king to involve himself in all but the most important cases, and his councillors began to hear numerous suits in his absence. They sat either at Westminster under the chairmanship of the lord chancellor – increasingly known as the council in Star Chamber from the room with a starred ceiling in which they met – or at the itinerant royal court under the chairmanship of the lord president of the council, as the council attendant. The records of conciliar jurisdiction are too thin to be absolutely sure that Henry VII's reign was the crucial stage in its rise, but the evidence of institutional and procedural developments suggests that it was. Much that became stereotyped under Wolsey was still experimental or flexible under Henry VII, while much that was regular practice under Henry – even the appointment of a lord president of the council – had no visible Yorkist precedent.[9]

Henry's retention of personal oversight of every aspect of government, his enthusiasm for justice, and his tendency to move around the country (at least until the last years of his reign) combined to make the council attendant the more active of these two incarnations of conciliar justice. By 1504 it was hearing more than 200 suits a year, far more than the council in Star Chamber, but from 1509 the situation was reversed. As executive control of government passed first to the surviving councillors of Henry VII and then to Wolsey as chief minister, the Star Chamber became the centre of government and with it, first under Warham but far more dramatically so under Wolsey, the centre of justice. The council attendant withered as a judicial body, apparently ceasing to operate at all from 1512 to 1514, but star chamber boomed, propelled by Wolsey's regular orations on the importance of imposing 'thindifferent ministracion of Justice' and his promotion of the 'lawe of the Stere chambre' as the means to that end.[10]

Like chancery, star chamber proved more attractive than the common law courts in various ways, using the English bill, the subpoena, depositions by witnesses under oath, and interrogatories (lists of questions furnished by the parties to be put to their opponents or to the witnesses). Again like chancery, it aimed at rapid equitable settlements, frequently compromises, which could be enforced with the full power of the crown. But as in chancery, the availability of a more effective route to justice made litigants try to lure the council into interesting itself in their cases by arguing that some great man was obstructing the course of justice to their detriment, or more commonly that their opponents had gained some advantage against them by riotous disorder. Just as they played on chancery's special interest in plaintiffs unjustly disabled by the technicalities of the common law, over contracts, uses, and the detinue of deeds, so they played on star chamber's special interest in violence and judicial corruption. Here too it was disputes over land that swamped the court, which was not shy of ordering defendants under massive penalties not to contest a plaintiff's possession of land even when it did not – as it sometimes did – formally award title. Land disputes already accounted for more than half the suits in star chamber under Henry VII, and few of the accusations of riot used to bring them into court look circumstantial enough to make them more than a convenient formula. By Wolsey's time some 41 per cent of suits were purely about title to land. The cardinal's enthusiasm for accessible justice made it easier than ever to bring suits before star chamber, as he relaxed various earlier restraints on frivolous litigation which in due course had to be reimposed or improved upon by his successors. As business increased, efficiency and flexibility went down, and star chamber suffered the familiar problems of overlap with the common law courts, until Edward VI's councillors resolved in 1551 that it should not concern itself with matters that might be settled at common law. That left Heath – more effective here than in chancery – and his Elizabethan successors to develop a new star chamber with purely criminal jurisdiction, punishing riots, forgeries, or abuses of justice, but refusing to settle the questions of property that underlay them.[11]

Wolsey's substitute for the council attendant took a different path. One aspect of its jurisdiction, at least since Richard III's reign, lay in hearing suits from those too poor to sue in other courts; for such business the dean of the chapel royal presided over a small gathering of councillors. In 1520 this body was reconstituted as a tribunal sitting in the White Hall at Westminster, which was to pass through several reconstructions and emerge after 1538 as the court of requests. Unlike star chamber, it rapidly lost its links with the royal council, as the comparatively trivial nature of many of the suits it heard, and the lesser political weight of its judges, made inevitable.

By the 1590s only antiquarian research into its origins could justify its right to exist at all. The legally trained clerics who had once manned it were replaced by a team of laymen trained in the civil law – two of whom headed the court as masters of requests – and at least one common lawyer, but it seems to have pursued equity into Elizabeth's reign with a freer hand than chancery could do. It functioned like the other equity courts, and faced their usual difficulties: efforts to raise the speed and lower the cost of litigation were necessary by the 1540s, poignantly so in a court designed for the poor. Yet it did play a specialised role in protecting the property rights of copyhold tenants, the majority of the English peasantry, whose tenures could not be reliably defended at the common law until the 1570s or 1580s. At a time when landlords might be tempted to exploit this weakness to enclose land or convert copyholds into more profitable leaseholds, the court of requests' use of manorial records or the testimony of aged tenants to establish the customary rights of copyholders was an important achievement, one backed up by chancery's efforts in the same direction from Wolsey's time onwards and later by those of the equity side of the exchequer. Such cases met the court's original moral intention, as the king's power protected the poor and weak. In the long run they also served more political ends, helping to make rural England a less disorderly place by defusing potential enclosure riots and similar popular unrest.[12]

The Impact of the Equity Courts

Three significant features of the equity courts which we have yet to examine help to explain their success. The first is their relationship to the characteristic late medieval supplement to, or substitute for, the workings of the common law courts, arbitration. Fourteenth- and fifteenth-century noblemen, bishops, gentlemen, lawyers and urban guilds regularly negotiated compromise settlements in disputes between their social equals or inferiors, and the councils of the greatest magnates operated like local equity courts. When the parties could not be brought to a mutually acceptable compromise, arbitrators turned themselves into umpires and imposed an equitable solution in the interests of keeping the peace. In this context the law of star chamber and chancery was often no more than arbitration settled by the king's councillors and backed by the king's authority, an extension of the king's personal arbitration between great men as Henry VIII still occasionally practised it.[13]

Henry VII's conciliar justice overlapped with his frequent appointment of individual councillors or trusted noblemen to arbitrate disputes. His mother Lady Margaret Beaufort wielded an equitable jurisdiction from her palace at Collyweston in Northamptonshire, often over cases referred to her by the king's council, much as Edward IV's regional lords Gloucester, Stanley and Hastings imposed arbitrated justice on the north, the north-west and the Midlands at Edward's behest. Under Henry VII and Henry VIII noblemen also continued to arbitrate disputes without explicit royal invitation, particularly when their tenants or gentry followers were involved. Their justice was not inherently worse than the king's. Considerations of practical power as a 'good lord', perceived status or 'worship' among the wider local community, and royal approval for actions likely to maintain the peace had encouraged Yorkist peers to try their best to arbitrate fair and lasting settlements, rather than merely backing their closest dependants to the hilt. Such considerations still applied, especially to peers who aspired to any sort of local pre-eminence. But increasingly arbitration took place under the aegis of the equity courts. Wolsey settled star chamber cases as often by setting up an arbitration – by noblemen or lawyers from the council, judges from king's bench or common pleas, civil lawyers from chancery, members of his own household, or local peers, gentlemen, lawyers or clergy – as by a full court hearing. In 1526 he even tried to clear the backlog of cases by wholesale referral to compulsory local arbitrations. By Elizabeth's reign more than half the completed cases in chancery were settled in the same way. Royal equitable justice won such ready acceptance because in execution it so resembled and subsumed private arbitration. While peers and gentlemen supplied the local knowledge and social weight to make such justice effective, it was the crown that placed its authority behind the judicial process and took the credit for its success.[14]

A second key to that success was the sense that the royal equity courts brought the king's power to bear effectively in every locality. They overrode franchises to hear cases from every part of the crown's dominions – Wales, County Durham, Calais and sometimes even Ireland – and they increasingly used local commissioners – peers, bishops, abbots, gentlemen and lawyers – to interview witnesses and extract answers from recalcitrant defendants. Thus, as

Tudor government often sought to do, they harnessed the prestige and talents of the local elites to the crown's service, especially when those talents included legal expertise: from Audley's time each such commission normally included at least one trained common lawyer. This fits well with the impression that the standards of behaviour enforced by the council courts over the use of violence or judicial perversion were not radically opposed to the values of fifteenth-century local society. Outrageous violence or extreme manipulation of the legal system met with disapproval in the gentry communities of later medieval England, and those who indulged too readily in such activities found themselves ostracised. What star chamber did was to tighten somewhat, and enforce with the crown's power, the norms to which previous generations had aspired, and which they had sought in their way to implement.[15]

Thirdly, the equity courts reflected and reinforced the growing political strength of the Tudor monarchy in their techniques for enforcement. As in the Yorkist council and chancery, but on a wider scale, bonds and recognisances were taken to ensure that plaintiffs were genuine in their complaints, that defendants continued to attend after their first appearance, that parties kept the peace towards each other during litigation, and that they obeyed the courts' decisions. The more people sued in the equity courts, the tighter the king's grip on his subjects became; the tighter the king's grip on his subjects became, the more attractive it was to sue in the equity courts. The high political profile of equitable justice was equally reflected in the close personal involvement of the crown's chief ministers in its promotion. Although Cromwell avoided Wolsey's time-consuming role as chancellor and chairman in Star Chamber, he was active there and as a dispenser of arbitrated justice through his own household. Protector Somerset likewise received petitions, asked local commissioners to investigate or arbitrate disputes and wrote letters on behalf of plaintiffs, though directing most suitors into requests or other courts. Even those who did not deal directly with a Cromwell or a Somerset knew that their opponents would have to stand before the most powerful men in the kingdom wielding royal power in its most effective forms.[16]

The equity courts did have their weaknesses, however. Their dependence upon delegated arbitration testified to the fact that their judgments were not as terrifyingly final as one might think. One case successfully arbitrated by two members of the council in the Marches in 1511 had passed through chancery, the council

attendant and star chamber between 1493 and 1509, but each tribunal had failed either to reach or to impose a settlement. Subtler
limitations came from the courts' reliance on local elites. Of course
the chancellor or the council could make efforts to choose trustworthy men in appointing commissioners to investigate or arbitrate, but
the writ used to appoint them – *dedimus potestatem,* 'we have given
power' – symbolised the extent to which bias and corruption could
seep into this system as it had into the common law. Over time there
was a clear shift in the social rank of those appointed as arbitrators,
as the great peers of Henry VII's reign – Oxford, Daubeney,
Bergavenny and so on – gave way to gentlemen JPs and lawyers
under Elizabeth. This both reflected and helped to advance changes
in the distribution of power in local society, but we must not fall into
the trap of assuming that gentlemen were any less tempted to abuse
that power than noblemen had been. As the equity courts matured
and ossified, such abuses became harder to control than in the days
of innovation and flexibility.[17]

The flexibility which marked the rising courts of equity was paralleled by their pervasiveness. The terms of appointment of successive
lord admirals from 1525 conferred ever wider equitable jurisdiction
over maritime cases on the court of admiralty, though a statute of
1536 stopped criminal trials of pirates under the civil law. From the
mid-fourteenth century the chancellor's powers to supervise the legal
system and intervene in sensitive cases were steadily expanded by
statute, but in Henry VII's reign conciliar tribunals, albeit led by the
chancellor, began to multiply at the boundary where justice and
administration met. Experimental conciliar courts were set up by
Henry VII to punish maintenance, retaining and riots and to punish
conspirators within the royal household in 1487, and to punish
corrupt juries in 1495. In 1539 a similar body was created to enforce
royal proclamations. None of these had a very lively existence, but
others did. The council learned in the law was a specialised offshoot
of Henry VII's council designed to enforce the king's claims against
those in breach of the feudal land law and other offenders, but it also
heard suits between parties. The general surveyors, charged with overseeing Henry's landed income, heard suits between crown tenants,
and the court of duchy chamber did the same for those who held
land from the Duchy of Lancaster. All used English bills, subpoenas,
recognisances, depositions, arbitration by commissioners and so on.[18]

Their role in Henry VII's fiscalism cost several of these courts their
powers or even their existence at the start of Henry VIII's reign, but

the court of general surveyors gradually revived and was joined by new administrative courts providing equitable justice for suitors in their area of competence: augmentations, wards and liveries, and first fruits and tenths. By 1543 the heads of these three new courts – Sir Richard Rich, William Paulet, Lord St John, and Sir John Baker – all sat in the remodelled privy council. All were able common lawyers, and two of the three had experience in the central administration of the Duchy of Lancaster, the seedbed of so much Tudor administrative practice. Each passed cases freely from his court into those of his colleagues as appropriate. The system had a good deal in common with that operated by the leading lawyers of Henry VII's council, in which Empson in the council learned (using the Duchy of Lancaster's clerk and offices), Southwell at the general surveyors, and Dudley, Empson and other councillors acting alone or in small groups heard suits and referred them to one another. It was fitting that Southwell's three nephews all held senior posts in augmentations or general surveyors by the 1540s. When augmentations was absorbed by the exchequer in 1554, its equitable jurisdiction went with it, expanding the exchequer's own equity side (which had been developing in an unspectacular way since the fifteenth century) into one of the great courts of Elizabethan England.[19]

Equitable justice spread geographically as well as institutionally. At first this was by duplication of central courts within the greater liberties. The royal palatinate of Lancaster had its own chancery court just as the bishop had his for County Durham, and the warden of the Cinque Ports fired off subpoenas and injunctions from his St James's court at Dover. All these courts survived the 1530s. This was partly because the crown realised their convenience: the Durham courts were adjudged in 1553 'very commodious, easy and profitable to the inhabiters and dwellers within ... the said County Palatine'. But it was partly also because those who came under their jurisdiction valued the protection they provided against the full force of the central equity courts: already in 1467 the Cinque Ports urged their warden to protest against the penetration of their franchise by chancery subpoenas. Such conflicts were inevitable, and in the end the central courts, wielding royal authority more visibly and immediately than their rivals, were bound to win; thus County Durham cases in chancery and the conciliar courts increased steadily from the 1540s. But bitter contests over such issues continued to 1600 and beyond.[20]

Equally controversial by the late Elizabethan period were the newer regional equity courts. In these the continuity with noble arbitration was at its clearest, for Edward IV's creation of a council at Ludlow in 1473 to supervise justice and government in Wales and the Marches in the name of his son Edward, prince of Wales, was the counterpart of his elevation of Gloucester, Hastings and other regional magnates. The council's re-establishment by Henry VII and his successors gave it an ever larger role as an equity court for Wales and the border counties. Wolsey repeatedly tried to clear the log-jam in star chamber by remitting all Welsh suits to the council, and by the 1570s it was hearing some 1200 cases a year. By the 1590s its northern equivalent, based at York, had reached almost the same level of business. Wolsey directed many suits towards it and it too built up a useful regional jurisdiction. Inevitably, though, both councils were popular mainly with those who did not have the money to pursue litigation at Westminster. The rebels of 1536 asked that all subpoenas sent to those living north of the Trent should be answerable at York, and by 1543 the council of the north was indeed given power to stay chancery subpoenas directed to northern residents. Such provisions were less popular with those who could afford the Westminster courts and lost in the regional councils. Thus much business, even that specifically ordered out by Wolsey, reappeared in due course to fill up star chamber or chancery. At least less flowed in from Ireland, where the council and the chancellor developed similar equitable jurisdictions to their English equivalents under the impact of Henry VII's reforms of 1494–6.[21]

Innovation in King's Bench and Common Pleas

Many of the equity courts were manned wholly or partly by common lawyers even before More began the run of common lawyer chancellors. Thus five common lawyers balanced five civil lawyers on the council of the north in 1525. But the common lawyers had a third response to the rise of equity beside infiltration and complaint: to improve the remedies available to litigants in the common law courts. It is easy to ridicule the deficiencies of those courts in the later fifteenth century. The standard procedure to secure appearance, 'mesne process' as it was called, running through distraint of goods and arrest by the sheriff to outlawry, took at least a year and a half to run its course. Even the state of outlawry no longer held much terror and could be readily terminated by the purchase of a pardon. Edward IV tried to strengthen its deterrent value but failed; Henry VII chased up outlaws with characteristic thoroughness, but with the intention not of making them attend court but of making them pay much more heavily for their pardons; Henry VIII approved acts to make outlawry more effective but then offered general pardons so wide that he virtually eliminated its force. This decay affected not only the minor outlawry which was designed to enforce attendance in civil suits, but even the major outlawry which prescribed immediate and total confiscation of the lands, goods and chattels of those failing to appear on indictments for felony or treason.

The sheriff often took the minimum possible action over the thousands of writs a year which flowed through the office of his deputy (usually an attorney in the Westminster courts, who kept and returned all the writs for convenience' sake but sent him a note of their contents). In mesne process, for instance, it was safest to report that the goods of someone who had failed to appear in court were worth nothing; that way the sheriff would not have to try to confiscate them, and would owe the crown no money if he failed in the attempt. It was normal to reply *non est inventus* ('he cannot be found') even when writs concerned people whom he was quite able to find when they were needed to sit on juries. In the 1460s one common pleas writ in five was never returned at all. And when a case did get to court, it could be lost on the most outrageous technicalities, such as mistakes in the wording or spelling of a writ. Less than one case in ten reached a judgment, though then as now many disputes were settled out of court once the first few writs demonstrated one's seriousness in pursuing legal redress.[22]

These failings must have contributed to the rise of arbitration in the fifteenth century and of the equity courts thereafter. It is true that the volume of business lost by common pleas in particular – where two-thirds of cases concerned debts of one sort or another – was probably determined as much by the general health of the economy as by the competence or otherwise of the court. Hence the fifteenth-century slump and the fluctuations of the Wolsey years when epidemics, dearths, taxation and war unsettled economic life. But the lawyers who ran common pleas – and even more so king's bench – certainly saw the need to win back lost business, and set about doing so by accommodating the pressure from litigants for new actions better suited to whatever their problems might be. King's bench began to entertain some 39 new actions between 1498 and

1549, mostly under the influence of two go-ahead chief justices, Sir John Fyneux and Sir Edward Montague, and an efficient prothonotary (chief clerk), John Roper. It was a successful family enterprise: Roper married Fyneux's daughter, Montague married Roper's, and they all prospered on the fees that extra business brought them. The most important innovations were actions on the case. These were unlike most common law actions, where one's problem had to be fitted into one of a limited range of rigid categories defined by the set wording of the different writs with which one might begin a suit. In the action on the case, on the other hand, the writ formula was brief and non-specific, and the plaintiff could state his problem in all its particularities in a declaration rather like an equity court bill. Lawyers could be relied upon to exploit the flexibility of these actions in their clients' interest as long as the judges would allow it. Thus actions on the case developed to deal with various areas of contract and debt which had been chancery matters, and by 1560 they accounted for 19 per cent of king's bench business.[23]

With the new actions came new procedures, cleverly exploiting a set of jurisdictional quirks and legal fictions which had been gradually combined over the course of the fifteenth century. If one's opponent had already made an appearance as a defendant in a current suit in king's bench, one did not have to start from scratch but could sue him directly using a bill, even if he were on bail rather than actually in the court's custody. One could ensure that he was a defendant answering a suit in king's bench by accusing him of a trespass in Middlesex, the county in which king's bench permanently sat, and over which it exercised an immediate jurisdiction activated by bills rather than writs. And one could solve the difficulty that he lived miles from Middlesex by using the writ *latitat* ('he is lurking'), which enabled him to be extracted from any other county. Once one's opponent was in the court's clutches, the fictitious Middlesex trespass – by the 1540s it always involved breaking into enclosed land at Hendon – could then be quietly dropped in favour of the bill concerning the real point at issue. This device, the 'bill of Middlesex', did not solve all the problems of the king's bench, for the success of one's case remained at the mercy of sheriffs and jurors, but it was faster, cheaper and more effective than mesne process. Together with the actions on the case, it explains why king's bench expanded its business more spectacularly by the 1550s than common pleas, whose judges were more conservative in their attitude to such innovations.[24]

From the 1480s onwards, king's bench and common pleas also nibbled successfully at the business of the church courts. Their two major targets were defamation and debt. The latter especially was an area in which the later medieval compromise between the two jurisdictions was wearing thin, as litigants exploited the fact that a debt involved a will or a broken promise to try their luck before the church courts. These were at hand in every diocese and combined swift, efficient procedures with ecclesiastical sanctions, culminating in excommunication, to enforce attendance and compliance. By 1495, 200 of the 350 instance causes (suits between parties) in the Canterbury consistory court involved the action of *fidei laesio*, breach of promise, mostly for debt or contract. Writs of prohibition existed to forbid the church courts from hearing suits which should have come under the common law, but the canon lawyers had evolved counter-measures which were usually successful in preserving their jurisdiction. Under Henry VII, however, a new weapon came into play. King's bench began to hear a rash of suits under the statute of *praemunire*, denying the jurisdiction of the church courts as though they were foreign (which, from the common lawyers' point of view, perhaps they were). These were mostly actions brought by aggrieved individuals trying to undo church court judgments that had gone against them, but as the judges of king's bench allowed more and more of them to succeed, large areas of church court business were destroyed in a few decades. The rise of actions on the case for debt – whose form aped the canon law actions they were replacing – neatly matched the decline of *fidei laesio*. Some enthusiastic bishops kept up the volume of business in their courts in the 1520s by an increase in office business (prosecutions), regulating such matters as the care of church buildings and clerical conduct. But it was only under Elizabeth that the church courts expanded their instance business once again, relying on litigation over tithes and defamation which did not impute a crime triable at common law (for instance calling someone a 'false knave' rather than a 'strong thief').[25]

Borough Courts and Manor Courts

The church courts' losses to the Westminster courts were paralleled by those to local tribunals, especially borough courts: the city of

London had to set up a new petty debt court in 1518 to hear the suits draining out of ecclesiastical jurisdiction. Meanwhile they seem to have found themselves under further pressure from laymen who found them too lenient. It was apparently in response to pressure from litigants that the London commissary court began to try far more cases of defamation using witnesses to the facts, and cut its acquittal rate by two-thirds, in the early sixteenth century. This factor even applied where moral regulation was concerned. Sexual offences always loomed largest amongst the London church courts' office business. But the church courts, which aimed to prompt the sinner's penitence and reintegration into society, cut insufficient ice with pimps and prostitutes to satisfy the respectable citizens of London. They turned to the mayor's court for large-scale drives to repress prostitution in the 1520s.[26]

While the borough courts gained on the one hand, they lost on the other. As the church courts found, the threat that a verdict in one tribunal might readily be undone in another that claimed superiority over it tended to make litigants go straight to the superior court. This combined with at least four other factors to draw business from local courts into Westminster, driving on judicial centralisation even when there was no coherent policy on the part of government to implement such centralisation. One was inflation, which brought the sum at stake in more and more cases over the limit of £2, thus removing them from the cognisance of most local courts. Similarly, economic expansion created more and more business relationships, and thus debts, which crossed jurisdictional boundaries, while changes in the distribution of industry and commerce often took place at the expense of older towns and thus lessened the business in their courts. A third force was the spread of trained common lawyers as increasing numbers of ambitious young men trained at the inns of court, and the more general dissemination of legal knowledge, doubtless accelerated by the popularity of legal texts among early printed books. By 1500 almost every town had a recorder, steward or town clerk trained at one of the inns to oversee its courts, whereas few had done so in 1400. Such men upheld the right of king's bench to review local verdicts, and imposed due common law procedure on what had once been flexible courts for merchants, thus helping to strangle them. Meanwhile local attorneys with enough scraps of legal learning to manage their neighbours' lawsuits at Westminster, and solicitors who linked provincial litigants to metropolitan attorneys, were starting to proliferate and, so contemporaries argued, to egg on aspiring suitors.[27]

Lastly, there may in many instances have been suspicion of the town oligarchies or manorial lords whose courts these were. Increased demand for land made it easier for some manorial lords to use their courts as a source of added income by fines and amercements, and this must have been resented. At a higher level than the individual manor, the stewards of great noblemen struggled to impose the jurisdiction of their soke courts and honour courts on litigants, not only for the sake of the fees and profits that always attended the doing of justice, but also to extend their masters' power. All too often, however, we know of their efforts from cases against them in the equity courts, where the noblemen's aggrieved inferiors gained a ready hearing against those they could represent as over-mighty subjects. Town and manor courts often made efforts to forbid those under their jurisdiction from suing elsewhere, but, faced with competition from the Westminster courts and the regional councils, the general trend in their volume of business was irrevocably downwards, just as the Irish local courts were losing out to the central Dublin courts at the same time. There was enormous variation from place to place. The bishop of Worcester's manorial courts had lost most of their private suits by 1450, but that at Redgrave in Suffolk held up well until the 1560s, only to decline steeply by the end of the century. In Northumberland and Durham some manor courts were still thriving on small claims in 1841. But even the royal manor of Havering (Essex), equipped with wide liberties by a charter of 1465 and run efficiently by the crown's leading tenants in the area, found a boom in manor court business under the Yorkists succeeded by a run of chancery and king's bench cases which dented its local supremacy. Predictably enough, they were mostly initiated by outsiders or residents excluded from the dominant circle, who claimed the court discriminated against them.[28]

The area in which the manor and borough courts held their own much better was that of economic and social regulation. The pressure of population growth bit at different times in different places, but everywhere it drove local authorities to regulate vagrancy, prostitution, gambling, alehouses, and unauthorised cottage-building, fishing, and wood-gathering by the poor. They devised new punishments – the stocks, the pillory, the cucking-stool and so on – to punish those too indigent or mobile to be fined. Where such problems had had to be addressed even through the demographic slump of the fourteenth and fifteenth centuries, as in London and Westminster, prosecutions intensified. Elsewhere in lowland England they generally appeared for the first time (at least for the first time since the Black Death) between the 1460s and the 1520s, and boomed thereafter. Such use of the courts for social control was in full swing long before puritan ideas arrived to gloss it with a peculiarly suitable theological framework and a sharpened sense of moral and governmental vocation for local elites.[29]

Alongside such activity there survived the traditional roles of the local courts in regulating the economic life of village or town. As open-field agriculture declined, so the number of manor courts producing detailed by-laws about the prescribed dates for sowing and reaping declined too, but problems like sharing the cost of drainage arrangements or controlling the number of animals each tenant could pasture on the commons remained; it was no coincidence that in suits between parties manorial courts were generally more active in arable-farming areas than in those dominated by pasture and woodland. Likewise borough courts controlled weights and measures, prices, building, industrial pollution, sanitation and so on. Together with jurisdiction over petty assaults, the moral and public nuisance business of local courts kept up their total caseload remarkably well, even after vagabondage, alehouse-keeping and other offences came under statutory control and thus within the purview of the royal courts. In Kent as late as 1600–2, nearly three times as many individuals appeared in criminal cases before manorial, borough, hundred and marsh courts as before assizes and quarter sessions combined: 22 per cent of the charges against them were personal (usually assault), 26 per cent moral, and 29 per cent public nuisances.[30]

Jurors and Communal Justice

The manor courts provide the extreme example of the participatory nature of much of the judicial system. The balance between lord and tenant varied widely: the abbey of St Edmund's power over the town courts of Bury St Edmunds was still tightly exercised at a time when the abbot of Battle held only nominal control over the Battle manor court, through which the leading townsmen ran the town. But it does seem that in most such courts the leading tenants played an influential role as the jurors who reported on offences and assessed appropriate amercements on those who had committed them. In a wide-ranging jurisdiction like that of Havering they also arbitrated settlements in many of the cases brought before the court. Their dominance explains why, under the strain of population growth, manor courts tended to protect the interests of established residents against outsiders and the poor. Their role in producing by-laws even gave them at times the status of a miniature local parliament.[31]

In the seventeenth century the grand juries at county assizes took on a similar role in articulating local opinion. There was no sign of that in early Tudor England, but wherever there were juries there was room for participation in the judicial process. In all the common law courts juries judged the facts in criminal and civil cases alike, and in criminal cases it was juries of presentment who first indicted each offender. This lent considerable flexibility to the community's response to crime, or so the detailed evidence available for the early seventeenth century suggests. The victim, his friends and neighbours, and the parish constable played the key roles in detecting and apprehending criminals. At indictment and trial, jurymen used their ability to reject charges out of hand, to try but acquit the suspect, or to convict him of a less serious crime than that with which he was charged, for example by deliberately undervaluing any goods stolen. Thus they modified the stark rigour of the law, which prescribed hanging for all felonies. Professional criminals such as horse thieves and burglars were treated harshly, as were vagrants and other strangers; the local poor who stole to eat or on impulse were effectively let off with a series of increasingly sharp warnings, though they might be hanged in the end. A similar scale of values was applied by juries in fifteenth-century East Anglia, where crimes of violence and repeated thefts of high value were punished more severely than other offences notionally carrying the same penalties. Once again the village elites were in charge: constables and jurymen at assizes and quarter sessions in early seventeenth-century Sussex tended to be yeomen farmers, substantial husbandmen or well-established artisans, just as they had been in mid-fifteenth-century Gloucestershire. Meanwhile many criminal cases never reached the courts at all because local gentlemen, clergy or yeomen arbitrated a settlement between victim and accused.[32]

All this fits with what we can reconstruct of the early Tudor situation, with one telling difference. Appeals of felony, in which the victim or his kin directly initiated the case against the accused almost as though in a civil suit, rose in number through the fifteenth century but were in decline by the mid-sixteenth. Their rise and fall probably reflects the perceived weaknesses of the more normal (and always more common) procedure by indictment and its increased reliability under the Tudors, but their very existence is a reminder of the extent to which the prosecution of crime remained a matter between the victim of a misdeed and its perpetrator. The use of trespass suits initiated by the victims of theft as a substitute for indictments for felony had a similar effect. The role of the aggrieved party was fundamental even in star chamber, where Henry VII and Wolsey relied largely on the petitions of those wronged by great men to expose their offences against public order and local justice. Conversely, in Elizabethan Essex one suspected felon in three was freed without trial because no victim or witness appeared in court.[33]

One corollary to this sensitive interaction between local communities and the king's courts was a dislike of informers or promoters, those who used penal statutes which promised a share of the fine to the informer to instigate prosecutions for their own financial benefit. A number of those associated with such prosecutions in London in Henry VII's reign were arrested in 1509, and George Whelplay, who tried to make a career from the late 1530s out of detecting smugglers and retailers of substandard or overpriced goods, was denounced by one customs officer as a 'false knave, polling and promoting knave'. Even the staff of the exchequer, where such prosecutions were brought, seem to have tired of Whelplay after a while, but informing for profit prospered from the mid-1540s, as it was the best means successive governments could find to regulate marketing offences and thus try to lessen the impact of inflation and dearth. Only in James I's reign did mounting criticism of the system's many abuses bring its effective abolition. Similar, albeit less justified, distaste for those who took upon themselves to report crimes of which they were not the victims probably underlay the complaints in the parliaments of 1529 and 1532 against the promotion of prosecutions by the 'summoners and apparitors' of the ecclesiastical courts, 'being very light and indiscreet persons'.[34]

In fact, despite their use of judges rather than juries to decide cases, the church courts were also heavily influenced in their office business by lay participation. Churchwardens, constables and other parishioners brought offences before the courts more often than clergymen or court officials. Neighbours might swear to the good character of the accused in order to secure his acquittal by compurgation, a procedure which seems to have worked fairly well in rural communities but to have been abused by persistent offenders in London. Punishments, as in many courts, involved community participation to exploit the shame of the guilty party. To perform public penance for one's sins was sufficiently embarrassing for more than half of those sentenced to it in London to choose to make a donation to charity instead. In borough courts offenders had no such option, and the element of shame in punishments such as the pillory and the cucking-stool was sometimes elaborated by making convicts process through the town accompanied by a crowd banging pots and pans in an organised version of the spontaneous popular demonstration of moral disapproval known as 'rough music' or the 'skimmington ride'. From Wolsey's time star chamber joined in, punishing perjury and similar offences with treatment like that meted out to the man who had to ride through Westminster in 1556 facing backwards and wearing pieces of paper which detailed his misdeeds, before being branded on each cheek with the letters FA for false accusation. The large crowds that turned out to witness public executions made even death by hanging a communal sanction of sorts.[35]

Justice with community participation – though perhaps without public executions – has an engaging ring to the modern mind. But contemporaries often regarded juries as one of the weakest points of both the civil and criminal sides of the common law system. 'I durste as well trust the trouth of one judge as of two juryes', said Sir Thomas More, and those who took their suits before him in chancery or star chamber presumably agreed. The trouble with juries in civil cases was that they were susceptible to 'labouring', as contemporaries called the almost universal (and perfectly legal) efforts of litigants to explain to jurors outside the formal proceedings in court why they were in the right and their opponent in the wrong. In criminal and civil cases alike, juries were vulnerable to 'maintenance', by which powerful men used their influence to protect their servants or allies from indictment or conviction, or forwarded the suits of their dependants. Maintainers might well employ threats or inducements to the jurors, or to others involved in the legal process. Jurors might also be so selected by the sheriff that they could be relied upon to find for the party with whom he sympathised. Fifteenth-century regimes extracted repeated oaths against maintenance – 1429, 1433, 1434, 1461, 1485 – from the great men of the realm and sometimes of each shire, but it is not clear that they had much effect. Nor did the comprehensive remedies against main-tenance or embracery (labouring juries to pervert justice – which was illegal) available in the Westminster common law courts from the later fourteenth century. Labouring and maintenance might be subtle and almost passive affairs. A great man might be thought of as likely to provide a more satisfying dinner than his opponent for a jury that found in his favour; or he might be the landlord of so many people in a certain area that it was hard to find a jury which did not feel that loyalty towards him demanded a decision that would meet with his approval. In neither case, nor in many where intervention was more active, would deliberate perversion of justice be easy to prove. And the terrible penalties provided for jurors whose verdicts were adjudged corrupt under the common law procedure of attaint made other jurors understandably reluctant to convict them.[36]

Henry VII attacked the problem from three sides – sheriffs, jurors, and maintainers – and also tried to bypass it altogether. Statutes con-demned sheriffs who selected jurors corruptly and jurors who were corrupted, and set up conciliar tribunals to prosecute all the parties to perversions of justice. There is little sign that the new statutes were put into effect in the common law courts, but at least a dozen juries and one sheriff came before the new tribunals. More radically, Henry's legislation greatly expanded the range of offences that could be dealt with summarily by the JPs without indictment or trial by jury, especially in sensitive matters like riots and retaining. Juries were too well entrenched in England to wither away as they had in many continental legal systems, and the summary procedure was significantly never introduced for felonies, which carried the death penalty. Further statutes against bad jurors were passed under Henry VIII, but the most promising option was conciliar control. Some 9 per cent of civil cases in Wolsey's star chamber alleged perversions of justice, usually involving juries, and the proportion of such business there increased to 27 per cent by 1601–2. By the 1540s star chamber, absorbing the functions of Henry VII's separate conciliar tribunals, was also taking on an increasing criminal workload, punishing by fines corrupt juries and contempts of court throughout the judicial system. In this function of star chamber one among Henry VII's many experimental responses to perversions of justice had come of age, though the frequency with which star chamber still dealt with such matters in the seventeenth century should be sufficient antidote to the idea that the problem was readily or rapidly solved.[37]

Sheriffs and Justices of the Peace

Sheriffs and other officers in the judicial system might abuse their powers in other ways, and here too Henry VII and his successors attacked on a broader front than earlier kings. Statutes against the abuses of sheriffs had been passed regularly since Edward III's reign, and under Henry VII freelance informers loosely linked with the king's legal councillors used them to bring actions against sheriffs who took bribes. A statute of 1504 made sheriffs clearly responsible for the upkeep of county gaols and enabled them to be fined if they let prisoners escape. Wolsey had new instructions for sheriffs printed, ordering them to execute writs, oversee their subordinates, and select juries properly. Henry VII set the JPs to watch over the sheriffs; Wolsey set the assize judges to report back to star chamber on the behaviour of the sheriffs and JPs, and his successors continued the practice. The sense that royal favour depended on due performance of one's duties, and that such performance was being monitored, was probably more important in keeping sheriffs and JPs from conspicuously abusing their powers than the threat of prosecution. Still the threat of prosecution remained significant. Wolsey humiliated a number of corrupt JPs and sheriffs in star chamber, and the proportion of cases there involving official corruption of one sort or another ran at 8 or 9 per cent both in his day and at the end of Elizabeth's reign.[38]

One of the greatest sanctions available in dealing with such offenders was loss of office. This was especially relevant to the JPs, whose role as the crown's major judicial agents at county level had been established in the fourteenth century but was steadily expanded from the later fifteenth: nine Yorkist statutes and twenty-one of Henry VII's bestowed new powers upon them. They tended not to try major crimes at quarter sessions, leaving those for the touring assize judges, and indeed the humdrum nature of much quarter sessions business may explain why only a handful of JPs usually attended each session, generally those who lived nearest the town where it was held. (Each county had its own system for rotating the quarter sessions round a number of different centres.) It was the office's growing prestige and the powers it conferred to act outside the sessions that made it so attractive. JPs could arrest suspects or bail them, and could take bonds from troublemakers to ensure they kept the peace towards each other, or from sureties to guarantee a suspect's good behaviour or appearance in court. They were also often prominent in local arbitrations. Marian statutes consolidated their role in investigating crime, taking depositions from witnesses and suspects and binding them to appear in court, where the justice's paperwork formed the basis of the indictment put to the grand jury. This legislation set the seal on the developments of the preceding century and a half, which resulted in a conviction rate in homicide cases roughly double that of the thirteenth century when juries presented felons on the basis of their own knowledge, like a manor court jury. One testimony to the increasing role of the JPs was the rise of a printed literature on how to do the job, necessary because, as Anthony Fitzherbert put it in his *New Boke of Justices of the Peas* in 1538, 'the more parte of suche persons as shulde execute and mynister the same lawes and actes have not the perfyte knoweledge and rememberance of the same as they shulde have yf they were collecte and compiled together in a lytle boke and volume'. Thus private enterprise followed up the efforts of fifteenth-century regimes to educate the JPs by circulating to them sets of the statutes relevant to their office.[39]

Whether ignorant of their powers or not, JPs were not slow to use them in their own interests and those of their friends, as complaints in the equity courts suggest. Elizabethan assize records show the advantage to an accused felon of being the tenant or well-liked neighbour of a JP. But as local justice and administration became increasingly reliant on the commission of the peace, so governments became bolder in manipulating its membership. Dismissals for misconduct were exceptional under Edward IV and Henry VII. At least Henry regularly injected new blood into suspect commissions, and showed good intentions by a statute denouncing JPs' 'neglygence, mysdemeanyng' and 'favour' and inviting complaints about them. But Wolsey was much readier to purge rogue justices, and the more assiduous of his successors in central government followed his example.

The size of the commissions grew steadily throughout the period, and the proportion of resident gentry on each commission also grew. This testified both to the increasing enthusiasm of gentlemen to occupy the post, and to the increasing value of situating a JP in each corner of each county as their investigative role expanded. A statute of 1542 built on this trend to institute local sessions by JPs in addition to quarter sessions, and though the scheme's inconvenience brought its repeal in 1545, such petty sessions developed spontaneously in many counties by the 1590s to cope with an ever increasing administrative and judicial workload. Meanwhile central direction of their activities was intensified: Wolsey, Cromwell and Audley all gathered JPs in Star Chamber to instruct them on the doing of justice, and the cardinal even set them a 21-point question-naire on the state of justice in their counties in 1526. The regional councils were also instructed to oversee their local justices, and at assizes the JPs were expected to defer to the wisdom of the assize judges, who were encouraged to instruct them in the law.[40]

The appointment of JPs involved sharing the crown's authority with the county gentry, as had been obvious from the enthusiasm with which the parliamentary commons had pressed for their establish-ment in the fourteenth century. That had its disadvantages, as shown by Bishop Lee's reluctance to solve the problem of Welsh justice by appointing JPs. He argued that they were bound to abuse their powers, as gentlemen holding office in the old marcher lordships had done in spectacular fashion. But Lee was overruled, and Wales and Cheshire were given JPs just as chartered boroughs and other liberties had had them for some time. JPs were far from perfect, but they were the most practical means available to Tudor governments to keep the peace at the local level. Indeed, their proliferation seems to have improved their performance, as justices drawn from the wider county gentry might use their powers to restrain the corrupt dominance of the narrower elites who had sat on the fifteenth-century commissions. Only in Ireland, where the settled Pale shires relied on the Dublin courts and those under less secure governmental control were toured by itinerant royal judicial commissioners, did the JP not become the linchpin of Tudor government.[41]

The Judicial Achievement and its Ambiguities

The greatest single problem in the maintenance of order in late medieval England, and thus the sorest test of Tudor justice, was the use of violence in disputes over land. Four main reasons made it so. The law of landownership was sufficiently complex that it was often genuinely unclear who had the best title to an estate. Land was the major source of wealth and status and thus worth considerable effort to obtain. Those who quarrelled over it included the most powerful men in local society, on whom the king had to rely to conduct local government. And the law made physical possession of land or the exercise of certain rights as landlord – collecting rents or holding manorial courts – among the best proofs of title, thus provoking attempts to enter property or exercise such rights in the face of opposition from one's rival, despite the legal penalties for forcibly taking possession. Technically no violence had to be used to commit the offence of riot: three or more people had merely to join together to perform an illegal act. Certainly physical violence was normally used in a calculatedly limited way, and murder was comparatively rare, as it was more generally in late medieval and early modern England. But these qualifications were little consolation to late medieval governments, who regularly drew the connection between violent riots over land, illegal retaining to raise the forces to participate in such riots, and subsequent perversion of the legal system by those involved to escape prosecution. They can be forgiven for not sharing historians' sang-froid over the fact that all-out private warfare normally broke out only under exceptional conditions of governmental breakdown, personal bitterness and contested local hegemony, ás in the 1450s and 1469–71.[42]

Special judicial commissions issued to great local men had been a characteristic response to riotous feuding until Henry VI's reign, but their flagrantly partisan use then caused them to fall out of favour. Instead the suppression of riots headed the agenda for conciliar jurisdiction as it developed through the fifteenth century, as it did that of Richard III's northern council and of the court of Duchy chamber's judicial interventions in Lancashire under Henry VII and Henry VIII: the same flexibility and forcefulness that made the equity tribunals thrive more generally made them the best weapon available against riot. Many of the riots alleged in Henry VII's council and Wolsey's star chamber were fictitious, but some were not, and when proven they were severely punished. Riots and forcible entries continued to come before the courts for many years, but there are clear signs that the crown's initiative and the response it evoked amongst local elites made the typical Elizabethan riot a smaller affair, led by men of lesser social standing, than its fifteenth-century equivalent. A reputation for riot and maintenance could ruin a career more certainly by the mid-sixteenth century than in the mid-fifteenth, and that in itself was a success.[43]

If governments could take effective but limited steps to impose the law, they could also take effective but limited steps to improve it. Statute after statute tinkered with details of the law and of court procedure. Some were inspired by notorious individual cases. Some were probably the result of initiatives from the numerous practising lawyers who sat in the commons. Others, like the package of seven measures introduced in parliament by Audley in 1540, plainly came from the crown. That, however, did nothing to guarantee their successful passage, since the 'learned men in the laws' who were 'rulers' in the commons blocked anything that might affect 'their own singular lucre, wealth and profit', as a petitioner (perhaps a man of straw to support officially sponsored moves to legal reform) complained to Cromwell. The conservatism and self-interest of the common lawyers may indeed explain why sweeping plans like that of 1535 for a new land registration system stalled, while most of the major law-reform statutes of the period brought business more clearly within the purview of the common law courts, as the statutes of uses (1536) and wills (1540) did for the land law, an act of 1542 did for bankruptcy, and acts of 1487, 1495 and 1545 did for usury.[44]

Confrontations between crown and common lawyers were rare, however, not least because so many of the crown's leading ministers – Cromwell and Audley among them – were themselves steeped in the common law. They found it natural to enforce the king's powers so long as they did so within the framework of the common law, and frequently their enthusiasm to turn the law to the king's service brought them close to what their fellow subjects regarded as injustice. The clearest instance came in the cooperation between Henry VII and his legally trained councillors – Bray, Lovell, Hobart, Empson, Dudley, Belknap and others – to strengthen the crown's political control of the localities and increase its revenues by exploitation of the king's rights as supreme fount of justice and feudal landlord-in-chief.

We shall consider this programme's financial implications later, but its impact on law and politics ties together many of the themes we have examined so far. The weaknesses in procedure and sanctions of the common law affected the crown as much as any private plaintiff, but Henry found the means to avoid them. Early in his reign his inventiveness and good intentions were sometimes greater than his success: two cases of the abduction of heiresses, for example, prompted a new statute against the offence in 1487 which was scarcely used thereafter. But from an early stage swift and flexible application of overwhelming royal power to solve individual cases was his hallmark: in the second abduction case, the local JPs were afforced by the king's solicitor, the lord chief justice and two local noblemen to have the perpetrators indicted within nine days of the offence. As Henry's idiosyncratic style developed, he regularly intervened in prosecutions – for example, those for retaining – at an early stage, after or even before indictment, offering to sell a pardon for a punitive sum or to dictate the terms of a recognisance. Such interventions, paralleling royally sponsored arbitrations and conciliar justice, were a powerful means to exert royal control over disputes of importance in local politics, though like many of Henry's initiatives they ran close to the strict definition of tyranny as rule outside the law, and they could prove counter-productively offensive to local opinion. Indeed, when they were applied to the benefit of the councillors who administered them (Empson in one well-documented instance), they ran the risk of making the rivals of individual councillors into critics of the Tudor regime.[45]

The common lawyers' dominance of Henry's council also raised the possibility that they might focus royal power on an assault on the privileges of the church. Attorney-general Hobart apparently provoked a political crisis, ending in his own resignation or dismissal in 1507, by his *praemunire* attacks on the jurisdiction of the bishop of Norwich's courts. Yet for most of Henry's reign and beyond, the civil and canon lawyers who ran the church courts and the chancery worked alongside the common lawyers to advance royal power. They were prominent both as great office-holders – Morton, Warham, Savage and so on – and as active councillors without portfolio, such as Christopher Urswick. Their cosmopolitanism and their familiarity with the Roman law's high regard for imperial power predisposed them to aid in the assertion of royal authority. Just as equity courts and common law courts combined despite jurisdictional tensions to fulfil the king's duty to do justice, so the civil lawyers and common lawyers of the royal council combined to serve the king. These men were individuals as well as professional archetypes. Their experience often spanned a number of different institutions and approaches to the provision of justice, thus enriching each and setting it in a wider context. To take four lord chancellors or lord keepers of the great seal, John Alcock (1485–7) had been president of the council in the Marches, Henry Deane (1500–2) had been chancellor of Ireland, Thomas More (1529–32) had been undersheriff of London (and thus a judge in the borough courts) and chancellor of the Duchy of Lancaster, and Thomas Audley (1532–44) had been town clerk of Colchester. Such experience might be pooled in the royal council or in the Exchequer Chamber, where the entire common law judiciary gathered to discuss difficult or controversial cases; this was a forum much used by Henry VII for advice of a quasi-political nature. The combined inside knowledge of early Tudor councillors gave royal government considerable insight into the legal system and its problems and possibilities.[46]

To focus on individual careers is also to remember once again that doing justice was a matter of profit for all involved. The profit might come from royal reward for those seen to be advancing the crown's reputation for justice: an unknown chief justice told his fellow judges in Henry VIII's reign that by the pursuit of good justice they would win the love of their fellow men 'and of the kinge him self, who is no slyght ponderer of mene's good qualities and service and yet a better rewarder of the same'. Still there was always a temptation to profit from injustice. Henry VII himself came dangerously close to selling justice, as when three of his councillors secured an undertaking from the earl of Derby in 1506 to give the king land worth £50 a year if Henry found in his favour in a lawsuit pending before the council. Judges at all levels, in the church courts as much as the equity and common law tribunals, were showered with presents, dinners, drinks and other inducements to look kindly on litigants. There were some safeguards against their hearing cases in which they were personally interested. In Henry VII's council, for instance, councillors were asked to leave the room in such circumstances. But the opportunities for corruption were immense, and it is less wonder that Empson, Warham, Wolsey, Audley and many others were accused of favouritism than that substantiated charges of perverting justice for profit were so few. John Beaumont, master of the rolls (deputy to the chancellor) under Edward VI, was found to have accepted the evidence of forged documents in one case in return for a share of the winner's proceeds, but his corrupt practices in his earlier career in financial administration were far more spectacular and successful than those in judicial matters. Though lawyers in general enjoyed a bad reputation among contemporaries – as they often do – their standards of professional probity seem generally to have been high.[47]

Part of the problem was that profits from fees, whether for court officials or counsel, were dependent on the volume rather than the quality of justice. As we have seen, this was a driving force in the reform of king's bench, and the expansion of chancery's mercantile business was likewise welcomed because the highly trained civil lawyers who manned the Yorkist and early Tudor chancery expected to command the high incomes that litigation between wealthy merchants generated. Despite the efforts of Wolsey and others, the cost of justice also meant that by the end of the sixteenth century the social status of litigants varied with the prestige of the tribunal. Yeomen or husbandmen had provided about one-third of the litigants in Wolsey's star chamber, and gentlemen another third or so, but the Jacobean star chamber was full of gentlemen's and even noblemen's suits. Chancery likewise seems to have become more exclusive. Manor courts and other local tribunals were left to cater for those too poor to sue elsewhere. But this pattern was broken by king's bench and common pleas, where litigation became cheaper in real terms as the century progressed, and yeomen, richer husbandmen and artisans made up a very significant part of the clientele. Village elites shared in Westminster justice as much as they shaped justice locally by their role on juries and in parochial and manorial office.[48]

By 1606 the rate of litigation in the central courts per head of the population was higher than it had ever been before or would ever be again. This statistic symbolised a trend to the centralisation of justice which had far wider importance than the mere growth of litigation in the central courts. The ever clearer judicial supremacy of those central courts, asserted first by the equity tribunals but soon by the reviving king's bench, was matched by the efforts of monarchs and ministers to oversee and, where possible, improve the administration of justice at all levels. The logic of the campaign was simple. Chief Justice Fyneux summed it up in 1519, arguing for royal supervision and, if needs be, abolition of inferior jurisdictions: 'the king must see that justice is executed, since he is the head of justice'. As this chapter has tried to show, the forces that made for its success, failure or modification were many and varied, but centred on the interests of the lawyers and officials who made the legal system work and on the men of power in local society, from noble arbitrators and gentlemen JPs to jurymen and parish constables, who implemented, used and shaped the king's justice. Each advance of the royal power to do justice facilitated other advances, as seeking that justice became more worthwhile and falling foul of it more unpleasant.[49]

By combining the centralised power of the equity courts and the reviving king's bench and common pleas with the local effectiveness of arbitrated settlements and accessible JPs, Tudor justice enjoyed considerable success. Many of those most tempted to use their local influence to ignore or abuse the law were exposed to royal disapproval or the threat of it in the conciliar courts. Even the patchy surviving records show about one in three of the peerage appearing

before Henry VII's council in one or other of its judicial manifestations, nearly all as defendants. Under Wolsey the dominant families
in various regions – the Stanleys, Percies, Dacres, Savages and
Breretons – were disciplined in star chamber. In theory at least, and
very probably in practice, the more such great men were forced into
seeing better justice done locally, the more the judicial system as a
whole improved. Such imposition was a matter of continual vigilance, for there was every danger that the concurrent devolution of
local judicial and administrative control onto a wider circle of gentry
would produce many petty tyrants instead of a few great ones. The
omnipresence of centralised equitable justice, however, made such
vigilance much easier. That put a further onus on continual reform
in the equity courts, as vexatious complaints and suits to exploit convenient fictions repeatedly clogged them up. But a legal system too
effective for its own good was far preferable to one too ineffective to
attract litigants or repress crime. Tudor ministers were well aware of
the problem that the laws might remain no more than hot air at
Westminster. As Audley complained in 1542, 'Many laws remain perfectly unknown, to the no small hurt of the republic'. But in two or
three generations they had done a good deal to bring the king's law
more effectively to every corner of the realm.[50]

3

LIVELIHOOD

Financial breakdown was one of the central features of the failure of Henry VI's monarchy, as mismanagement fatally exacerbated an underlying, albeit temporary, weakness in the crown's financial base. By the 1440s, Henry's average annual revenue was half that of Richard II or Henry V, yet the costs of his household were rising sharply; he was quite unable to meet his debts to his leading subjects for their service in war and government, yet he continued to alienate his resources to unpopular courtiers. By the 1450s, parliaments repeatedly urged him to bolster up his bankrupt crown by resuming the grants he had made of royal lands and revenues, but he ended his reign a king who, in the words of one chronicler, 'helde no Householde ne meynteyned no warres'. By the 1470s, when Sir John Fortescue, former chief justice of the king's bench and chancellor to the Lancastrian government-in-exile in the 1460s, completed his treatise on *The Governance of England,* Henry had lost three kingdoms, France once and England twice (in 1461 and 1471), and Edward IV had been deposed and then returned to power by the vagaries of noble faction. It was no wonder that Fortescue thought it an urgent priority to pursue the commons' call for resumption much further, to strengthen the crown with a livelihood, an assured income. With such an endowment, he argued, the monarch could meet the costs of government, impress his subjects with his kingly living – for instance, building palaces 'ffor his pleasure and magnificence' – encourage loyalty by rewarding those who served him well, defend himself against sudden attack and make himself more powerful than the greater subjects who might threaten his position.[1]

Fortescue did not maintain that wealth was the answer to all the problems of government, or that only wealthy kings could rule well: in the light of the successes of Henry V, who was under-resourced by his criteria, he could not have done so. Nor did he make the case that a popular king who could secure obedience by good rule did not need to find security in riches, which would have been a basic assumption of many of his contemporaries. But he did argue that many remedies to the king's poverty were more dangerous than the disease itself. Kings with insufficient livelihood might alienate their subjects by inventing 'exquysite meanes of geytinge of good', often by the 'perversion of Justice': Richard II and Edward II, deposed after tyrannous extortions, must have been in Fortescue's mind. Foreign kings, he noted, made themselves rich by heavy taxation, often levied without consent: even as he wrote, Louis XI was more than trebling the tax burden in France, Charles the Bold doing the same in Flanders. But in so doing, Fortescue claimed, they lost the love of their people, at least of the common people who shared neither the French nobility's exemption from taxation nor its slice of the fiscal cake in royal pensions and wages of war. In England, where the commons, braver than the French, would rebel rather than pay exorbitant taxes – as, he doubtless recalled with a shudder, they had in 1381 – that would never do. So the answer was land: the king should have 'is livelihod ffor the sustenance off his estate in grete lordshippes, maneres, ffee ffermys, and such other demaynes, his people not charged'.[2]

Fortescue's was a very English view: in England the consensus that taxation should be raised only with the consent of representatives of the community of the realm grew and remained strong through the fourteenth and fifteenth centuries, whereas in France it waned. Thus it became a key element in Fortescue's favourite distinction between the 'dominium politicum et regale' ('politic and royal lordship') of England and the 'dominium regale' ('royal lordship') of France. Fortescue's was also a lawyer's view, all in favour of a strong king as long as he played by the rules – the rules of which the common lawyers were the referees – and all in favour of a centralisation of power that would prevent noblemen, even loyal noblemen, becoming 'myghty in thair contraes to do what them liste'. Fortescue's plans have long been seen as a blueprint for the monarchy of the Yorkists and early Tudors, and it is instructive that they had much in common with the advice given by his contemporary George Ashby to Henry VI's son, Edward, prince of Wales, in his *Active Policy of a Prince* of about 1470. But to what degree the kings who seemed to implement the policies advocated by such writers actually shared their views is hard to say. They do seem to have thought that wealth brought power, and to have sought it determinedly. One ambassador reported that Henry VII liked 'to be thought very rich, because such a belief is advantageous to him in many respects', and Thomas Cromwell was widely rumoured to have promised to make Henry VIII the richest king in Christendom. They did not pay much attention to Fortescue's warnings about 'exquysite meanes of geytinge of good'. Henry VII's concern for money gave him an unpleasant reputation for avarice which faded only as it became convenient to contrast the way in which he 'enhanced his riches by wisdom and mercy' with his son's more spectacular exactions.[3]

Ordinary and Extraordinary Income and Expenditure

Early Tudor kings could not afford to observe Fortescue's neat distinction between an ordinary endowment of steady value, designed to fund the normal needs of government, and extraordinary levies raised with consent to fund warfare. Throughout the early Tudor period efforts to endow the crown with a generous landed revenue combined with efforts to refine and expand the systems of direct and indirect taxation, to the point where it could be said of Henry VII, in a phrase to strike a chill into Fortescue's English heart, that he 'would like to govern England in the French fashion, but he cannot'. The main reason for the crown's insatiability was war. The loss of some major records of crown finances and the complexity of those that survive make many of the figures available for a discussion of early Tudor finance no more than estimates, but it seems that Henry VIII's three major wars with France and Scotland might be costed at around £1 million, £0.5 million and £2 million respectively. (In comparison, the much-lauded achievement of Henry VII was to raise his peacetime annual revenue to something over £100,000.) To compete among the European powers even without making war was remarkably costly, as Henry VII found in making loans of between £226,000 and £342,000 – money he was unlikely ever to see again – to his allies the Habsburgs in 1505–9.[4]

Such costs rose steadily as the budgets of the continental monarchies with whom the Tudors competed continued to expand, as armies grew larger, and as firearms, fortifications and the training of troops became more sophisticated: all these problems were combined in the financial nightmare of Protector Somerset's attempt to control lowland Scotland in defiance of French and Scottish forces, using fortified garrisons manned partly by foreign mercenaries. Meanwhile in practice much expenditure relating to foreign policy, such as Henry VII's loans to the Habsburgs, Henry VIII's large programme of ship-building, the subsidies paid to the Swiss in 1515–16 and the French in 1527–9, or the fortification of the coastline that prompted the rapid dissolution of the greater monasteries in 1538–40, was not of the irregular and clearly defined sort suitable for presentation to parliament. Regular charges were inflated by the maintenance of a large navy from Henry VIII's reign, costing some £20,000 a year even in peacetime by 1551–3. Furthermore, the dynastic insecurity of the Tudors made the provision of liquid financial reserves to combat rebellion a priority. (Fortescue had recognised that diplomacy, internal security and the maintenance of a navy needed regular funding, and intended his livelihood to cover them, but he could make no provision for an expansion in the costs of such activities.)[5]

Finally, as early as the 1520s the growing scale and cost of warfare began to outgrow parliament's preparedness to fund military ventures. By Edward VI's reign, in consequence, parliamentary taxation met only some 22 per cent of military spending. Thus in the short term the needs of war made early Tudor financial history a series of swings from increasingly vast overexpenditure to increasingly severe retrenchment, while in the long term the costs of internal and external security drove the expansion of the state's budget in England as elsewhere, not only through the traditional route of parliamentary taxation but also through the maximisation of other forms of income. The development was made explicit for contemporaries when the commissioners dissolving the chantries were told to defuse local opposition by explaining that the process would relieve the king's subjects of taxation to maintain his wars.[6]

War had also been the major source of Henry VI's financial problems, for at least in the 1430s his income apart from parliamentary taxation should have been sufficient to meet his non-military costs. Tudor governments' difficulties were further exacerbated by another factor: the crown was especially vulnerable to the inflation which began to be noticeable in the 1520s. All three of its main sources of income were unlikely to react sensitively to price inflation, since land rents were fixed for the length of each lease, customs were assessed on the fixed official values of goods rather than their market price, and individuals tended not to volunteer to adjust their tax assessments upwards to take inflation into account. Thus inflation and royal inclination combined to drive the peacetime costs of the crown upwards almost as steeply as its military charges. The royal household, which had run on around £13,000 a year under Henry VII, attracted the cost-cutting attention of Wolsey, who dismissed large numbers of staff under the Eltham Ordinances of 1526, and of Cromwell, who followed Edward IV's measures of 1471–2 and 1478 in tightening the control over the household's internal budget of the board of greencloth, the committee of the household's senior financial officers. But by the 1550s, the household took more than £50,000 a year, twice what Henry VI's household had cost at its most bloated; with the advent of King Philip in 1554–5 expenditure passed £75,000. By then the extravagant palace-building campaigns of Henry VIII were a thing of the past, but they had involved the outlay of more than £100,000 on Hampton Court and Whitehall, and as much again on some 50 lesser houses. Meanwhile the subsidies necessary to shore up English government in Ireland grew larger as the Reformation and attempts at direct rule complicated the situation there: they peaked in 1552 at £34,700, then fell back to average £21,400 in 1555–65.[7]

Historians' discussion of early Tudor finance has tended to focus on questions of central administration, whether on the maintenance of the Yorkist 'chamber system' of financial administration, or on the degree of administrative modernisation involved in the creation of new financial institutions in the 1530s and 1540s. But there is a danger of missing the wood for the trees. The expansion in the state's budget and the consequent search for politically acceptable ways to tap the national wealth were of more fundamental importance than the details of the paperwork that kept track of the king's money or of the institutions that produced the paperwork. Before examining the administrative structure of the early Tudor financial system, we should investigate the sources of royal income.

The Crown Lands

Land came first, both chronologically and in its value as a tool of government. Fortescue advocated a landed endowment because he knew that land was far more than a source of income. As we have

seen in chapter 1, the expansion of the royal demesne under the
Yorkists and early Tudors was a central element in the spread of
royal lordship throughout England and in the cultivation of a new
relationship between the crown and the county gentry. Edward IV
led the way, combining his own Yorkist family estates with the Duchy
of Lancaster and the older crown lands, then adding lands
confiscated from political enemies, and even some purchased with
the proceeds of taxation, to create by far the most extensive royal
demesne in medieval English history. Richard III went further, and
Henry VII further still, as Table 3.1 shows. Edward IV promised the
parliamentary commons in 1467 'to lyve uppon my nowne, and not
to charge my Subgettes but in grete and urgent causes'; the enlarging demesne made it more feasible for him and his successors to do
so than it had been for Henry VI. But the political costs of maintaining a demesne as large as Henry VII's were considerable, both in the

Table 3.1 Estimated Net Annual Income from the Crown Lands
(to the nearest £1000, not including Duchy of Lancaster or sales of land or
monastic goods)

Henry VI	£8,000	(1433)[a]
Richard III	£22–25,000	(1483)[b]
Henry VII	£40,000	(average 1502–5)[c]
Henry VIII	£25,000	(1515)[d]
Henry VIII	£48,000	(augmentations average 1536–46)
(post-Dissolution)	+ £38,000	(general surveyors 1542) = £86,000[e]
Mary	£83,000	(1555)[f]

Approximate Net Yield of Crown Lands in Ireland[g]

Henry VII	£600	(c.1500)
Henry VIII	£2,650	(1537–8)

[a] B. P. Wolffe, *The Crown Lands 1461 to 1536: An Aspect of Yorkist and Early Tudor
Government* (London, 1970), p. 38.
[b] Ibid., p. 64.
[c] Ibid., p. 69.
[d] Ibid., p. 85.
[e] W. C. Richardson, *History of the Court of Augmentations 1536–1554* (Baton Rouge, LA,
1961), p. 130; the figure for augmentations is calculated from P.A. Cunich, 'The
monastic spoils: reinterpreting the accounts of the first court of augmentations'
(forthcoming), and represents the average rental income of the court (about £85,000
p.a.) multiplied by the percentage of the court's total income spent on purposes
other than those internal to the court's operations such as repairs, fees, annuities and
pensions (57 per cent).
[f] D. M. Loades, *The Reign of Mary Tudor* (2nd edn, London, 1991), p. 239.
[g] S. G. Ellis, *Reform and Renewal: English Government in Ireland, 1470–1534*
(Woodbridge, 1986), p. 78.

ill-feeling caused by his appropriation and retention of his subjects' estates on the grounds of their supposed idiocy, political unreliability or incapacity to pay large fines for various offences, and in his refusal to deploy the stock of royal land as it had been deployed in the past, to endow loyal noblemen who might control local affairs in the king's interest. His son, at least, judged the costs too high, and dispersed nearly half Henry's estates to aggrieved claimants and new magnates in the first few years of his reign, until Wolsey's advent and the costs of the war of 1512–14 brought tighter husbandry to the crown's estates as to many other areas of finance.[8]

Henry VIII had traded the financial benefits of an enlarged demesne for the political benefits of an enlarged fund of patronage, for kings, it seemed, could not have their cake and eat it. However, by the 1530s the example of the German and Scandinavian Lutheran princes (and perhaps the resonance of English disendowment debates running from the mid-fourteenth to the mid-fifteenth century) offered a way to do just that, by confiscating the landed wealth of the church. Even the old rhetoric of resumption could be called into play, Henry talking by 1533 of resuming the crown lands alienated by his ancestors to the religious orders, though it soon became clear that so many of his subjects claimed to be the heirs to monastic benefactors that dissolution by statute in the king's interest was the easiest way to proceed, at least to sweep up the smaller houses in 1536. The monastic estates were so extensive that Henry could both endow his crown with a new livelihood even larger than his father's, and reward those he favoured with outright gifts or favourable sales of church land. In its sacrilegious radicalism, this operation also had a political cost, but it was a cost which the process of dissolution made it possible to pay. The revolts of 1536 were suppressed by noblemen well rewarded with monastic land, leading troops paid from the proceeds of new clerical taxes and the confiscation of monastic goods. Those who fell foul of the king over their involvement in these revolts or in the turbulent politics of 1538–47 saw their estates added to the royal fund, often for redistribution to those judged more loyal.

In addition, as the monastic estates entered crown ownership (especially those of the larger monasteries induced to surrender in 1537–40), they carried a large burden of fees and pensions to laymen, from local lawyers and gentry to Cromwell and his fellow-councillors, granted by the expiring religious houses in the hope of protection. Those fees continued to be paid, giving the crown an enormous – albeit rather inflexible – pay-roll of annuitants like that maintained by earlier kings to enhance their influence in local society. By 1550–1 the annual bill for pensions and annuities paid by the treasurers of the revenue courts totalled more than £63,000, 23 per cent of the courts' aggregate income, and less than £4500 of that went to ex-monks. Even this figure underrates the sums involved, because many annuities were paid by receivers before they forwarded their net receipts to the treasurers. In the first ten and a half years of augmentations' operation, £58,380 was paid in annuities by the receivers in addition to the £21,986 paid out by the treasurers, just as £24,353 was spent by the receivers on fees to the court's officers in addition to the £12,408 spent by the treasurers. Of course the crown's cash income from its new estates was lower because of these payments than it would otherwise have been, but the burden would lessen as the beneficiaries died off – at Buckfast Abbey it declined from over 50 per cent of gross revenue in 1539 to over 40 per cent in 1559 – and in the meanwhile the political return was considerable. In Ireland the compromise with the local laity was even more naked, for there the Dissolution statute was rejected in parliament in 1536 and passed only when the gentry and lawyers of the Pale were convinced that their interests as lessees and administrators of the monasteries' lands would not be sacrificed to those of incoming English government servants.[9]

This second landed livelihood was at least as important to mid-Tudor royal finance as Henry VII's had been to him, and some of those who administered it still hankered after Fortescue's vision of an inalienable landed endowment sufficient to meet all the crown's regular needs, as the recommendations of the revenue commission of 1552 showed. By 1550–1 the court of augmentations, managing the bulk of landed revenue, accounted for 59 per cent of the crown's gross income from regular sources (not including taxation, sales of land and so on), and in 1555 Mary's clear landed income was calculated at £82,741 out of a total revenue (excluding taxation) of some £132,000, whereas Henry VII's £40,000 constituted rather less than half of his annual income (excluding taxation) of some £91,000 in 1502–5. Even at the end of the sixteenth century the balance had only returned to roughly where it stood under Henry, for the crown lands probably contributed some 39 per cent of Elizabeth's income in her last years. Accumulation did not stop with the monastic lands: the collegiate churches followed in 1540–8 and the chantries in 1545–8, and from 1536 bishops were forced into ever more unfavourable exchanges of land with the crown. Much of this land was sold or given away by Henry VIII. More was dispersed by the predatory councillors of his son, who not infrequently gave it to themselves or short-circuited the process by pressing bishops to exchange lands with them directly. But far more remained in the crown's hands than is often realised. By Henry's death his income from ex-monastic lands, at £90,296 in 1545–6, was only a quarter below its peak of £126,296, attained in 1540–1. Even the Edwardian goldrush was mitigated in effect by the subsequent disgrace of several of its greatest beneficiaries. In Somerset the crown estate was still some three times larger in 1570 than it had been in 1536: nearly one-third of the monastic land there remained in royal hands.[10]

The efficacy with which the royal estates were exploited is harder to assess than their sheer scale. It does seem that the Yorkist kings and Henry VII pressed their administrators and tenants hard to max-imise the crown's income from each estate, as indeed Henry IV and Henry V had done in the Duchy of Lancaster. But even there, in the hothouse of later fifteenth-century administrative efficiency, the raising of rents, renewal of rentals, threats to turn out tenants in favour of those who would pay more, revival of seignorial rights, col-lection of arrears, removal of unreliable officials and disallowance of expenses which marked the chancellorships of Sir Richard Fowler (1471–7), Sir Reynold Bray (1485–1503) and Sir Richard Empson (1505–9) succeeded in raising the crown's gross income from the duchy's lands only 17 per cent above that achieved by Henry V, though this was a great improvement on the slump of Henry VI's reign. The duplication of these methods of direct management – rather than farming out each manor for a lump-sum rent – through-out the administration of the crown's estates, the elimination of sinecure offices and of many annuities, and the insistence on cash payment did produce dramatic increases in the value of other blocks of lands. The gross yield of the Duchy of Cornwall rose from £2789 in 1433 to £4173 in 1503–4, but more startlingly its net yield rose over the same period from £151 to £3572, and the cash delivered to the treasurer of the chamber in 1503–4, including arrears, totalled £4284, just as cash deliveries from the Duchy of Lancaster to Henry VII's chamber were 57 per cent higher than to Henry V's.[11]

The consideration of cash yields alone, although important for contemporary perceptions of the king's wealth and power, obscures the fact that much of the gross income of the Lancastrian crown estate which never reached the centre of government as net cash income did not simply disappear, but was being spent locally to some effect, especially in the payment of annuities to the crown's political supporters. Moreover, the improvements implemented by the Yorkists and Tudors may have owed as much to the general upswing in the rural economy beginning in the later fifteenth century as to administrative ruthlessness. They could meet with successful resist-ance from well-organised tenants, like that which culminated in a stand-up row in the manor court of Havering in Essex in 1497 between Queen Elizabeth of York's rent-collector and the tenants' leader Sir Philip Cooke. At times they ran ahead of the economic recovery, as on the Duchy of Lancaster estates in Derbyshire, where rent increases advocated by commissioners in 1497 could not be implemented until the local depression of 1485–1505 gave way to the renewed growth of 1505–20. Initiatives to improve the revenues of individual estates would have availed comparatively little had the volume of lands in the crown's hands not been deliberately and hugely increased by successive monarchs. And, almost inevitably, the larger and more complex the crown's estate became, the more lethargy crept into its administration.[12]

One problem was that the practices of private estate management which Edward, Richard and Henry had generalised from the Duchy of Lancaster and the Yorkist family estates were not wholly suitable to the agglomeration of monastic and other lands held by the crown in the mid-sixteenth century. Each block of estates – those of the earldom of Warwick or the earldom of Suffolk under Henry VII for instance – was administered separately by a team of receivers and auditors wherever the individual manors lay, rather than being inte-grated into a single system of estates divided county by county. This made some sense when the additions to the demesne still consisted of comparatively few large blocks of estates, each traditionally run as a unit. Indeed Henry VIII developed this policy in a characteristic way from the 1520s, creating honours – feudal collections of manors ranging across county boundaries – dependent on a central royal palace and partly designed as hunting complexes. Superficially the arrangements made by the court of augmentations to administer the monastic lands were more rational since, at least after 1547, each of its receivers had responsibility for one or more counties, but even here the honorial system was remarkably persistent. Until 1547 each receiver took charge of all the lands, wherever they lay, of each monastery whose site lay in his circuit, and even after that date the lands of each religious house within each county were accounted separately, rather than taking all the crown's estates in each parish together. When the courts of general surveyors and augmentations were merged in 1547 the county system was finally applied to nearly all the crown's lands, though some of the financial benefit was lost because all the local officials now surplus to requirements had to be compensated with pensions equal to their previous fees. Here again political needs balanced those of finance, for these officers constituted a royal affinity in the provinces as well as an administrative team. In any case, such administrative restructuring offered no sure solution to the more general problems afflicting the system by the 1560s. The arrangements for detailed local supervision of the crown estates remained ramshackle, and as the great blocks of noble or monastic estates were augmented or replaced by scattered parcels such as the chantry lands it became harder to keep track of the crown's holdings or to assess their proper rental value.[13]

The officials of the augmentations and other revenue agencies seem to have been generally honest but rather conservative in their estate management. Such conservatism was entirely in tune with the policy of the crown's ministers from the 1550s to the 1590s: they aimed to increase net income, by waiting for pensioners and annuitants to die and transferring repair costs to the tenants, rather than to force up gross income by rent increases. They succeeded, for net estate income was some 40 per cent higher in the 1590s than in 1552, but they left rents well below the market value and bequeathed to the generation of Robert Cecil the problem of introducing a more dynamic policy in response to inflation. In other ways the crown improved its exploitation earlier, though still without the vigour of the sharpest contemporary landlords. Fowler and Bray capitalised on the manorial rights of the Duchy of Lancaster, chasing up bondmen – who could be made to pay all manner of fines – and raising profits of court; by the 1540s commissioners were touring all the crown estates selling crown serfs their freedom. Fowler and his successors also began to step up sales of timber from the Duchy's woodlands, and these sales accelerated through the 1510s and 1520s until specialist surveyors of woods were appointed in each of the land revenue agencies in the 1520s and 1530s. From 1547 the augmentations instituted a network of woodwards in each county, though timber sales in 1550–1 still accounted for only 6 per cent of the court's revenues.

Such casualties (unfixed revenues) were always vulnerable to the desire of the crown's local officers to hedge their fixed fees against inflation by selling the crown's possessions for their own profit, or selling without proper authorisation, paying part of the price to the crown and keeping the rest as an inducement to sell. In the sales spree of the Dissolution it is a wonder (and a tribute to the tight supervision of Thomas Cromwell and Richard Rich) that as much money from monastic goods, lead from monastery roofs and so on reached the government as it did, though much bellmetal and lead was effectively bought on account and still unpaid for in the 1550s. The confiscation and sale of the goods of parish churches was a greater and more long-drawn-out fiasco. Rumoured among the rebels but denied by the government in 1536, contemplated by the privy council in 1545, and heralded by inventorying of church goods in 1547, 1549 and 1552 in a vain attempt to forestall embezzlement or diversion to other parochial needs, it was finally decreed in 1553 when the second English prayer book had rendered most of the ornaments of worship redundant, only to be overtaken by Edward's death and the restoration of catholicism.[14]

Centralised attempts to collect and export monastic lead were even more unsuccessful than local sales, since they glutted the market at Antwerp, and an ingenious plan to barter lead for Spanish alum, to be resold to English clothiers, failed in 1545 because the government found itself with about seven years' worth of alum at the normal rate of national consumption. But in general it was at the local level that the crown's financial managers faced most frustration. The sophistication of the augmentations' system of regional auditors was blunted by the tendency of receivers and bailiffs not to turn up to their fortnight-long annual audit, or to arrive with excuses rather than cash. At regular intervals from 1515 to the 1550s pressure had to be renewed to persuade local receivers neither to hold onto the crown's revenues as a source of personal credit, nor to give priority to the payment out of their receipts of fees and annuities to the locally influential rather than the delivery of cash to the crown. As in other areas of government, what was needed was continual revolution, as Wolsey realised in maintaining the pressure from above exercised by Henry VII to produce increases in cash deliveries from the crown's Welsh estates in the 1520s. But the crown's local agents were a significant part of the political nation, and could not be pushed too far. By 1554 more than £125,000 was owed in arrears by the local officers of the court of augmentations – much of it, to be fair, probably uncollectable from those who owed it to the crown in the first place – yet bills enabling the crown to recover such debts from the widows, heirs and executors of defaulting accountants were rejected in the parliaments of 1546 and 1558.[15]

When land itself was sold, the crown took more care to realise the price in cash immediately, as was imperative when the sales came in response to financial emergencies such as the wars of 1542–50 and 1557–9, and feasible when purchasers dealt directly with the central staff of the augmentations. The market for land was so bullish, except in the economic crisis of the later 1550s, that there was little difficulty in finding purchasers for each tranche of estates placed on the market and few buyers secured great bargains at the crown's expense. Except when part of the estate involved was explicitly treated as a gift from the king in reward for service, the standard price was twenty times the annual value, and sometimes this was pushed as high as thirty times the annual value to take account of opportunities to increase the current rents. Altogether, it has been calculated, the crown realised £1,103,239 1s. 10d. from sales of land through the court of augmentations over the period 1536–54; and at the peak of the monastic sales in 1542–5, and again in 1548–50 when many of the chantry lands were sold, the receipts made a crucial contribution to war finance. On the other hand, as many historians have pointed out, once they were gone, they were gone, and with them the possibility that a landed livelihood might be maintained sufficient in itself to sustain government. From 1548 even the attempt to keep some financial interest for the crown in the shape of a reserved rent of 10 per cent on all property sold was abandoned.

Henry VII, and perhaps even Fortescue, might have been happy with the major contribution towards the regular costs of government which the property still in the crown's hands made under Mary; the problem was that the need for sales and the urge to disperse lands in patronage recurred in her reign and in those of her successors. Even the prudent Elizabeth, who cut the proportion of outright gifts amongst her alienations in Somerset to 1 per cent (where her father had freely given 49 per cent of the land he distributed in 1536–9), nevertheless disposed of about a fifth of the crown estate there between 1558 and 1573, long before the exigencies of war finance enforced the sales of the 1590s; and in substituting leases on favourable terms for full alienation as a means of reward, she cut back her income from those crown lands that did survive.[16]

The Customs

The second great pillar of crown finance was the customs revenue (see Table 3.2), derived from a range of import and export duties built up over the thirteenth and fourteenth centuries. To some extent its yield was beyond the crown's control, since it depended on the volume of trade and thus on the overall health of the economy. Part of Henry VI's problems sprang from the combination of Europe-wide economic depression and a changing balance within English exports as manufactured cloth, comparatively lightly rated for customs duties, replaced the much more heavily rated raw wool. These changes made his revenue from the customs less than half that enjoyed by Edward III in the second half of his reign, when it had proved the mainstay of war finance. In this respect, as in the rural economic revival which facilitated the exploitation of landed income, monarchs from the 1470s were fortunate. Henry VII in particular saw trade boom in the 1490s and 1500s, producing a rise in average annual cloth exports of 61 per cent over his reign as a whole (though at the expense of a continuing decline of 30 per cent in

Table 3.2   Annual Customs Receipts
(to the nearest £1000)

Henry V	£49,000	(average 1413–18)[a]
Henry VI	£30,000	(average 1441–52)[b]
Edward IV	£34,000	(average 1471–83)[c]
Henry VII	£37,000	(average 1485–1509)[d]
	£48,000	(peak year 1507–8)[e]
Henry VIII	£38,000	(average 1509–47)[d]
	£51,000	(peak year 1519–20)[f]
Edward VI	£26,000	(1550–1)[g]
Mary	£29,000	(1556–7)[g]
Elizabeth	£83,000	(1559–60)[h]

[a] J. H. Ramsay, *Lancaster and York* (2 vols, Oxford, 1892), i, 313.
[b] R. A. Griffiths, *The Reign of King Henry VI: The Exercise of Royal Authority, 1422–1461* (London, 1981), p. 396.
[c] C. D. Ross, *Edward IV* (London, 1974), p. 385.
[d] W. G. Hoskins, *The Age of Plunder: King Henry's England 1500–1547* (London, 1976), p. 179.
[e] G. Schanz, *Englische Handelspolitik gegen Ende des Mittelalters* (2 vols, Leipzig, 1881), ii, p. 46.
[f] Schanz, *Englische Handelspolitik*, ii, p. 59.
[g] F. C. Dietz, *English Government Finance 1485–1558* (Urbana, Ill, 1921), p. 208.
[h] G. D. Ramsay, *The City of London in International Politics at the Accession of Elizabeth Tudor* (Manchester, 1975), p. 50.

wool exports). Meanwhile imports increased as the domestic economy grew, the yield of the customs on non-sweet wine rising by 47 per cent and on other classes of imports by even more.[17]

Henry was not merely lucky, he had in part made his own luck. His foreign policy aimed consistently at encouraging trade – except when the demands of dynastic security required the use of English trade with the Netherlands as a diplomatic weapon, when he was ruthless in cutting it off – and securing advantages for English merchants abroad and at home. He tried to revoke or deviously reinterpret the privileges granted by Edward IV at the expense of English traders to those of Spain and the Hanseatic towns, though in both cases the needs of his dynastic diplomacy eventually made him relent. Such concern for trade was certainly not disinterested, either politically – the support of London and its trading interests had been of great assistance to those who could command it during the Wars of the Roses – or financially. In Henry's later years he lent some £87,000 to English or Italian merchants, doubtless expecting a return like that pursued more directly by Edward IV, who conducted a considerable import/export business on his own account. Henry also maximised the crown's income from trade by improvements in the levying of the customs, following on those initiated by Edward. From the very start of the reign royal commissioners hunted out corrupt customs officers, and chastened customs officers prosecuted smugglers: over three-quarters of the 1806 crown prosecutions in the exchequer in his reign were for customs evasion, and 40 per cent of such actions were concluded, a high rate by the standards of the contemporary legal system. Large fines were levied on London merchants for such offences, and by the end of the reign Edmund Dudley was threatening that the king would suspend trade if the Merchant Adventurers, who dominated the cloth trade, did not cooperate in further investigations 'for the Custume'.[18]

Henry's other initiative was the book of rates. This had been introduced by 1502–3, at least in the port of London, which dealt with half the nation's external trade and would soon deal with two-thirds of it. It gave official valuations of goods on which the customs due could be assessed, to prevent merchants from claiming that their wares were worth less than they really were. From the 1530s the use of such books was extended throughout the realm, but they became a liability when inflation set in. By 1552 it was estimated, for example, that imported silk cost £1 a yard on the open market, but was rated at only 7s. 6d. a yard in the book of rates, so the crown's income from poundage (the relevant customs duty) at 5 per cent was 4^{1}/2d. where it should have been 1s. A new book was needed, and was recommended by the royal commission on the revenues of 1552. The Marian government provided it in 1558, with valuations on average 75 per cent higher than those current since Henry VII's reign, and sometimes higher still: thus red herrings, rated at £4 a thousand as recently as 1545, were fixed at £8 a thousand in 1558.

Mary's councillors, led by the veteran financial minister William Paulet, marquess of Winchester, also tackled the other major difficulty of the customs system, the underrating of cloth. Without consulting parliament, which controlled the grant of most of the other customs duties but had obligingly voted them without interruption since the 1380s, various extra duties were imposed in May 1558. Some discriminated against French goods, and these were largely dropped once peace was made in 1559, but the new imposition on cloth was much too valuable to lose, for it increased the duties payable on each cloth about five times over. Even though the merchants contested its validity in the law courts, they soon reached a compromise in negotiations with the crown, leaving the duty in place to generate more than half the London customs in the 1560s. Together with the new book of rates, it had more than doubled the customs revenue and opened the way, through the continued expansion of trade and the increasingly controversial use of unparliamentary impositions, to the fundamental role played by the customs in early Stuart finance, equal to that of Henry VII's day if not quite to that of Edward III's.[19]

Feudal Revenues

The third area of crown income on which Henry VII's attention was closely focused was that derived from his position at the head of the feudal system of land tenure. Because land held directly from the king by his tenants-in-chief technically passed back into the king's hands at the death of each tenant, he could charge money for its restoration to the heir (livery, or special livery which cost more but protected the tenant against subsequent royal claims that the process had not been properly carried out), take its profits in the period between the tenant's death and the heir's livery (primer seisin), retain control of it until an underaged heir reached 21 (wardship), arrange the marriage of an heir in wardship, or refuse to give the tenant's widow her dower portion of the estate unless she married the man the king chose, or bought a licence to marry another. Similar profits might be drawn from the estates of bishoprics at each change of bishop and religious houses at each change of head. The original military rationale of these arrangements soon gave way to financial and political exploitation, and kings from the Angevins to Edward II sold wardships or added wards' lands temporarily to the royal demesne, when they were not using the system to reward their favourites.

The use of such resources was, however, a very sensitive political issue – a central point, for instance, in Magna Carta – for it opposed the financial interests of the king directly with the financial interests, and often the personal happiness, of his most powerful subjects. Thus Henry V sent out commissioners to investigate and maximise his feudal rights, and sold wardships and licences for widows to marry, personally striking bargains with his leading nobles in such matters, but he was careful not to push his terms tyrannously high. Only frenzied and, with hindsight, doomed regimes like that of Edward II in the 1320s squeezed feudal incidents for all they were worth either in revenue or in rewards. The unpopularity of wardship in particular, and of the inflexibility in the deployment of landed inheritances which went with primogeniture, was such that most landowners had taken since Edward III's reign to entrusting their lands to feoffees, who technically held the land from the king to the use of the landowner and thereafter his nominee (usually the heir). Thus even when the landowner died, the king's tenant did not, and the opportunity for the most devastating exactions – though very rarely the whole range of feudal incidents – was lost to the king.[20]

Some royal counter-measures had already been devised by 1461, and were applied by Edward IV and, with extreme intensity, by Henry VII. Special commissioners were used to seek out lapses or evasions of the king's rights, pressure brought on the escheators who held local inquisitions into the land held by each tenant-in-chief at death, minute investigation made of the livery of land to each heir to see whether his estates had been perfectly redeemed from the king's hand. The requirement that each alienation of land (including those to feoffees) must be licensed by the king was utilised to insist that a little of each estate be kept by the original landowner as a tenancy-in-chief, and that any division of estates should always make each new tenant a tenant-in-chief. Those who alienated land without such licences might be heavily fined, and those who took them on the king's terms and thus remained tenants-in-chief, if only of one acre of ground, were exposed both to royal control of the ward's marriage, and to prerogative wardship, by which the king, as the senior lord with rights of wardship, claimed control of all the ward's lands, whether held directly from the crown or not. Prerogative wardship, which had been largely abandoned before 1485, was the subject of intense discussion amongst ambitious lawyers from the 1490s, as in many areas of the feudal law they sought to equip the crown with ever more ingeniously generous interpretations of the thirteenth-century 'statute' *Prerogativa Regis* which defined the king's rights. Counsel for the crown – often the same men – argued in the lawcourts for the application of those same interpretations, earning one of them the rebuke from an opposing pleader that 'You and your fellows will say anything to earn your fee from the king'.[21]

Since Henry sold more or less anything that could be sold, from appointments to office to decisions in lawsuits, it is no surprise that he freely sold the marriages of wards and widows and at times personally drove hard bargains with potential purchasers, meticulously recorded in his chamber accounts; touchingly, Henry at least resisted the temptation to sell his own mother when the earl of Derby's death made her a king's widow in 1504. Alongside sales went fines: for entering one's lands without proper livery or marrying a royal ward without permission, just as for involvement in rebellion, hunting the king's game, letting prisoners escape, or failing to take up knighthood if one were a landowner of a certain level of wealth (distraint of knighthood). After about 1503, as the king lost his personal control through illness and his earlier ministers, notably Bray, through death, administrative elaboration reflected the range of incidents Henry was exploiting. To Empson's council learned, and Edmund Dudley's more freelance dealing in fines and recognisances, were joined a master of wards and a surveyor of the king's prerogative who pursued king's widows as well as outlaws and convicts through a network of county surveyors.[22]

The policy's financial success was marked: by 1504–6 wardship and livery alone raised nearly a tenth of royal income (see Table 3.3). Fines yielded much more, at least in the bonds for future payment which Henry collected systematically in the last years of his reign. Dudley took more than £30,000 in cash and £189,000 in bonds in 1504–8. But, as the programme's connection with Henry's

Table 3.3 Annual Crown Income from Wards and Liveries
(to the nearest £1)

Henry VII	£9,409	(average 1504–6)[a]
Henry VIII	c.£7,000	(average 1541–6)[b]
Edward VI	£11,027	(average 1546–52)[b]
		35 wardships sold p.a.[c]
Mary	£15,423	(average 1552–8)[b]
		49 wardships sold p.a.[c]
Elizabeth	£14,677	(average 1558–1602)[b]
	£29,551	1561[d]
		64 wardships sold p.a. 1558–68[c]

[a] H. E. Bell, *An Introduction to the History and Records of the Court of Wards and Liveries* (Cambridge, 1953), p. 7n.
[b] J. Hurstfield, 'The profits of fiscal feudalism, 1541–1602', *EcHR*, 2nd series 8 (1955–6), 55.
[c] Bell, *Wards*, p. 114.
[d] Bell, *Wards*, p. 48.

rule by recognisance suggests, it was politically controversial, too close for comfort to Fortescue's 'exquysite meanes of geytinge of good'. Henry's attempt to secure a feudal aid in 1504 for the knighting of his eldest son and the marriage of his eldest daughter was strenuously and successfully resisted in parliament, where Henry was in effect bought off with a peacetime subsidy. His subjects' fear was that the register of tenants-in-chief which the assessment of the feudal aid would generate might be used to intensify royal exactions still further.

Individuals had more immediate cause for grievance. Sir George Tailboys had to pay Henry more than £500 not to have him declared a lunatic and his lands taken into wardship (he was presumably sane enough to see the virtue of paying up). The duke of Buckingham had to pay £2000 for a pardon for his mother's remarriage without licence (his mother should have been fined, but he had money on that scale and she did not, and in any case she was dead before the fine was levied). Dudley's list of Henry's unfair exactions, compiled in 1509, included large fines for marriages, liveries and the restitution of temporalities to religious houses which should have been exempt from such charges. It was no surprise that when Henry died, the surveyorship of the prerogative disappeared along with Empson, Dudley and the council learned, and the more spectacular exactions ceased. However, the principle of county-level supervision continued with the appointment of county feodaries for the office of wards in 1513, many debts for liveries and other fines were reduced or suspended rather than cancelled outright, the surveyors of crown woods, established in 1521, were charged with pursuing the king's widows and fines for the violation of statutes, and wardship administration too was tightened in the 1520s. Distraint of knighthood, much used by Henry VII (in one year to the tune of £1125 in fines), survived to be exploited again by Cromwell, Protector Somerset, and Mary. And by 1529 Henry VIII was preparing to tackle the issue which even his father had not confronted head-on, that of uses.[23]

The result was an eleven-year struggle, in which Henry eventually combined his father's methods with his own. Initially he cajoled the peerage into an agreement that the crown might take into wardship one-third of the lands of a tenant-in-chief, uses notwithstanding, but a bill based on these terms failed in parliament in 1532. Henry then resolved to 'serche out the extremitie of the lawe', as he told MPs. Cromwell, Audley and Henry himself did so by exerting enormous pressure on the common law judges to find that Lord Dacre's disposition of his lands (held in use) by will was invalid, thus undermining all uses and indeed almost every title to land in the country. This opened the way to the statute of uses of 1536, which made uses ineffective as a device for evading feudal incidents or bequeathing land by will, but aroused frequent protests among the rebels of that year, and set lawyers – even royal office-holders, when sufficiently well paid by private clients – to work devising ways to avoid the new regulations. By 1540, with the removal of Cromwell's firm and legally nerved hand, Henry was back to compromise, and the result was the statute of wills, which allowed tenants-in-chief to devise two-thirds of their land by will but retained the crown's right to wardship over one-third.[24]

For the moment this was a politically stable solution, though wardship itself would become increasingly unpopular as the Tudors gave way to the Stuarts. From Henry's point of view the retreat from the high point of 1536 was the more acceptable because the Dissolution of the Monasteries was rapidly expanding the number of lay tenants-in-chief subject to feudal incidents, at least until the weakness of his son's regime led to the peculiarity of 'Greenwich tenures' for purchasers of crown lands to spare them the inconveniences of tenure-in-chief. In any case, the multiplication of tenancies-in-chief as monastic estates were resold among the gentry, and the specialised oversight of the court of wards from 1540, drove the number of wardships found and sold steadily upwards through the reigns of Edward and Mary and into Elizabeth's early years, and with them the crown's profits. Only then did the potent combination of Elizabethan moderation and Cecilian corruption allow the crown's income from its feudal prerogatives to stagnate to the point where desperate and controversial efforts at renovation proved necessary after 1603.[25]

Pensions, Coinage and Purveyance

A range of other financial expedients was available to early Tudor rulers without recourse to direct taxation, parliamentary or otherwise. One useful source of ready cash was the pension paid by the kings of France to buy English acquiescence in their pursuit of conquests in Italy and elsewhere. First negotiated by Edward IV in 1475 and renewed by Henry VII in 1492 and by Henry VIII at the conclusion of each of his wars with France, it ran at around £10,000 a year until surrendered by the chastened Edwardian regime in 1550. Further payments from the French followed the restitution of Tournai in 1518 and Boulogne in 1550, raising the annual cash receipts in some years as high as £50,000, but these did not meet the costs of fortifying and garrisoning them since their capture in 1513 and 1544 respectively, let alone the cost of conquering them in the first place.[26]

More lucrative but more dangerous was manipulation of the coinage. Medieval English kings had largely avoided the temptation to profit from a reduction in the precious metal content of their coins of a given face value, though Edward IV foreshadowed his grandson's depredations in the profitable recoinage of 1464–5. Henry VII even waived his normal profits from the mints – less than £100 a year – in order to raise the quality of the coinage, an act of concern for the image of kingship his coins projected as much as for the health of the economy. Henry VIII was more reckless, at least in his later years. He was debasing the Irish coinage in the 1530s, but it was only from 1544 that he began to release smaller coins with a lower silver content in England. Once started, it was hard to stop, because the only way to continue to draw in silver to the mints and still profit from debasement was to raise the price the crown offered for old coin or plate, and lower still further the quality of the recoined issues. Somerset continued relentlessly, and Northumberland, though bent on stabilising the coinage, indulged in one last burst of debasement and then bungled the revaluation of debased coin necessary to counteract inflation and protect the new coinage. Before 1542 the silver content of English coins was 92.5 per cent; by April 1546 it was 33.3 per cent; by April 1551 it was 25 per cent. Four times as much coin had been minted between 1544 and 1551 as between 1526 and 1544, and the increase in volume and decrease in quality of the coinage had caused rapid inflation, driven sterling down on the foreign exchanges, and induced an unhealthy sequence of booms and slumps in the export of cloth. Full revaluation and recoinage of the debased coins to restore proper stability would be painful for the poor, and the Marian financial reformers took up again the plans made by Northumberland but interrupted by Edward's death, but dared not implement them in the dearth year of 1557, leaving it to Elizabeth, who brought the sorry tale to an end in 1560–1. The only extenuating circumstance was that the crown had drawn profits of £1,270,684 from the debasement, about a third of the cost of the wars, fleets and fortifications of 1542–50.[27]

Monarchs could profit more directly at the expense of their subjects' economic well-being through purveyance. This was the right to requisition supplies for the royal household or the armed forces at a price named by the crown. By the 1590s the price was only about a quarter of the market price, while earlier in the century, though less unreasonable, it had often been paid months or years late. The activities of the king's purveyors, whose recurrent vice was to 'bye iij tymes asmoch as seruyth the kyng, and selle it agayn to their oun aduantage' as Henry Brinklow put it in about 1542, were restrained by more than 40 statutes from the thirteenth century to the mid-sixteenth – some of them gathered in a handy printed volume in about 1505 for those who wanted to confront errant purveyors with chapter and verse – and by sections in the household ordinances of 1478 and 1526, but complaints never ceased. The true value of purveyance cannot be calculated, but it was substantial enough that successive governments sought to reform it rather than abandon it altogether, all the more so as inflation raised the costs of the royal household: the royal commissioners of 1552 hoped that 'the kinges prerogative in prises [purveyance] … must nedes helpe muche, to the decrease of this chardge'.

Cromwell tied purveyors more closely to the household departments they serviced, and tried to make them intermediaries with regular contractors rather than licensed looters; he also cut back many of the exemptions from purveyance granted in the past. The

Edwardian social reformer John Hales engineered purveyance's experimental suspension in 1549, aiming to transfer the burden of supporting the household from poor farmers to rich sheepmasters and clothiers who would pay the taxes on sheep and woollens which were his replacement for it; but the scheme soon proved even more unpopular than purveyance, at least with the parliamentary classes, who first mutilated his legislation and then withdrew it. Instead the Marian government turned to sharper statutory limits on purveyors and the extension of late Henrician composition arrangements. Under these, shires near the court, led by their JPs, negotiated a quota, usually of wheat, to be supplied to the household at the queen's price; then they levied local taxes to pay the farmers the full price for their produce. Such schemes were generalised under Elizabeth, largely converting purveyance into one of the various forms of local taxation – militia rates and so on – with which her regime tried to compensate for the deficiencies of national finance.[28]

Parliamentary Taxation

Elizabeth's problem was that she and her ministers lacked the political will, or perhaps the desperation, to reinvigorate the nation-wide system of direct taxation; it took the parliamentary side in the Civil War to do that. Henry VII and Henry VIII, faced with a similar task, proved bolder and more successful than would Gloriana (see Table 3.4). In 1485 the standard form of parliamentary taxation was the fifteenth and tenth, a property tax with a yield frozen into fixed local quotas in 1334. Since then the Black Death, the rise of the cloth industry, London's growing commercial predominance and the beginnings of enclosure for sheep- and cattle-farming had radically altered the distribution of wealth in the country, but no acceptable and efficient substitute for the fifteenth and tenth had been found, despite experiments with poll taxes and taxes on landed incomes from the 1370s to the 1470s. The former had provoked popular rebellions, the latter sharp debate in parliament, under-assessment by local commissioners, and blunt refusal to pay. None had raised more than the £31,411 of Edward IV's tenth on incomes of 1472, little better than the fixed £30,000 or so of the fifteenth and tenth. High annual rates of taxation using multiple fifteenths and

Table 3.4 Annual Crown Income from Direct Lay Taxation (to the nearest £1000)

	Parliamentary	Non-parliamentary
Henry V	£60,000 (average 1415–20)[a]	
	£75,000 (peak years 1415, 1417)	
Henry VI	£13,000 (average 1436–45)[b]	
Edward IV	£8,000 (average 1461–83)[c]	>£21,000 (1474–5)[d]
	>£31,000 (peak year 1474)	c.£30,000 (1481)[e]
Henry VII	£12,000 (average 1485–1509)[f]	>£48,000 (1492)[g]
	£90,000 (peak year 1497)	
Henry VIII	£27,000 (average 1509–46)	£204,000 (1522–3)[h]
	£48,000 (average 1512–17)	£112,000 (1542)[i]
	£69,000 (average 1524–5)	£120,000 (1545)[i]
	£89,000 (average 1541–6)	>£100,000? (1546)[i]
	£194,000 (peak year 1546)	
Edward VI	£44,000 (average 1547–53)	
	£126,000 (peak year 1547)	
Mary	£73,000 (average 1554–8)	£109,000 (1557)[j]
	£163,000 (peak year 1558)	

[a] *Henry V: The Practice of Kingship*, ed. G. L. Harriss (Oxford, 1985), p. 145.
[b] Griffiths, *Reign of Henry VI*, p. 384.
[c] C. D. Ross, *Edward IV* (London, 1974), pp. 215–18, 371, 385.
[d] R. Virgoe, 'The benevolence of 1481', *EHR*, 104 (1989), 26.
[e] Ibid., p. 38.
[f] These and all following figures for parliamentary taxation are calculated from R. Schofield, 'Taxation and the political limits of the Tudor state', in *Law and Government under the Tudors*, ed. C. Cross, D. M. Loades and J. J. Scarisbrick (Cambridge, 1988), pp. 231–2 and F. C. Dietz, *English Government Finance, 1485–1558* (Urbana, Ill, 1921), pp. 225–6.
[g] Virgoe, 'Benevolence of 1481', p. 43.
[h] J. A. Guy, 'Wolsey and the Parliament of 1523', in *Law and Government*, p. 1.
[i] Dietz, *Finance*, pp. 165–6.
[j] D. M. Loades, *The Reign of Mary Tudor* (2nd edn, London, 1991), p. 342.

tenths had proved possible under Henry V with victories abroad, visibly prudent financial management and careful wooing of the commons in parliament, but even his success was waning by the last years of his reign.[29]

Accurate, directly assessed taxation of landed incomes, preferably combined with a poll tax or tax on wages, was the aim of both Henry VII and Henry VIII in their continuation of the complex dialogue of the English crown with its subjects, a dialogue conducted as much through popular unrest and non-cooperation by local elites as in parliament. Henry VII's success was very mixed. In 1489 he secured from parliament a directly assessed subsidy intended to raise £75,000 and renewable in succeeding years should his war in Brittany continue, but unsurprisingly, given its overtones of regular taxation without consent, it was declared not to be a precedent for future grants; out in the counties incomes were widely underassessed, and the final yield was only some £24,000. In 1497 and 1504 parliament would agree only to raise the same quota for each county as a fifteenth and tenth, apportioning the sum among individual taxpayers by direct assessment of their incomes and property. Nonetheless, the coupling of these new taxes with simultaneous fifteenths and tenths gave Henry's taxation in war years an intensity greater than that of Henry V, and the result was disorder: the Yorkshire Rising in 1489 (preceded by intensive lobbying for local exemptions), a smaller revolt in Yorkshire in 1492, the Western Rising in 1497, repeated delays in payment or refusals to pay in Yorkshire and Lancashire, and a string of attacks on tax collectors to rescue goods distrained for non-payment.

In the next reign all three dams – parliamentary haggling, elite non-cooperation and popular resistance – were broken, but briefly and incompletely. In the parliamentary sessions of 1512–15, a succession of subsidy acts provided increasingly effective directly assessed taxes on incomes and goods, one of which even incorporated a 4d. poll-tax on everyone over 15 not otherwise assessed; from 1514 taxpayers might be put on oath to declare their wealth truly if the commissioners were not satisfied with the returns made by the assessors they appointed for each township. The change from the fixed quotas of the past was drastic. In 1515 the total assessment in counties grown rich since 1334 was sometimes eight times higher than under the fifteenth and tenth, and in London it was nearly fifteen times higher. The subsidies were the product of careful parliamentary management, not least in 1515 when Wolsey used an act of resumption like those of the fifteenth century to convince the commons that the king was not being careless with their money. But again the levy met with trouble in some areas, Ripon and Richmond in the North Riding of Yorkshire mounting a significant revolt in 1513, and Craven, in the West Riding, manifesting non-cooperation with assessment, very belated payment or non-payment, and protests to the local magnate Lord Clifford. Like Henry VII's subsidy of 1489 and several of Edward IV's experimental levies, these subsidies raised in practice far less than had been intended, and indeed the grants of 1515, made after the conclusion of peace with France, were expressly designed to make up this shortfall.

Next time Henry went to war, in 1523, there was trouble in parliament, where the session dragged on long into the summer as Wolsey went bullyingly but unsuccessfully beyond the standard tactics of asking for much more than he hoped to get. Nonetheless, the subsidies voted in 1523 and collected in 1524–5 were so successful – taxing perhaps 90 per cent of households in rural areas and a half to two-thirds in towns – that they provided the model for all future Tudor lay subsidy acts, though the rates of assessment and thresholds for exemption remained usefully flexible. These subsidies also saw the first use of anticipation, by which richer taxpayers were asked to pay some months before the date specified in parliament in order to help the war effort at a crucial moment. Popular resistance to taxation was not yet dead. Problems with assessment and collection in parts of Yorkshire and Lancashire continued into the 1520s. Opposition to taxes both real and rumoured marked the rebellions of 1536, and tax-strikes continued into 1537, discouraging further attempts to reform the fifteenth and tenth as Cromwell had tried to do. Likewise, John Hales's ill-conceived sheep tax had to be withdrawn after complaints in the Western Rebellion of 1549. But in the wars of the 1540s parliament and populace alike finally bowed to Henry's awesome will, voting and paying enormous sums over an extended period. It is true that debasement and the consequent increase in the money supply made Henry's achievement look more striking than it was. Estimates suggest that Henry V was drawing his taxes out of a money supply of about £639,000, Edward IV his out of £700,000, but that by 1544 the figure had reached perhaps £1,190,000 or £1,230,000, and by 1551 debasement may have pushed it up to £2,660,000. Nevertheless, even as a proportion of such totals, the yields of Henry's direct taxes are impressive, and the less intimidating Edwardian and Marian regimes maintained very respectable average yields from direct taxation. Thus the total annual tax burden on London in the period 1540–59 in real terms was nearly twice as high as that in Elizabeth's later years, even when the various local levies of Elizabeth's reign are taken into account.[30]

As such figures suggest, all this effort bore less fruit in the long term than its immediate effect might have promised. The high direct taxation of Henry VIII's reign and those that followed acted in part to compensate for the declining yields of the customs in real terms, so that all that resulted was a change in the sources of royal income rather than a major increase. And when the yields of direct taxation are adjusted for inflation, the middle decades of the sixteenth century represent a slight rise in a fairly level trend running from the 1490s to the 1640s, a rise soon smoothed out after about 1570.[31]

The rot which would ruin Elizabethan subsidies was already setting in by the 1540s. The great success of the reformed subsidy was its accuracy of assessment. Even the peers – examined on oath about their incomes in 1523 by commissioners led by Cardinal Wolsey and Archbishop Warham – were taxed realistically, and at local level commissioners with the eyes of the government upon them tried their hardest to be equally effective, if needs be at the cost of truthfulness. In Craven and parts of the North Riding, commissioners in 1524–5 eventually forged the assessments and tried to cover up their difficulties with the taxpayers, rather than face the kind of punishment Lord Clifford had taken for passing on complaints to the government in 1515. Even in the 1540s the Craven assessments were still to some extent works of fiction, but now they overrated individuals' wealth as often as they underrated it, and they certainly generated larger total yields than those of the 1510s and 1520s; across Yorkshire and Lancashire, the tradition of resistance dating back to the 1480s seems finally to have ended. Yet as subsidies became more frequent and more familiar, and as the tight management of local politics exercised by Henry VII, Wolsey and Cromwell began to fade, the accuracy of assessment wilted. Among the peerage there was a clear fall in 1547, when several noblemen revised their statements of their income downwards by £500 or more now that the old king was no longer breathing down their necks; by 1558 the average assessed landed income of the peers was down to £685 from the £921 of 1534. Where the nobles led, the gentry who staffed the county commissions of assessment followed. One sample suggests that subsidy assessments fell from recording nearly half each taxpayer's wealth as shown in probate records in the period 1524–42, through one-third in the later 1540s, to little more than a quarter in the 1550s and just over a fifth in the 1560s. The effects of this decline were all the more serious because the poor were throughout the period far more accurately assessed than the rich, the friends and relations of the commissioners: between 1524 and 1572, those rated at under £10 in goods were assessed at 59 per cent of their wealth as valued for probate, while those worth £100 or more were taxed on 10 per cent.

Collusive underassessment, one of the three bugbears of late-medieval taxation, had overcome the concerted political pressure of the early Tudor kings where parliamentary quibbling and popular upheaval could not. The effect was reinforced by the elimination of the progressive rates of taxation on higher incomes which were introduced in the subsidy of 1523 and continued in those of 1544–57, and consciences were eased by the abolition of assessment on oath in 1563. Elizabethan subsidies could be voted with remarkably little fuss and even in multiples of three or four, because by the end of the reign, even at face value, they cost the country as a whole little more than half what they had done at its start – after decades of inflation, far less in real terms – and because they cost the parliamentary classes proportionately even less.[32]

Non-Parliamentary Taxation

Despite being short-lived, Henry VIII's success in raising levels of parliamentary taxation was the more striking because it was accompanied by very large extra-parliamentary levies (see Table 3.4). Forced loans were as old as parliamentary taxation, and were often requested to enable the crown to spend the proceeds of such taxation faster than it could be collected. Thus Henry VII, for instance, raised £40,000 in 1496–7 to begin preparations for his Scottish expedition, promising to repay it from taxation by the end of the latter year. Such loans were justified by invoking national emergencies in the instructions sent out to the commissioners who negotiated with individuals to determine the sum they were prepared to lend the king, and in the royal letters sent directly to those known to be wealthy, suggesting an appropriate figure. At times the requests were strengthened by securing the promises of the peers or councillors to contribute generously before the rest of the population was approached, or even by using the great council as a quasi-parliamentary body to grant consent, as Henry VII did in 1496. It was difficult to refuse help to the king on theoretical grounds, but many might plead poverty or haggle over the sum requested, and strong regimes drew far more from such loans than those already in financial or political straits: Henry V in 1421 raised the largest general loan before Henry VII, but a rare surviving return from one area in 1446 shows that sixteen out of twenty people approached declined to contribute, and five of those did not even bother to turn up to meet the commissioners.

The leap from the £9000 raised in 1421 to Henry VII's £40,000 was facilitated by Edward IV's introduction of benevolences, levies raised like a forced loan but with no expectation of repayment. Taxpayers were told that paying the benevolence was a substitute for their compulsory military service in campaigns to be led by the king in person, and those approached were the comparatively well-off whose wealth Edward's parliamentary income taxes had failed to tap. Edward himself was active in negotiation with contributors in 1474–5, his royal clerks and household men were prominent on the commissions, and in 1480 he probably obtained the consent of a great council. All this added to the pressure that produced a handsome yield, but generated sufficient ill-feeling for Richard III to agree to a statute abolishing benevolences in 1484. The statute was neatly side-stepped by Henry VII in 1491–2 with a 'loving contribution' even larger than Edward's benevolences, backed by a great council and retrospectively validated by statute.[33]

Throughout, the limits on such levies – beyond that of the government's general ability to persuade people to pay – were primarily those of the information available about the wealth of those approached. Wolsey breached such limits in spectacular fashion in 1522. First he conducted the most minute survey into the landholding and individual wealth of the English population since Domesday Book, aiming to assess the country's military strength and improve the machinery for raising troops: the information was gathered by carefully chosen and tightly supervised commissioners and given on oath. Then he used the statistics from this 'general proscription', sharpened by a second round of enquiries, to levy a forced loan in two stages from all laymen worth £5 and over, at progressive rates four times higher than those of the subsidies of the 1510s. The yield was astounding, but at the cost of grumbling reflected in John Skelton's obsessive concern with the loans in his satire on Wolsey,

'Why come ye nat to courte'. The grumbling turned to dismay when it became evident that the king was not invading France in person and that, despite promises made as late as the parliament of 1523, there was no possibility of repayment.

Such dismay – and the real hardship produced by the impact of war on trade and the heavy subsidies of 1524–5 – helped sink the 'amicable grant', Wolsey's euphemism for a benevolence, in 1525. Like the loans this was to be assessed using the returns of 1522 and progressively rated, at top rates more than 50 per cent higher than those of the loans. However, the commissioners, even the fearsome Wolsey dealing in person with Londoners, met such reluctance to pay the allotted sums that the rating system was abandoned in favour of negotiating for voluntary contributions, and when riots broke out in Suffolk the scheme was dropped entirely. Like Henry V and several other predecessors, Henry VIII had run into the problem that high rates of direct taxation, whether parliamentary or extra-parliamentary, could be maintained only for a limited number of years: one clear sign of this in the 1520s was the tendency for each successive levy to be paid further and further behind the appointed date.[34]

In loans and benevolences as in parliamentary subsidies, Henry pushed the limits of the possible still further in the 1540s. In 1542 he took another forced loan (confident that he could always secure a retrospective statute authorising its non-repayment, as he had done in 1529 for the loans of 1522–3), in 1545 a benevolence and in 1546 a 'contribution', and all to considerable effect. The demands were driven home hard – one London alderman reluctant to pay the benevolence was sent north to fight the Scots *pour encourager les autres* – but, equally significantly, they used the subsidy assessments (which were at least intended for purposes of taxation) rather than those of the general proscription, were fixed at lower rates than those of the 1520s, and began their incidence at higher thresholds of wealth than had the amicable grant. In such exactions, as in parliamentary taxation, the triumph of Henry's will was facilitated both by the more measured ambitions of his ministers in the 1540s and by the circumstances in which they operated: visible success in the capture of Boulogne in 1544, visible danger in the French fleet sailing up the Solent in 1545, visible opportunity in the plans to marry Prince Edward to Mary, Queen of Scots, a run of good harvests (excepting that of 1545), general economic trends favouring those, from substantial husbandmen upwards, who came above the thresholds of these later loans and benevolences, and perhaps the first flickerings of a kind of protestant nationalist political theology. These successes were also testimony to the political strength of Henry's government, as the sequel showed. The Edwardian regimes made no attempt at extra-parliamentary levies, and Mary took a limited forced loan in 1556 only to repay it from the proceeds of the larger forced loan of 1557. The latter was enforced with Henrician thoroughness and ferocity, but was raised as a substitute for parliamentary taxation, rather than an adjunct to it, by a government that dared not face the commons.[35]

Peacetime Taxation

The overwhelming majority of these levies, whether approved by parliament or not, were made in wartime, but the minority which were not have excited the attention of historians. No Tudor government quite fulfilled Fortescue's nightmare of permanent direct taxation in England, whether the country were at war or at peace, though in Ireland, where military emergency was the norm, subsidies were reformed in assessment in 1477 and collected every year between 1494 and 1527 and between 1532 and 1576, sanctioned by parliamentary grants every five or ten years. But the allocation of extraordinary revenues to extraordinary purposes and ordinary revenues to ordinary purposes was especially difficult to maintain as inflation and the strains of war hit home, and government finance became again the hand-to-mouth business it had been under Henry VI: by Edward VI's reign, a quarter or even a third of revenues from parliamentary taxation was spent on the regular charges of government, much of it on the household, and under Elizabeth subsidies were voted regularly in peacetime, twice explicitly because of the insufficiency of her ordinary resources.

There were later medieval precedents for peacetime taxation and for the appropriation of wartime taxation to the general costs of government, though the first was uncommon and the second unpopular. Even Fortescue stressed the intermittency of taxation rather than any narrow link with warfare, stating vaguely that it should be requested when the king 'hath nede ffor the gode and defence off his reaume'. But well into Elizabeth's reign it remained safest to describe external threats to English security and invoke royal expenditure on defensive purposes, including fortifications, the navy and the suppression of rebellion, when approaching parliament for peacetime supply. Henry VII did so in 1504, when the preamble to the supply bill cited not only the feudal justifications for raising an aid (for which the subsidy was a substitute), but also the king's 'gret and inestimable charges for the defense of this his Realme' and his establishment of peace with England's neighbours 'to the gret wele comfort and quietnes of all his Subjettis'. Henry VIII also mentioned the costs of past defence in 1529 when cancelling the repayment of the forced loans. On the latter occasion, when passage of the bill was 'sore argued', Henry stored up trouble for himself by undertaking to request no more taxation in his lifetime 'oonles right urgent causes move hym (which shalbe evident to all his said subgiectes)', a promise on which the rebels of 1536 tried to take him up. In 1534, determined not to repeat the débâcle of 1532 when a subsidy was refused despite rumbling conflict on the Scottish borders, Cromwell followed the example of the second top-up subsidy of 1515 and of some medieval acts, to add a general eulogy of Henry's government to the rather thin instances of defensive expenditure in the preamble to the subsidy bill; although it was passed, it was weakened by provisos added in debate, was levied at low annual rates and only above a high threshold, and, together with the fifteenth and tenth attached to it, still provoked fury in the revolts of 1536.

Further peacetime subsidies were passed in 1540, 1553 and 1555, but they tended to stress the costs of defence past and present, as well as incorporating the debt of gratitude for good government used in 1534 and repeated even in the wartime subsidy acts of 1543 and 1545, and in the act of 1544 to excuse Henry from repaying the forced loan of 1542. With this parliamentary dialogue went the broader dialogue with the taxpaying public: the thresholds of these peacetime subsidies were again higher than those of the wartime taxes of the 1520s and 1540s. The 1555 bill said least about national defence, perhaps because the last thing Mary's councillors wanted the commons to think was that she was about to drag England into her husband's war against France, perhaps because it crystallised a growing and partly humanist-inspired perception that the duties of government embraced Fortescue's 'gode' as well as his 'defence' of the realm. Whatever the reason, it met strong resistance. Many MPs argued that the crown's ordinary resources should be strengthened to meet regular expenditure, for example by not returning to the church the revenues which Mary was simultaneously surrendering as she undid her father's Reformation, rather than that taxation should be used to make up the shortfall. In the end the commons passed only the subsidy, and not the three fifteenths and tenths which the councillors had also requested. Peacetime parliamentary taxation, like non-parliamentary levies, was as much a test of the political strength of individual regimes at particular moments as of the evolution of a general principle; Mary's government, after all, had nearly as much trouble securing a wartime subsidy in 1558. Like benevolences and forced loans, it remained a feasible option for governments throughout the period, but one suitable only for sparing use, and one which would necessitate under Elizabeth the combination of the cultivation of MPs' fears of an international papist conspiracy against queen and realm, and the repeated submission of the details of the queen's policy to the test that she was acting in the visible interest of the nation rather than in pursuit of any personal or dynastic ambition. The legacy of that combination would ultimately prove counter-productive for her Stuart successors.[36]

Clerical Taxation

The effectiveness of lay taxation under the early Tudors was surpassed by that of the taxation of the clergy. In the fifteenth century the granting of clerical tenths by the convocations of the provinces of Canterbury and York – each levy raising about £15,200 and £2000 respectively – was similar to the granting of lay fifteenths and tenths in parliament, and followed a similar track, Henry V taxing the clergy in 1415–20 with unmatched intensity. Here too Henry VII sought to innovate, securing grants of specific sums from the Canterbury convocation in 1489 (£25,000) and 1496 (£40,000). The clergy were also called upon to contribute to his forced loans and 'loving contribution', and were mulcted in other ways. Henry moved his bishops from see to see to profit from his rights to the bishoprics' revenues during vacancies and the fines for restoring their temporalities, fined them heavily for breaches of the statute of *praemunire* by their church courts, and charged religious orders large sums for confirming their privileges. These exactions probably eased after

1509, but the intensity of taxation continued to grow, Wolsey assessing the clergy at higher rates than the laity for the loans of 1522–3 and calling a special legatine council in 1523 to vote a swingeing subsidy payable every year for the next five years at annual rates of between 5 and 10 per cent of clerical income: the loan raised some £56,000 and the subsidy perhaps £120,000.

Worse was to come as clerics' ability to negotiate levels of taxation with the crown was drastically reduced by Henry VIII's assault on the church. First Wolsey's taxation and Henry VII's legal fiscalism were mixed in the demand in 1531 for another five-year subsidy totalling £118,000, ostensibly granted by the convocations to offset the costs to which Henry had been put in resolving his marital difficulties, but in practice extracted by threatening to prosecute the entire church under *praemunire* for their collusion with Wolsey's legacy. Then, in 1534, the suspension of payments from the English church to Rome – which had averaged some £4816 a year in the period 1485–1532 – prompted the amalgamation of papal taxes on new incumbents into a royal levy known as first fruits; simultaneously, clerical tenths were made a permanent, annual tax, their impact sharpened by a new survey of the church's wealth, the *Valor Ecclesiasticus*, compiled by royal commissioners in 1535. Clergy among the rebels of 1536 demanded a lightening of the burden, but to no avail. From 1540, clerical subsidies voted by the convocations were revived alongside the annual tenth, stepping up the annual average income from the church to some £47,000 over the period 1535–47, about three times the pre-Reformation yield. Additional pressure on the richer clergy for loans, benevolences and the anticipation of subsidy payments meant that many bishops paid a quarter of their gross incomes to the crown in 1540–7. Mary eased clerical taxation to the consternation of her commons; Elizabeth restored it but failed to revise the *Valor Ecclesiasticus*, thus allowing inflation to soothe away the effects of her father's predatory instincts among the clergy as among the laity.[37]

Borrowing

When land, customs, feudal dues, debasement and taxation all left a gap between income and expenditure, the answer was borrowing. Making war on credit had a long though not very honourable history in England – Edward I and Edward III had each managed to bankrupt entire Italian banking houses – but the Tudors fortunately never threw themselves on the developing international banking market of the sixteenth century with the vigour of the Spanish and French kings. After the first few years of his reign, Henry VII seems to have avoided borrowing entirely, except in using forced loans to anticipate the yield of his intensified taxation. By the 1520s Henry VIII had returned to Edward IV's practice of taking large loans – around £20,000 – from the citizens of London, negotiated through the corporation, and in the 1540s also through the livery companies. Somerset, Mary and Elizabeth all did the same, and after 1574 Elizabeth managed to confine all her borrowing to London and to loans requested from her individual subjects by letters under the privy seal and conscientiously repaid.

Before that date she had had to clear up the legacy of the wars of 1542–59, a huge debt on the Antwerp money market. Henry borrowed nearly £1,000,000 there between 1544 and 1547, though all but £75,000 was repaid by his death. The loans were short-term, usually for six months, so each soon needed replacement by another; English credit was not good, and competition from merchants and from Antwerp's Habsburg masters sometimes drove the real interest rates as high as 18 per cent, but Antwerp was the only source in northern Europe of credit on such a large scale, and was especially useful when money was needed on the continent to buy arms and pay mercenaries. When Edward died, the crown still owed £61,000 at Antwerp, though Northumberland had begun to employ the self-consciously brilliant financial manipulator Thomas Gresham to eliminate the debt. His techniques included negotiating down the interest rate on new loans to around 12 per cent, and, most importantly, controlling the exchange rate to the crown's advantage by taking the foreign currency earnings of the Merchant Adventurers' sales of English cloth, using them to repay the king's debts, and repaying the merchants in sterling at London; to facilitate the operation of this scheme, and compensate the Merchant Adventurers, successive English governments had to concentrate exports in the company's hands by abolishing or seriously diminishing the privileges of the Hanseatic merchants. Both Mary and Elizabeth borrowed heavily at the start of their reigns, and Mary complicated matters by a scheme to borrow money from Genoese bankers in Spain rather than at Antwerp; Mary had total foreign debts of more than £150,000 by autumn 1554, and Elizabeth reached the peak of royal indebtedness at Antwerp in 1560, at £279,000. Gresham was employed by both queens, and had indeed used large subventions from Mary's retrenching financial ministers to liquidate her debt by 1557, only to see her die in debt at Antwerp to the tune of £92,000 or so, borrowed to pay for the war in 1558. He then worked with the same domestic financial experts as in 1556–7, led by Lord Treasurer Winchester, to clear Elizabeth's debts as he had cleared her sister's, and thereafter the new queen's prudence and the decline of Antwerp as an entrepôt during the Revolt of the Netherlands combined to end the money market's temptation.[38]

Financial Administration

The administrative means devised by the early Tudors to control the gathering and expenditure of these financial resources were the product of many forces. One of the most basic was a tension between the need for security and the need for flexibility in collecting royal revenue and controlling its expenditure. The more an institution operated along traditional, well-established lines, generating records which the law courts recognised as authoritative, and operating checks and balances on individual officials, the more likely those who dealt with it were to feel that they knew where they stood, and the less vulnerable the king was to peculation or the build-up of uncollectable arrears. Such an institution, broadly speaking, was the late-medieval exchequer: it ground slowly at times, but it ground small. Yet kings who needed to gather and spend large amounts of cash in a hurry, if needs be at their own verbal command – most obviously, kings at war – needed something different. For such purposes many rulers in the thirteenth, fourteenth and fifteenth centuries used their wardrobe or chamber as a major spending department, and some even used it to collect specific revenues, as Edward II made his chamber a land revenue office in his last years.[39]

Different types of revenue were peculiarly suited to different styles of administration. Throughout the Tudor period, most parliamentary lay taxation continued to be collected by the exchequer, even though Henry VII sometimes drafted its proceeds across into the chamber; the pursuit of odd pounds, shillings and pence due from the hundreds of minor gentry and yeomen who served as subsidy collectors was the sort of task for which the exchequer was well equipped. Likewise, the exchequer always dealt with the sheriffs, for their revenues were in part ancient and regular and came in dribs and drabs (such as castle-ward), and in part closely linked with the operations of the other long-established central law courts (such as the profits of distraint or of the confiscation of the goods of condemned criminals). Thus when, in 1519–20, Wolsey appointed a commission to investigate the revenues and expenses of the shrievalty, it met in the exchequer and was headed by a justice of common pleas; there was no thought of transferring the sheriffs' accounts to the chamber system. The exchequer's predictability was also a reassurance to those who dealt with it, offering security to the subject as well as to the ruler: this was symbolised by the publication in Henry VIII's reign of at least fifteen editions of a printed handbook listing all the fees payable by accountants at different stages of the exchequer's process.[40]

When the royal demesne was expanded and run like a large private estate, on the other hand, something was called for much more like the domestic administration of a great nobleman: which was of course what the Duchy of Lancaster, centre of operations for Fowler, Bray and Empson, had begun as. Receivers-general, in this case hand-picked royal servants, could be appointed to supervise each block of estates, paying their cash receipts into the chamber and accounting before *ad hoc* teams of lawyers and financial experts, overseen by the lord himself. One-off payments from individuals on terms negotiated with the lord or his leading administrators – such as those generated by the intensified exploitation of the king's feudal rights – were also natural material for household finance.

Both elements, the need for flexibility and the dependence on estate revenue, were very visible in the Yorkist and early Tudor elevation of the king's chamber. This originated in Margaret of Anjou's financial administration in the later 1450s. Retreating to the Lancastrian heartlands in the Midlands and thus distancing herself from the exchequer at Westminster, apparently awaiting renewed civil war at any moment, she squeezed her dower lands and her son's principality of Wales for all available cash and concentrated it in the royal households, where it was both on hand and in the control of her trusted partisans. For Edward IV, moving around the country subduing his enemies and drawing on the revenues of his own estates and those he confiscated, it was natural to operate in the same way; likewise for the equally troubled Richard III and Henry

VII. Each time the crown changed hands, however – in 1483, 1485 and 1509 – exchequer control was reasserted, as the traditional and dependable institution tidied up the loose ends left by the emergency supremacy of the chamber, only for each new monarch to duplicate the chamber system with more or less variation from his predecessor. (There may also have been political virtue in a brief return to traditional ways by each ruler, especially for Henry VII, keen to stress his Lancastrian credentials.) The trend was certainly to give the chamber control over an ever wider range of revenues, culminating in Henry VII's use of his treasurer of the chamber, John Heron, as supreme national treasurer in the last decade of the reign; but then the exchequer's tidying-up was ever more forceful. Edward IV and Henry VII alike, even at the end of Henry's reign when less than £13,000 a year was being both collected and spent by the exchequer without passing through the chamber, continued to keep the exchequer's accounts in order by issuing warrants to cover money received and spent by the chamber, and to pass accounts on to the exchequer for filing once the auditing process was complete. But by 1509–10 clearer steps than these had to be taken in council and parliament to regularise the relationship between exchequer and chamber.[41]

What had complicated matters was the administrative consolidation inevitable within the chamber system as it controlled ever more royal income, and as Henry grew older and less able to supervise everything in person. The greatest sign of this was that once Heron became a national treasurer, and everyone with financial dealings with the crown needed to be able to find him, he ceased to follow the king around on progress and fixed himself in an office in Westminster Abbey. The particular problem in 1509 was that the general surveyors, the group of councillors directing the administration of the crown estates and auditing the accounts first of the receivers of land revenue and then of an increasingly wide range of other royal accountants, had grown into a court. It summoned accountants by writs under the privy seal, bound them to appear, sometimes on penalty of several hundred pounds, arrested them, imprisoned them, bound them to carry out its orders, sent out commissions of inquiry and settled cases between the king's tenants. It was operating rather like the council of a great lord, indeed like the duchy council in the Duchy of Lancaster or the shadowy conciliar court of audit active in 1508–9 controlling the affairs of Prince Henry's lands in Wales, Cheshire and the Duchy of Cornwall. But it

was doing so not in a clearly delineated and traditional field like the
Duchy council, but across the whole range of royal finance and
national life.

Doubtless this maintained efficient flexibility, uncomfortably so
for the victims of Henry VII's exactions. But since the general surveyors, the council learned, and other 'by-courts' set up by Henry, were
not courts of record like the exchequer, king's bench, common
pleas or chancery, whose recorded judgments carried authority
recognised throughout the legal system, they were felt not to offer
the necessary security to the king or his subjects. As the council
resolved on 11 October 1509, they should be abolished because if
they continued 'the king's right and title in process of time should
perish for lack of matter of record in court of authority', and
because 'the king's subjects cannot be discharged by any of the said
by-courts' and were therefore 'troubled contrary to his laws to their
utter undoing'. An awkward search then began for a new compromise between flexibility and security. Heron was accorded by statute
a new though short-lived title of general receiver of the king's revenues, and his warrants and acquittances were given full legal
authority; the general surveyors were deprived of access to the privy
seal and effectively incorporated within the exchequer. But this
proved unsatisfactory, and stage by stage from 1512 to 1536 most of
the independent powers of Henry VII's general surveyors were
restored, this time prescribed by successive statutes in order to avoid
the uncertainties raised in 1509, and kept under the overall
supremacy of the exchequer.[42]

Meanwhile the exchequer had been adapting itself to add flexibility to its security. Between 1485 and 1514, the culmination of a longstanding process of reform improved its cash flow, internal auditing
and record-keeping, and provided the king with annual statements
of the financial situation. Such changes fitted the exchequer well to
operate within the system coordinated by Heron, as was hardly surprising when many of the officials of the Yorkist and early Tudor
exchequer were themselves key figures in the chamber's financial
operations and the exploitation of land revenues. Edward IV's
under-treasurers included Sir John Say and Sir Richard Fowler, both
chancellors of the Duchy; two early sixteenth-century exchequer
tellers were simultaneously clerks to Heron; Sir John Daunce began
his career as a teller in 1505 but by 1515 was receiver-general of
wards and a general surveyor; and so on. The same was true of the
methods these men used. The exchequer's formal accounts were

kept on parchment, in Latin, with figures in Roman numerals, but their rough accounts used paper, English and the handier Arabic numerals; and as the newer institutions grew in age and institutional pretensions, they too adopted parchment, Latin and Roman numerals for their formal accounts. True, there were those who argued in Henry VIII's reign, as there would be in Elizabeth's reign, that the only way to security for the king's money – and, dare one suspect, for the jobs of those writing the memoranda – was a full return to the 'ancient course', the elaborate procedure of the medieval exchequer. But in general, divisions between old and new were a matter of the administrative compartments bureaucrats had to create to make the system work – and of the distinctions imposed by the need of the lawcourts and their clients to have everything cut-and-dried – rather than of any fundamental rivalry of personnel or institutional spirit.[43]

This was even the case in what has been seen as one of the crucial differences between the exchequer and the newer agencies, the degree to which they dealt in cash rather than making payments by assignment. In the fifteenth-century exchequer, assignment was the norm: the crown's creditors were directed to a debtor, say a customs officer, and told to take what the crown owed them from him. However, except where it suited both parties to conduct the transaction locally, the result was usually an exchange of cash and bonds for future payments at Westminster, and regimes in need of cash for war – as in Henry V's reign, or during the reforming treasurership of Ralph, Lord Cromwell (1433–43) – managed on occasion to make large proportions of the crown's income available in cash at the centre using the exchequer machinery.[44]

The Yorkist and early Tudor chamber was more clearly oriented towards cash collection and payment than the exchequer had been, but many payments were still assigned by royal warrant, and revenues were allocated *en bloc* to fund the royal household and the garrisons of Calais and Berwick; in the former instance it was politically advantageous to show that taxation was not being diverted to the household, and in the latter it made practical sense to collect revenue at the edges of the kingdom and spend it there. Henry VII even applied the same principle to direct taxation, having the bishop of Carlisle, who acted as a regional surveyor for feudal incidents in the north, collect taxes from the clergy and laity alike in Yorkshire in 1496–7, and either spend them on the war against the Scots or pay them into the chamber as need demanded. The practicality of assignment made it a feature of the court of augmentations' opera-

tions too, at least for recurrent expenditure. The most startling dis-
covery in a recent re-examination of augmentations' activity between
1536 and 1546 is that during that period the receivers disbursed
£209,108 by assignment in pensions to the ex-religious, such that
they were paid in total nearly a quarter of the income reaching the
receivers, far more than had been assumed when only the central
accounts compiled by the treasurers were examined. Nonetheless,
part of the exchequer's adaptation in the early Tudor period was a
shift towards cash: more than 50 per cent of its transactions were
made by assignment in 1480, 25 per cent in 1509, 16 per cent in
1512. By the 1550s about 95 per cent of the exchequer's revenues
passed through in cash, and its rapid cash flow lent it a reputation
for giving less opportunity than the other revenue courts for money
to stick to the hands of its officials.[45]

The huge task of absorbing the new estates confiscated from the
church in 1536 demanded a more radical solution to the problems
of flexibility and security, though one based very much on existing
precedent. The result was the creation of the court of augmentations, a body for surveying and leasing monastic lands, collecting
and spending the income they generated, auditing the resultant
accounts, and settling any resultant disputes, in function not unlike
the general surveyors, but constituted by statute as a court of record,
explicitly free from exchequer interference. It was closely modelled
on the Duchy of Lancaster, both in its central administrative personnel and in its enjoyment of the autonomy the general surveyors had
lacked, symbolised by its own seals, a privy seal to summon accountants and a great seal under which the chancellor of the augmentations could make leases of less than 21 years' duration without any
warrant from the king. In its scale, in its consciously created autonomy and powers of enforcement and its carefully prescribed administrative routine, as in its partial application of the principle of a
national organisation divided by counties, earlier adumbrated in the
surveyorship of the prerogative and the office of wards, it was novel.
But its debts to the Duchy and these other institutions, and the fact
that its bureaucracy, although the product of creation rather than
evolution, was no more formal or efficient than that of the exchequer, make it hard to assign the augmentations the central role
in a shift from medieval to modern administrative structures that has
been suggested. Its importance was more practical. Firstly it served as
a model for other courts set up to administer new or expanding
areas of royal revenue: first fruits and tenths in 1540, wards in the

same year (expanded to wards and liveries in 1542), and general surveyors in 1542. Secondly the very size of its budget, especially after its
absorption of general surveyors in 1547, made it *faute de mieux* the
dominant institution in national finance in succession to the
chamber, where the shortage of funds by 1534 led the treasurer Sir
Brian Tuke 'almost totally in to extreme dispaire'.[46]

The chamber's precipitate decline – in the 1520s it had still controlled most of the king's money – highlights another central feature
of early Tudor financial administration. The interplay of institutions
– chamber, exchequer, revenue courts – conceals the very significant
role played by individual treasurers appointed by the monarch *ad
hoc*. Such officers were predictably given control of large sums of
unusual expenditure: treasurers of war are the most frequent
example. Under Henry VII, individual ministers also gathered substantial sums in specific types of income, such as Dudley's bonds or
the fines on the western rebels. More significant still, however, were
those charged with considerable volumes of income and expenditure, effectively making them independent elements in the financial
system. Ironically Thomas Cromwell, moulder of regular institutions
in the cases of the courts of augmentations and wards, was himself a
prime example of an irregular, personal treasurer. In 1532–5 he
handled between £32,000 and £46,000 a year in royal revenues, more
than the exchequer though rather less than the chamber. He did so
partly by dint of a selection of comparatively minor offices whose
roles he expanded, cuckoo-like, to dabble in both the household-
based financial system (as master of the king's jewels) and the exchequer (as chancellor of the exchequer); but mostly because he was
steadily gaining the king's confidence. He drew income from many
sources, ecclesiastical, feudal and otherwise, and spent it on anything
from Ireland, through the navy and the expenses of ambassadors, to
the building of palaces and the construction of the king's tomb. In
many cases he obtained the royal warrants necessary to approve
these expenditures only after he had made them, and a good deal of
the money he spent had been withdrawn from the king's private
financial reserves, the coffers: he was the sort of flexible financial
executive that Heron had once been to Henry VII. As he moved into
a more senior ministerial role, he had to replace himself with his
servant John Gostwick, formally treasurer of first fruits and tenths
from 1535, but in practice collecting and spending many of the mis-
cellaneous revenues accumulated by Cromwell, more than £60,000 a
year, including drafts from other revenue institutions, between 1535

and 1540. Here, as under Henry VII, extreme administrative flexibility – Gostwick never submitted a formal account – mixed inseparably with political loyalty as Gostwick, for instance, served as paymaster-general to the troops suppressing the rebellions of 1536.

Gostwick's position was regularised by the rather sudden creation of the court of first fruits and tenths on Cromwell's fall, but similar figures continued to arise. The role taken by Sir Edmund Peckham during 1554–5, when all the income of the revenue courts was temporarily channelled into his hands while they were incorporated into the exchequer, was an understandable expedient. So perhaps, in the context of the financial emergency of 1552–3, was Northumberland's creation of a treasury for 'special service and affairs' under the control of Peter Osborne, who received and spent nearly £40,000 in sixteen months. But Peckham's previous roles, as the occupant of a specially created post of high treasurer of the mint to spend the profits of debasement, then as the manager of a special fund for the proceeds of the sale of chantry lands, show less obvious reason for elevating the individual above the institutional. And the reassertion of exchequer supremacy in 1554 did not end such practices. One teller especially trusted by Mary, Nicholas Brigham, was allowed to bypass various procedural niceties to take personal control over 70 per cent of the money passing through the exchequer by 1557–8, some £290,000 a year. Under Elizabeth another teller, Richard Stonley, played a similar role, handling 52 per cent of the exchequer's revenues between 1558 and 1566.

Such elevation of individuals was entirely in keeping with the comparative informality of much financial administration. Although the court of augmentations had specially built offices with their own garden in the palace complex at Westminster, much of its business was conducted at Rich's house in London or even his country home at Leighs in Essex. Those who wanted payment from Tuke as treasurer of the chamber had to visit his house and badger his personal servants, since his departmental clerical staff, like that of most royal officers, was quite inadequate for the workload involved. Officials kept the king's money at home, where even highly trusted men like Brigham might leave it in unguarded coffers and run the risk of its theft. Those employed in the mint, the exchequer or even the augmentations often worked alongside kinsmen, neighbours and business partners as well as colleagues in an administrative department. Throughout the period bureaucratic structures tended to give way to the urge to find the right man for a particular task and then create a post for him, rather as Henry VII had tended to do: thus Sir Francis Englefield was given wide powers as general surveyor of the customs to oversee the new levies and new rates of 1558.[47]

Financial Coordination

The same stress on individual control and responsibility was evident in the overall coordination of the financial system. Royal oversight of the machinery as a whole was most intense under Henry VII, though rare survivals from the Bray papers suggest his ministers played a more considerable role than one might imagine, and many of his interventions can be paralleled from the activities of Henry V. Under Henry VIII, chief ministers had to take on more of the high-level coordination of the various financial agencies, although the obscure system of royal deposit treasuries centred on the jewel house and king's coffers may have been used by the king to exercise tighter control than has previously been thought, and it is noteworthy that even the officials of the augmentations kept travelling to and from court to check matters with the king, as their expense accounts show. Even Edward VI was taking over the authorisation of some expenditure in the months preceding his death. Still Wolsey and Cromwell each exercised supreme executive control over royal finances, intervening in the affairs of lesser royal officers, and transferring responsibilities from one individual or institution to another: it was to them, for instance, that commanders in the field wrote when they needed money. After Cromwell's fall, it was formally the privy council as a body that exercised such control, but when detailed coordination again became vital in Henry's last French war, it was Lord Chancellor Wriothesley who took up the reins, meeting the treasurers of all the revenue institutions every Saturday to discover where funds were currently available. Somerset took charge during his protectorate, Northumberland, albeit no financial expert, thereafter. Financial control, as we might expect, was a function of political supremacy rather than of a specific position within the revenue administration; and even the exchequer would find its way round procedural irregularities to carry out the orders of a Cromwell or a Somerset.[48]

Such factors added an extra level of complication to questions of administrative change. Before Edward IV's elevation of the chamber, it had been clear who was in charge of the crown's finances at the highest level below the king: the treasurer of the exchequer, suggestively also known as the treasurer of England, coming in the sixteenth century to be known as the lord treasurer. As financial policies or the regimes implementing them changed, so did the treasurers, and that the public held them responsible for fiscal policy – as the public seems to have held Wolsey responsible in the 1520s and Cromwell in the 1530s – is evident in the murders of Bishop Stapeldon in 1326, Sir Robert Hales in 1381, and Lord Say in 1450. (Although excessive, the reaction may not have been unjustified given the tendency of some late medieval treasurers to help themselves to large sums of the crown's money.) The political use made of the office by early Tudor treasurers – John, Lord Dinham (1486–1500), and the two successive Howard earls of Surrey and dukes of Norfolk (1500–46) – is unclear, though its patronage powers were vigorously exercised by the Howards, and their role as treasurers may help to explain their very intensive attendance at council meetings and in parliament. One might speculate further, for example that the reassertion of the exchequer in 1509 was not unconnected with Surrey's leading role among the councillors of the new king; but evidence is lacking.[49]

It is fuller at the other end of the period, where many of the machinations surrounding the restoration of exchequer supremacy in 1554 and the partial resurrection of the ancient course in the years that followed had as much to do with the political standing of Lord Treasurer Winchester, and personal rivalries among his subordinates, as with the practicalities of financial administration. Examples might be multiplied. Lord Chancellor Wriothesley bitterly opposed the strengthening of augmentations brought about by the reorganisation of 1547, partly to defend the crown against the Frankenstein's monster of an unduly powerful and autonomous revenue court, but also to defend the fees and jurisdiction of the chancery, and his own resultant influence. The apparently irrational preservation of the court of wards and Duchy of Lancaster outside exchequer control in 1554 is probably attributable to the fact that the recently appointed master of one, Sir Francis Englefield, and chancellor of the other, Sir Robert Rochester, were good catholics and faithful servants of Mary throughout Edward's reign. Against such men Winchester, the flexible Henrician and Edwardian survivor only reappointed treasurer by the skin of his teeth, could make little headway in the queen's favour.[50]

The personal, political and *ad hoc* were naturally prominent in another area of crown finance, that most intimate to the monarch. The men best able to spend money on the king's whim were those who attended him in his privy chamber, and by the end of Henry VII's reign his groom of the stool controlled a privy purse account directly funded by the takings of the surveyor of the prerogative. Henry VIII greatly expanded the privy purse's role as a spending department, at times threatening to make it fully the equivalent of his father's chamber, run by trusted servants and favourite courtiers, and responsive to his needs: in 1529–32 he even took the trouble to sign the privy purse account books. The range of its spending extended into areas untouched under Henry VII – jewels, building, and secret affairs of state – and the volume expanded too, to £18–20,000 a year in 1514–19. But, unlike his father's chamber, it was not the agency of royal supervision of the entire financial system, which was instead generally coordinated by the chief minister. Therefore for practical reasons, as much as out of political jealousy of the courtiers who managed it, Wolsey and Cromwell strove to limit its budget and deprive it of independent sources of income, like the French pension which was paid directly into it in 1529–32. However, Henry's taste for gold was too much like his father's for privy chamber finance to wither away. Henry VII had stored up reserves beyond Heron's control in the royal coffers, often in foreign gold coins: £10,000 of this hoard was still left in 1513. He also used the royal jewelhouse as a kind of deposit treasury, just as noblemen salted away and on occasion displayed their wealth in plate and jewels. Henry VIII built up similar reserves when he had the chance, filling an interconnected series of deposit treasuries based at various royal palaces.

He did so most conspicuously in the years between the start of the Dissolution and the outbreak of war in 1542, drafting 9 per cent of the total yield of augmentations in 1536–46 and half the yield of the subsidy of 1540–1 into the privy coffers. In charge of the privy coffers at their height was Sir Anthony Denny, keeper of Westminster Palace and one of the two chief gentlemen of the privy chamber from 1539; from 1546, when he took over as groom of the stool, he also managed the privy purse, which was funded partly from the coffers and partly by direct drafts from the revenue courts and the mint. Denny disbursed large sums during the war years – £246,404 17s. 2¾d. in 1542–8, to be precise – but most of this was still in some sense expenditure on the king's personal needs, whether furnishing palaces or funding the royal entourage on the invasion of 1544. Even

at their peak, then, the privy purse and privy coffers did not coordinate national finance as Henry VII's chamber had once done, except
in so far as Henry VIII's creaming-off from the revenue institutions
on which these household agencies were parasitic concentrated the
available surpluses under his control. Coffers and purse alike were
part of the loosely integrated system managed by monarch and ministers which characterised Henry's finances, so much so that Sir
William Compton, groom of the stool until 1526, moved his financial
experience across to the under-treasurership of the exchequer when
he relinquished control of the privy purse.[51]

The role of the privy chamber and privy coffers was one sign among
many that the changes of 1536–42 had consolidated individual
financial departments, endowing them with more clearly defined
responsibilities, routines, and records than the embryonic departments and freelance ministers of Henry VII's day, but had given no
clear shape to the system as a whole, bar giving the privy council the
ability to direct much expenditure by its own warrants. Such institutional consolidation was also evident outside the revenue collection
system, as in the administrative remodelling of the navy, a newly
prominent spending department placed in 1546 under a council for
marine causes manned by six officers with clearly defined responsibilities, the direct ancestor of the future navy board. The overarching
structural vagueness was evident from the need for numerous *ad hoc*
audit commissions in the 1540s. Henry VII's general surveyors or
other councillors had audited all manner of accounts under the
king's supervision, and Wolsey's reform proposals of 1519 promised
that Henry VIII would take over such duties, but he never did so.
Instead most accounts which did not naturally find their way into the
traditional workings of the exchequer (as those of the sheriffs or
customs officers did) were audited by individual veterans of Henry
VII's council under Wolsey's supervision in the 1510s, but came
before the general surveyors from the 1520s. In 1543 two auditors of
prests – cash payments to individuals or between institutions – were
appointed within the court of general surveyors to carry out such
audits. When incorporated within augmentations in 1547 they were
entrusted with regular checks on the drafts passing between the
various revenue courts as well as the auditing of accounts for royal
building, military expenditure and so on. Still auditing seems to have
remained haphazard, and accountants often had to beg for commissions to be appointed to audit their accounts in order to clear their
liabilities to the crown. As under Henry VII, however, informality of

structure was accompanied by continuity and experience in personnel: thus Walter Mildmay, an augmentations clerk from 1540, auditor
of prests from 1543 and general surveyor from 1545, served on at least
35 audit and investigative committees between 1547 and 1554 alone,
and went on to be one of Elizabeth's leading financial ministers.[52]

Meanwhile, the sort of overall coordination once provided by the
exchequer was sought first in enlarging the scope and powers of the
augmentations in 1547, then, in a scheme planned in 1552–3 but executed only after Mary's accession, in the absorption of augmentations
and first fruits and tenths into the exchequer, and thus the restoration of exchequer control over some 75–95 per cent of the crown's
centrally administered income. Both sets of measures were originally
recommended as means to cut costs by removing superfluous administrative duplication, and in 1552–3 even out of sheer atavism in a
desperate financial crisis, but their end result was to make possible
the coordination of Elizabethan finance by the privy council, lord
treasurer and chancellor of the exchequer, and even the creation of a
large cash reserve in the exchequer's central deposit treasury like that
in the coffers of Henry VII or Henry VIII, totalling £270,000 by 1585.
How beneficially these developments injected into the exchequer the
alien and more effective working practices of the newer institutions is
much more debatable, for the advantage of the retention of the
auditing practices of the augmentations for landed revenues, and the
considerable autonomy within the exchequer of the staff dealing with
first fruits and tenths, was outweighed by the application of the
obscurantism and personal feuding of the exchequer staff to such
large proportions of the crown's income, while the same flexibility
that had opened the newer revenue courts to gross peculation proved
too much of a temptation for a number of exchequer officials. Even
in financial administration, which, G. R. Elton contended, 'supplies
more, and more detailed, instances of the reforming activity of the
early sixteenth century than does any other aspect of government',
continual revolution was to prove necessary.[53]

Corruption

Vigilance was especially required in dealing with corruption, a
problem of two varieties, in each of which the limits of the accept-

able were rather ill-defined. The subtler and more widespread form was the acceptance by royal officers of inducements to favour individuals in their dealing with the crown. This was to an extent an accepted privilege of office, and had been rife in the late-medieval exchequer, where the order in which creditors' claims were met depended on their ability to curry favour with the king, the exchequer staff, and the accountants on whom payment was assigned. Henry VII's rapacity towards his subjects and niggardliness in rewarding his servants probably combined to encourage such practices, and the concentration of influence over the dispersal of the monastic haul in the hands of Cromwell, Rich and the senior officers of the augmentations gave them a new lease of life. From one point of view such men were providing access to the inside of the financial machinery, a service heavily in demand, at the going market rate; from another they were exploiting their position to get rich at the public's expense. The only known investigation into allegations of corrupt practices against Rich found them 'slanderously and untruely forged', but the rebels of 1536 seem to have shared Henry Brinklow's view that the augmentations men 'make many tymes the king to robbe his subiectys, and thei robb the kyng agayne'. Such practices would only become an overwhelming problem if the abuses of its officials dangerously lowered the reputation of the crown, or if such a large proportion of the money an institution's clients were prepared to pay for its services went in unofficial fees that the crown's own takings were seriously diminished. The first seems never to have reached crisis level under the Tudors, but the second clearly did by the latter part of Elizabeth's reign, when William Cecil, Lord Burghley, as master of the court of wards was probably making three times as much from the sale of each wardship as the queen.[54]

In the second category of corruption, outright peculation by financial officials – taking the crown's money for oneself with no intention of repaying it – was clearly thought to be wrong, but using such money for one's own purposes while it was in one's custody was generally accepted as part of the perquisites of office. Difficulties arose either when private investments made with royal funds went wrong, making repayment impossible, when officers died without sorting out their affairs, or when books were cooked successfully enough for it to be unclear just what had been going on. Unfortunately the flexibility of the newer institutions made such confusion ever more likely, whether deliberately created by profiteers at the crown's expense or not. Commissions set up to call in the crown's debts, especially that of 1552 which had a special brief to examine corruption in the revenue courts, found some notable instances. Richard Whalley, augmentations receiver in Yorkshire (1546–52), Sir William Sharington, vice-treasurer at the Bristol mint (1546–9), and John Beaumont, receiver-general of the court of wards (1545–52), had each made thousands of pounds by simple peculation, falsifying accounts and using the king's money for private speculations; Sharington at least had the good taste to spend his profits on a splendid new house at Lacock (Wilts) with avant-garde classical detailing. Bigger fish than these probably got away. Sir John Williams, treasurer of the augmentations from 1544 to 1554, had never submitted a final account though he was meant to do so annually; at the court's dissolution he was found to have – accidentally? – left more than £30,000 received for land sales out of his accounts, suddenly entering them as a lump sum some time in 1552–3 when investigations were closing in. Yet as one of Mary's earliest supporters in 1553, he was untouchable.[55]

Such embarrassments lived on beyond the Edwardian orgy of self-help, when such men had merely watched and imitated as best they could the Seymours, Dudleys and Herberts, on into the Elizabethan exchequer. Five tellers of the six who held office between 1567 and 1571 managed to lose more than £44,000 of the crown's money in the grey area between gainful employment of cash balances and downright theft; even Lord Treasurer Winchester's hands were not visibly spotless. Thus the basic problem evident at the lowest levels of the administration, that of extracting the crown's money from those entrusted with its collection and care, remained a problem at the top too. Of course undiscovered peculation is hidden from the historian, making the argument from silence a dangerous one, but it is noticeable that Henry VII not only fined several of his leading ministers or their executors for misuse of funds or similar offences, he also took large bonds from senior administrators for their performance in office, and bound them for the repayment of quite small and detailed sums. Only with such predatory supervision was the flexibility of the newer administrative bodies not a licence for laxity.[56]

The wider enforcement of the crown's financial demands under Henry VII, when the general surveyors, the council learned and ministers such as Edmund Dudley or the master of the wards, Sir John Hussey, had access to the privy seal for writs of summons and routinely took bonds from crown debtors and subordinate officers alike, seems to have been more efficient than what followed in the world of the autonomous national institutions, for all that they were equipped with their own seals and other legal machinery. To some extent the problem was one of the sheer scale and complexity of the crown's financial affairs from the 1530s, but there was also slackness. Although all officials in the augmentations were meant to give bonds for their performance, some omitted to do so and the procedure availed little. The concerns raised by the royal commission of 1552 on this score were met by a statute of 1553 insisting on the bonding of all those handling the crown's money, but it took another round of scandals before the policy was implemented in the 1560s in the case of those able to do most damage, the exchequer tellers. Calling in the crown's debts became a standard technique of post-war retrenchment from Wolsey's drive of 1514–16 to the rash of debt-hunting royal commissions of the mid-to-late 1540s and 1550s, but there had to be a large body of uncollected debt for it to work at all. By the 1550s such debts ranged from those for the purchase of crown lands or monastic lead, through those of minor local revenue or spending officials, to those owed by the major administrators caught out in drives against corruption or councillors fined for political offences; and by 1555–7 'debts upon obligations',, many of them the new bonds for repayment negotiated by successive royal commissions, were bringing in more than £30,000 a year. Many debts were never paid in full, as was perhaps inevitable when a large proportion of the crown's debtors were also its most prominent servants. Numerous Elizabethan aristocrats and courtiers died vastly in debt to the crown, but this was a symptom less of the crown's ruthless exploitation of their economic weakness than of the extensive credit which those in royal favour could command, if needs be at the cost of their descendants.[57]

The Financial Achievement and its Limitations

From the political point of view this situation was an enormous improvement on that of Henry VI's reign, when the crown was hopelessly indebted to its leading subjects and had to watch them feuding over the chance to claim some repayment. But the improvement was much less the result of administrative change than of successful appropriation by the crown of a much larger share of the nation's wealth in land and the proceeds of direct and indirect taxation. Those elements were not balanced quite as Fortescue would have liked, nor were they as permanently assured to the crown as he would have wanted. Indeed by the 1560s both the effectiveness of direct taxation and the breadth of the demesne were in serious decline. At times the early Tudor monarchs had come too close to 'exquysite meanes of geytinge of good' for the comfort of their subjects, devastatingly so for the regular clergy. On the other hand, as he had envisaged, a richer monarchy had proved a stronger monarchy, not only at home where wealth funded patronage, magnificence and the suppression of revolt, but also abroad, where Henry VIII had fought more successfully on the continent than any English ruler since Henry V.

The demands of war, however, tended not only to maximise income but also to maximise expenditure beyond the available income. Budgeting in the 1540s was woefully inaccurate. The 1544 campaign in France cost perhaps twice as much as had been estimated, and Somerset's policy in Scotland, which was meant to be a cheap alternative to that pursued by Henry, actually proved costlier. There were several extenuating factors: the lack of an omnicompetent financial body able to provide accurate figures as Henry V's exchequer had done for his wartime budgeting, the irrelevance (because of inflation, the widespread use of mercenaries, and so on) of the precedents drawn from previous campaigns of the sort Henry VII and his councillors had used in planning their invasion of Scotland in 1497, and the uncertainties of large-scale borrowing at Antwerp, quite apart from the strategic miscalculation that underlay Somerset's difficulties. The final result was the nearest Tudor England ever came to the run of official bankruptcies begun by the Spanish crown in 1557 and the French in 1558–9, the suspension of payments ordered by Northumberland in 1552, as the crown's total debts at home and abroad reached something between £200,000 and £250,000.[58]

That England hit the wall at the end of the path of escalating military expenditure in the same decade as her continental rivals should not surprise us, for it fits with numerous parallels in the fiscal development of the European states, as each tried to expropriate and deploy the fruits of demographic and economic expansion more effectively than its military opponents. Although neither France nor Spain broke with Rome, each levied increasingly heavy taxation on clerical incomes, and Francis I confiscated and sold the treasures of several cathedrals and abbeys; each multiplied and intensified direct and indirect taxes on the laity, took forced loans, and raised taxes without the usual consent when needs be; each exploited the crown's feudal prerogatives and customs duties; each sold crown land and rights (and famously in France also appointments to office) in desperate attempts to balance the books. Francis I investigated and fined corrupt officials, suffered from incompetent budgeting, and experimented with degrees of cash-based centralisation and assignment-based devolution in fiscal administration, including the use of royal coffers; over the course of his reign his administrative tinkering led to greater centralisation and uniformity in financial management, of the sort achieved by the 1570s in England. Intriguingly, he and his successors also met limits to fiscal expansion similar to those faced by the Tudors. In France in the early seventeenth century as in the multiple-subsidy wartime years of late Elizabethan England, the deflated profits of direct taxation were no higher than those raised in the 1520s. In both countries, though in different ways, attempts to increase these yields were resisted by ordinary taxpayers and political classes alike. This was fortunate: states which tried to push the rate of extraction much higher than this in the crisis produced by the peak of population growth and the onset of poor weather in the years before 1600, notably Castile and Muscovy, wrought havoc with their internal economies and depopulated whole areas of the countryside.[59]

Both the French and Spanish monarchies – ruling, it must be remembered, very much larger populations than that of England – were considerably more successful than the English state under the Tudors in establishing a livelihood, in their case in regular tax revenues. In this perspective England stood somewhere between the great continental states and Scotland, where James IV had pursued similar measures to those of his father-in-law Henry VII, expanding and exploiting the demesne, sharpening his feudal rights, and battening on the wealth of the church to triple royal income, but where regular large-scale direct taxation of the laity began only in the 1580s. For the most part, the efforts of Henry VII and Henry VIII succeeded merely in returning the crown's total income in real terms to about the level of the later fourteenth and early fifteenth centuries, before the collapse of Henry VI's reign. Only in the 1540s, with large contributions from debasement and sales of land, did the Tudors manage to extract a share of national income – perhaps 9 per cent in wartime – comparable to that taken by Philip II in Spain.

The less fleeting success of the French and Spanish kings was dangerous, however, because it led them beyond the temptation to sell capital assets into the mortgaging of future income, by the creation of funded debts which were to dog their financial managers in the following century, since, unlike the Dutch Republic with its booming economy or the English state in the 'financial revolution' after 1688, they were unable to maintain constant public confidence in their creditworthiness. Henry VIII's adventures at Antwerp suggest that, given the opportunity, he would have been quite prepared to follow his brother-monarchs down this road too, spending Elizabeth's revenues in advance as well as squandering her capital. Perhaps the ultimate failure of Fortescue's vision of an endowed monarchy was not only a blessing from the point of view of Whig historians, preserving as it did the necessity for taxation and thus for parliamentary consent; it was also a blessing in disguise for the early modern English monarchy. An English crown declaring regular state bankruptcies by rescheduling an ever larger consolidated debt would have made Chief Justice Fortescue turn in his grave almost as certainly as an English countryside blighted by unduly heavy regressive taxation, full of Englishmen eating apples, lard and offal like the unhappily overtaxed French.[60]

4

EMPIRE

'This realm of England is an empire …' asserted the act in restraint of appeals in 1533, 'governed by one supreme head and king having the dignity and royal estate of the imperial crown of the same'. It was a claim to the highest form of jurisdictional autonomy conceivable: as the Canterbury convocation put it in 1536, rulers exercising 'Imperium merum … have the whole entire supreme government and authority over all their subjects without knowledge or recognising of any other supreme power or authority'. Indeed it stretched the bounds of the authority of the secular state beyond what many of Henry VIII's subjects would previously have found conceivable, substituting royal for papal jurisdiction over the English church. Yet it purported to be doing nothing new. The act's preamble argued that 'divers sundry old authentic histories and chronicles' showed that England 'so hath been accepted in the world'. And it left the exact relationship between church and state and the nature of royal power unclear for generations to come. As such it may stand as a symbol of the expanding ambitions of those who governed Tudor England, of the sources of those ambitions and of the arguments used to justify them, and of the extent to which those ambitions were, or were not, realised in the extension of royal power into new areas of national life.[1]

Sovereignty and Empire

Imperial kingship was one element amongst several in a vocabulary of power developing fast in early Tudor England, and adroitly deployed by Henry VII and Henry VIII alike. In the background stood a revival in the language and rituals of twelfth- and thirteenth-century sacral kingship, evident perhaps from Henry VI's coronation and certainly from the Yorkist reigns. Meanwhile 'sovereign' seems to have been the word on Henry VII's lips from the first years of his reign. In 1485 he commissioned two ships for his navy larger than any built since 1422: whereas previous royal ships had usually been named after saints, Henry's were to be called the *Sovereign* and the *Regent*. In 1489 he issued a new gold coin, at 20s. the largest in denomination ever issued by an English king, and named it the sovereign. On it and on all his subsequent issues of coinage he was depicted wearing a closed, or arched, imperial crown, symbol of the claim to imperial kingship upon which his son was to build. Henry VIII latched onto the vocabulary of empire long before the Reformation, naming ships the *Henry Imperial* and *Mary Imperial* as early as 1513–14. But empire blended in his early years with sovereignty and with older conceptions of feudal overlordship, as in the unprecedentedly high claims made concerning the nature of his authority over the city of Tournai, captured from the French in 1513 and retained as an English possession for the next five years. Even in the 1530s the most noticeable and durable change in the language of royal proclamations and statutes derived only indirectly from the notion of the imperial crown. This was the habit, introduced permanently in 1534–5 though prefigured in 1526, of calling Henry VIII 'his majesty' – traditionally an imperial title – rather than just 'our sovereign lord', 'his highness' or 'his grace'. Here, then, was no clear single theory of state power, but a rich blend of ideas of varying origins and connotations, mingling to legitimate growing royal claims.[2]

Little in all this was strictly new. We might expect as much of 'sovereign', which had indeed been the personal motto of the diligently conventional Henry IV, and a term current for a century and more by 1485. But it was equally true of empire and majesty. In 1397 Richard II's chancellor called him 'le roy entier emperour de son roialme'. In 1393 obsequious MPs had referred to the same king's 'royal majesty'. Henry VI's reign saw the arched imperial crown depicted on Henry V's chantry chapel, and Henry VI himself referred to in one tract as his 'most imperial majesty'. All these usages hinted at a higher view of royal power than that implied by the more normal vocabulary of the fourteenth and fifteenth centuries. We might expect no less from the assertive kingship of

Richard II. But these innovations also shared a common origin in English emulation of France. Richard saw much to imitate in the hallowed kingly cult of his French father-in-law; Henry VI was himself king of France, and understandably extended his French titles into the usage of his English regime. His successors' claim to France encouraged the habit, such that Henry VII was regularly graced with the French royal epithet 'Most Christian King'. It was French royal lawyers, more consistently than any others in Europe, who had beaten back any external power's claims to jurisdiction in France ever since the thirteenth century with the dictum 'rex in regno suo imperator est' (the king is emperor in his kingdom). The king of France was 'sa majesté'; even the idea of the crown as an impersonal entity, as in 'the imperial crown', was much stronger in France than in England in the fifteenth century. Thus it was that notions of empire seeped into English political discourse across the period of the Hundred Years War, and revived with special force when Henry VIII revived the war and took over Tournai.[3]

Such terminology was not only vague but also second-hand. It was perhaps even devalued as rulers everywhere made increasingly extreme claims for their powers: by 1463 the duke of Brittany was displaying a kingly crown on his coat of arms, and in 1469 the Scottish parliament claimed 'ful jurisdictioune and fre impire within his realme' for their king. Yet its resonances among the sets of ideas on government current in the governing circles of early Tudor England were considerable. Civil lawyers were happy to follow their French counterparts in assimilating the royal power to the Roman imperial power of their textbooks: it was Cuthbert Tunstall who assured Henry VIII in 1517 that 'the Crown of Englond is an Empire off hitselff mych bettyr then now the Empire of Rome: for which cause your Grace werith a close Crown'. Humanists found it natural to use the classical term *imperium* for any supreme secular power, and tied England's heritage of imperial kingship neatly to the English birth of Constantine the Great, even though the purists among them balked at tracing it directly to King Arthur's supposed imperial hegemony over large areas of Europe. Perhaps most important of all, common lawyers found that for most purposes the imperial crown fitted well with their own preoccupations. Their reverence for the traditions of English kingship revelled in its repeated assertions of imperial supremacy over the other kings in the British Isles, Scottish, Welsh, and Irish. The earliest texts of their own discipline, notably Bracton's thirteenth-century *De Legibus et Consuetudinibus*

Angliae (*On the Laws and Customs of England*), represented the king of England as without equal or superior, the vicar of God. One might expect such high-flown language to seem unfamiliar to a generation raised on the more measured Fortescue, but interest in Bracton was reviving in the early sixteenth century. At a more partisan level, the notion suited their conviction that the king's common law was supreme within the realm, in particular superior to canon law or ecclesiastical custom. Only if the king's imperial attributes were taken to supersede the legislative functions of parliament – another aspect of English tradition and national jurisdictional coherence dear to common law hearts – might the common lawyers begin to have their doubts about the rhetoric of empire.[4]

Church and State

As the act in restraint of appeals suggests, imperial rhetoric found its fullest expression in Henry VIII's subjection of the church. This was the most obvious example of the growth of the state's power in early Tudor England. By the end of the 1530s, the king was supreme head of the church and governed it through a lay vicegerent in spirituals (Cromwell), the religious orders had been dissolved and their property surrendered to or appropriated by the crown, and taxation of the church was permanent and heavy. By the last years of Edward VI's reign, within two decades of the act in restraint of appeals, the chantries, the goods of parish churches and many of the bishops' estates had gone the way of the monasteries; bishops were being appointed by royal patent as royal delegates and deprived by royal commissioners; process in the church courts ran in the king's name; and radical innovations in liturgy were being introduced by parliamentary statute, radical innovations in doctrine merely by conciliar fiat. Not even Mary could put the clock back. She divested herself by statute of the supreme headship, though she had had to use it to start her recatholicisation programme. Thereafter she utilised the privy council to oversee the restoration of altars in place of communion tables, and to direct the persecution of heretics through royal commissions rather than directly through the old episcopal machinery. Most ironically of all, by the end of her reign she was engaged in a confrontation with the pope worthy of Edward III or Henry V, over

Paul IV's replacement of Cardinal Pole, the archbishop of Canterbury, by another legate whose letter of appointment Mary refused to allow into the country.[5]

The last point raises the problem of how great a change in relations between the crown and the English church the Reformation really represented. Fourteenth- and fifteenth-century kings had taxed the church hard and nominated bishops (though these were formally appointed by a combination of election by cathedral chapters and papal provision). They had encouraged liturgical standardisation to produce a more recognisably English church – promoting the celebration of St George's day and so on – and had used the church as a propaganda machine in the Hundred Years War. Their parliaments had legislated against papal intrusion in matters of patronage and jurisdiction, in the statutes of provisors and *praemunire*, and had established a legal framework for the suppression of heresy by the lay power. Thus there were strong precedents for royal leadership in the English church, and as we shall see they were growing stronger after 1485. Yet the Reformation was different. It separated the English church completely from western Christendom, and subjected it unequivocally to a king who appropriated even the right to pronounce on doctrine. Elsewhere in Europe Lutheran and catholic rulers alike were taking a tighter grip on the finances, patronage and privileges of their national churches in the late fifteenth and early sixteenth centuries. In the later sixteenth century, such state control was to be a standard element of what is inelegantly termed confessionalisation: the shaping of an aggressively catholic Bavaria, an aggressively Calvinist Rhine Palatinate, and so on. But in establishing the supreme headship Henry also went beyond such continental practice, shocking even Luther and Calvin.[6]

The divorce crisis was the trigger for the changes of 1529–36, and determined some of their central characteristics, such as the denial of papal jurisdiction. But even before the rhetoric of empire legitimated the decisive break in 1533–4, Henry's confrontation with the pope began to throw up forceful statements of his supremacy over the English church. From August 1530 his representatives at the papal court were arguing that English provincial privileges precluded any Englishman, Henry included, from being cited to Rome in a lawsuit; by the next month this claim had turned in the bluffer tones of Henry's noble councillors to the assertion that he was 'absolute both as Emperor and Pope in his own kingdom'. By 1531

Cromwell, rapidly emerging as the leading draftsman and parliamentary manager of the radical group among the king's advisers, was tinkering with additions to the king's titles to represent these claims. The pardon of the clergy of that year recognised Henry as 'protector and supreme head of the English church and clergy so far as the law of Christ allows'; the last phrase, moreover, was only inserted after a rearguard action by the king's clerical opponents.

Henry's fascination with his God-given supremacy over the church had begun to have a life of its own from the time he looked over, and carefully annotated, the materials generated by the teams of research scholars he set to work to justify his stance on the divorce. They provided historical evidence – mostly of doubtful authenticity – that previous English kings had exercised such a supremacy, as had Roman emperors. This doubtless caught Henry's imagination better than their sounder arguments that national churches had enjoyed a fair degree of provincial self-determination in the centuries before the high medieval heyday of papal centralisation. These findings expanded naturally on the already intensifying imperial traditions of English kingship. They gave the clerics trained in Roman law who would be called in to defend Henry's supremacy – notably bishops Gardiner and Sampson – the chance to align him with the great codifier of their discipline, Justinian. Such views also blended readily with the models of Old Testament kingship, directly accountable to God, available to Henry from Lutheran sources, and incorporated in some of his propaganda as early as 1531. Henry's identification with King David went far enough for David to be depicted with the king's features in Henry's personal psalter. It was probably also the case that many elements in Henry's Reformation that looked doctrinally protestant to his reformist ministers and subjects, in particular the assault on the monasteries and on popular 'superstition', appeared to the king as the duties of a purgative biblical king. In wielding the royal supremacy he did, as Cuthbert Tunstall put it, 'as the chief and best of the kings of Israel did'.[7]

There were precedents for such royal leadership in reform of the church, especially in Henry VII's reign. Like his contemporaries Ferdinand and Isabella in Spain and Louis XII in France, like the French and Breton rulers who had hosted him in exile, Henry saw support for reform, charity and the crusade as badges of christian kingship. As the humanists argued ever more eloquently for the need to return the church to its ancient pristine state, and delineated ever more clearly the model christian monarch whose service to the common weal would involve leadership in such reform, the moral imperative behind such action grew ever stronger. Henry VII apparently saw no contradiction between this and the intensifying fiscal exploitation of the church in which he also anticipated his son. Indeed, he happily charged the Cistercian order £5000 for confirming its privileges only eleven years after pledging enthusiastic support for its efforts at reform. Towards the end of his reign, Henry and his common lawyer councillors mulcted the church in three other ways: as a feudal landholder, through heavy fines for the restoration of estates on the succession of each new bishop or abbot; as a source of rival jurisdiction to that of the common law courts, through controversial actions of *praemunire* against the church courts necessitating the purchase of expensive royal pardons; and as the gaoler of convicted clerics, whose escapes from episcopal prisons cost Archbishop Warham alone £1600 in fines arranged by Edmund Dudley (albeit at a rate standard since the thirteenth century). Meanwhile Henry became increasingly reluctant to grant mortmain licences for the alienation of land to the church to support chantries. After 1500, he set the fines for such licences at up to ten times the annual value of the land involved (where in the mid-fifteenth century prices had varied between one and three years' value). In the last years of his reign, testators began to provide for the possibility of a statutory abrogation of their chantry provisions. Such an act was indeed to be passed in 1532, and the last known mortmain licence was issued in 1534.[8]

What seems to have alarmed churchmen still more than the financial aspect of these policies was the general threat to the church's liberties presented by an assertive king surrounded by aggressive common lawyers. There was no sign that Henry VII or his son would issue the sort of generously worded general confirmation of ecclesiastical liberties granted by Edward IV in 1462. Bishop Russell of Lincoln was in a state of some panic as early as 1492 over infringements to the liberties of the University of Oxford: 'for Godds sake', he warned the university authorities, 'persuade all our scolers to remembyr the tyme and condycion of this dayes that we be yn'. In particular, ecclesiastical encroachment on the criminal law – such as the university's jurisdiction over errant scholars – was an obvious target both for kings concerned to establish law and order and for partisan common lawyers. The right of criminals to take sanctuary in churches, especially those of monastic houses with especially extensive privileges of sanctuary, was one area of friction. The right of anyone who had ever taken clerical orders, even those of lesser rank than priest, deacon or subdeacon, to be tried in church courts (known as benefit of clergy), was another. The workings of sanctuary and benefit of clergy had been ever more closely circumscribed by the common law judges in the reigns of Henry VI and Edward IV, and statutory restrictions were the next step. Edward IV vetoed a bill infringing sanctuary, but an act of 1489 limited benefit of clergy to deacons and priests, and later legislation declared it inapplicable to certain offences. Over sanctuaries Henry VII was similarly firm but fairly restrained, ignoring their privileges on occasion when he was desperate to capture traitors lurking inside, but securing delegated papal powers for Cardinal Morton to review and regulate their operation.[9]

All this should not obscure the continuing cooperation between the two systems of courts in less controversial areas. Yet clerical reaction to Henry VII's policies was forthright. There were complaints in the Canterbury convocation of 1504 that the church's liberties were being infringed, and in Henry VIII's first parliament a bill for securing the church's liberties was introduced. It failed. By the early years of Henry VIII even senior churchmen in royal service were bitter critics of crown policy towards the church. The dean of Windsor, Henry VII's almoner, councillor and diplomat Christopher Urswick, took to praising Becket's stand against Henry II and circulating a Venetian treatise against state exploitation of ecclesiastical property. Still confrontations continued. Further restrictions on benefit of clergy in an act of 1512 met the zeal of clerical spokesmen inspired by the fifth Lateran Council (1512–17) head on in the clash of 1514–15, which ended with Henry, briefed by the judges, asserting that 'the kings of England in time past have never had any superior but God alone'. In 1519–20 the spotlight turned to sanctuary, when a series of debates in the king's council sparked by one especially prominent case led to a declaration by Wolsey that all sanctuaries existed only by royal creation. In the same case Chief Justice Fyneux, one of the most aggressive protagonists of common law supremacy, ruled that no sanctuary could offer protection for more than 40 days, one of a number of attacks on sanctuary from the bench in the years 1517–22.[10]

Over sanctuary and benefit of clergy, Wolsey tended to use his legatine powers to smooth over differences between the defenders of clerical liberties and their common lawyer critics, offering better regulation rather than radical change. After his fall, the pressure on both privileges revived. Benefit of clergy was further restricted by acts of 1531 and 1540, but survived into the Elizabethan period and well beyond as a blessing to any criminal who could read (since this was the only practicable test of clerical status). Sanctuary likewise limped on until 1727, despite Cromwell's note to himself before the 1536 parliament, 'Item specially to speke of utter destruction of seyntuaries'. But by an act of 1540 it was made inoperative for major crimes, and clearly limited to 40 days except in eight places carefully distributed about the country. The judges' agenda had more or less been fulfilled, though its corollary, the construction of a new code of canon law for the English church entirely congruent with common law, stalled in the 1530s and again in the 1550s.[11]

In other ways, Wolsey served to continue Henry VII's combination of rapacity and reform. As chief minister and papal legate, like Cardinal d'Amboise under Louis XII, he was able to promote reform on the king's behalf, especially amongst the monastic clergy. Again like Amboise, he was able to press the clergy for unprecedentedly high levels of taxation, raising an annual tenth on clerical incomes for five years in the 1520s. And as legate, he was able to set up the machinery for a centralised administration and financial exploitation of the church which Henry VIII and Cromwell began to reconstruct as early as 1531–2, often using the same personnel who had served Wolsey. Cromwell himself moved smoothly from dissolving monasteries to fund Wolsey's collegiate foundations in the 1520s, through arranging exchanges of land between monastic houses and the crown in 1531–2, to planning wholesale dissolution by 1534, and implementing partial dissolution in 1536. In clerical taxation (the *praemunire* fine of 1531, then the tenths levied annually from 1535), Henry and Cromwell again took up where Henry and Wolsey left off. Even Cromwell's vicegerential probate court was modelled on Wolsey's as legate. And when such legatine prerogatives as the right to issue dispensations were transferred to the archbishop of Canterbury rather than to the vicegerent, Cromwell and his men intervened constantly in their operation. In form the vicegerency in spirituals was radically new, but in content it looked alarmingly like Wolsey's legatine regime writ large. Neither was much comfort to most churchmen.[12]

There is of course a danger of forgetting that all these developments were dependent on political contingencies at every level. The pope might have looked to compromise, Thomas More rather than Thomas Cromwell might have won the struggle for Henry's conscience, and so on. As it was, the continued interaction of pressure from the common law interest with the other aspects of the rhetoric of empire, the momentum of Wolsey's centralisation, the urgings of protestant bishops and courtiers and the king's self-fashioning as Old Testament monarch, produced the distinctive Henrician reform. A church directed from Canterbury might have taken the place of one directed from Rome; national churches were quite capable of going into schism – as the French had done as recently as 1511–14 – without erecting new administrative hierarchies. In the event, those bishops who resisted Archbishop Cranmer's attempts to exercise metropolitan supremacy over their sees in 1534, in a replay of earlier struggles between Archbishops Morton and Warham and the other bishops of Canterbury province, found they had jumped out of the frying pan and into the fire. Henry responded by creating the vicegerency, and in September 1535 the degree of the church's subjection was made painfully clear. Cromwell suspended the bishops' powers and then restored them on terms that stressed that they were held under the authority of the king as supreme head.[13]

It was not only the bishops for whom the Henrician Reformation and its sequels made a daily reality of the crown's expanding powers. Every parish in the country found its worship regulated by Cromwell's injunctions of 1536 and 1538, and every individual found his or her birth, marriage and death recorded in the new parish registers at Cromwell's command (for purposes of taxation, it was widely suspected). From 1545, children and adults using a primer to learn reading and basic prayers all had to use the *King's Primer*, with its preface by Henry explaining his reforms in the church. From the start of Edward's reign, carved scenes of the crucifixion began to be replaced at the focal point of churches by boards painted with the royal arms. From 1547, clergy regularly read out to their parishioners the 'Exhortation concernyng Good Ordre and Obedience to Rulers and Magistrates' from the Book of Homilies issued in that year. Henry did his best to demonise England's favourite saint Thomas Becket, the champion of clerical privilege against royal power, though he could do little about the irritating fact that so many of his leading ministers – Cromwell, Audley, Howard, Wriothesley, Cranmer – were named Thomas. Henry gained increased powers of political persuasion and coercion: tighter control over the church's opinion-forming machinery, tighter control over ecclesiastical patronage, and a large harvest of church land and tax revenue. By his last years there are even signs that a nascent protestant nationalism, of the sort that would burgeon under Elizabeth, was starting to compensate for all the damage done to the stability of his regime by his decision to assault the church. That damage was considerable and lasting. Three of Tudor England's most threatening revolts – in 1536, 1549 and 1569 – were held together by disaffection over religious policy, and the turbulence of Henrician politics was bloodily greater once religious issues began to divide opinion at court.[14]

Franchises

Other manifestations of imperial monarchy were less problematic. The untrammelled power of the imperial crown had an internal as well as an external aspect: with the common lawyers' attack on clerical liberties came an attack on all jurisdictional franchises within the realm. At the inns of court, interest in Edward I's *Quo Warranto* legislation revived from the 1490s in parallel with the increasing attention given to other statements of royal power such as *Prerogativa Regis*. Little use had been made of *Quo Warranto* since Edward's great campaign against the jurisdictional claims of non-royal courts, but in the 1490s there were *Quo Warranto* investigations in Cheshire, Durham and Lancashire, partly to make money in fines, but partly also to impose royal regulation on franchises. Between 1512 and 1547 the king's bench heard 188 *Quo Warranto* cases. This did not constitute a coherent royal assault on lesser jurisdictions: the cases arose from a wide range of (mainly local) considerations, the crown rarely won, and individual judges – notably again Chief Justice Fyneux – were keener for radical change than most of the king's councillors. Ever tighter supervision, rather than wholesale abolition, was the keynote of Henry VII's policy, though it is noteworthy that unlike Edward IV he did not create extensive new liberties for trusted noble followers. However, the revival of *Quo Warranto* contributed to the climate in which it was natural for Cromwell to follow his note on abolishing sanctuary with 'Item for the dissolucion of all fraunchyses and liberties throughout this realme', and indeed to produce the act of 1536 which did just that. The instinct for sweeping statutory reform seems to have been Cromwell's own, but the general line of policy had been adumbrated by two generations of common lawyers, at the inns, on the bench and, with ministers from Edmund Dudley to Thomas Audley, in the king's council. Only in Ireland, where franchisal jurisdictions were still useful in bolstering the power of Anglo-Irish magnates on the military and political border with the native Irish, did early Tudor regimes preserve or renew them.[15]

Franchises had once performed just such a positive role in Wales, but under Henry VII and Henry VIII the marcher lordships saw the same progression as the English liberties, from supervision backed with the threat of change, to the general implementation of such change. The shiring of Wales in 1536–43, whilst distinctly haphazard in its progress, was an important part of the wider process of drawing the realm together under one law implemented through one administrative model, that of the lowland counties of England. Thus it did for Wales as a unit what Henry VII's charters of 1504–8, removing the civil disabilities and cumbrous Welsh land law which prevented their assimilation within the wider English realm, had already done for Welshmen as individuals. Shiring also does seem to have had some practical benefits for Welsh society, at least for its leaders among the gentry.[16]

The impact on English franchises is harder to judge. At its least, the change brought about by the act of 1536 could be literally nominal: JPs were appointed, writs ran and courts were held in the king's name rather than that of the bishop of Durham, the earl of Chester, or the abbot of Bury St Edmunds. Liberties less extensive than those of the palatine counties of Cheshire, Lancashire and Durham seem already to have been fairly well integrated with the wider common law system before 1536, though the greatest of them left indelible marks on county administration even after their demise, such as the division between West Suffolk (once the Liberty of St Edmund) and the rest of the county. The palatinates remained almost as self-contained after 1536 as before, and centrally dictated changes to their court systems had at times to be reversed because they were so inappropriate to local needs: effective change had to be the product of negotiation between central and local interests rather than the imposition of a central master-plan. Where significant change did occur for Cheshire and Durham, it was more by the piecemeal process of judicial centralisation, as plaintiffs took their cases outside the franchises into chancery or star chamber, and Wolsey or his successors gave them a ready welcome: in Cheshire this was already running strongly in the 1510s, in Durham it began to do so only in the 1540s. Subtler influences from the centre also anticipated legislative change, for the justices in the highest courts of the palatinates tended, from Henry VII's reign if not earlier, to include lawyers from the same pool from which members of the regional councils, assize judges and justices of king's bench, common pleas and the exchequer were drawn. Cromwell's statutes at times amounted to little more than blustering rhetoric and hamfisted repair of systems that were not obviously broken; but they chimed with the many other forces that worked at varying speeds for the unification of England under the crown.[17]

Those forces, and the irregularity of their effects, can be paralleled from the continental monarchies. In 1539, Francis I of France abolished sanctuary, with papal approval. In the same year he issued the ordinance of Villers-Cotterêts, ordering the substitution of French for Latin in all legal documents, the universal introduction of parish registers, and many other nationwide standardising reforms to the legal system. Latin remained in use for a century or more, parish registers were not kept in the form required, if at all, and the parlement of Rouen, Francis's own remodelled version of the ancient Norman sovereign court, left out sixteen clauses it did not like when it registered the edict, and hoped the king would not notice. The French experience points up both the scale of English success, and the favourable conditions – England's comparatively small size and heritage of strong government – in which English reformers operated. All over Europe in the later fifteenth and sixteenth centuries, legal and administrative systems were being made more homogeneous. New or more powerful royal judicial institutions were being created – French parlements, Castilian audiencias, the Burgundian parlement at Malines. Anomalous or newly conquered provinces were being absorbed. Yet each state operated at its own speed and in its own way, and the particularities of English development are as striking as its part in this common pattern.[18]

Social and Economic Policy

In general England moved ahead of the run of European states in the jurisdictional elements of state building. At least in comparison with other nation-states, it did the same in another significant area of state growth, the conception and implementation of social and economic policy. Sixteenth-century governments were even less successful than those of our own day in their attempts to shape economic development, but this was certainly not for lack of trying. Of the 458 royal proclamations issued between 1485 and 1553, 285 concerned economic and social matters. So did more than a quarter of Henry VII's 192 statutes, the second most significant group of acts (after those touching religion) in the Reformation Parliament, and a large majority of bills put into early Elizabethan parliaments.

Royal economic management of a basic kind already had a long history in England when the demographic and economic crises of the fourteenth century produced much more ambitious legislation to regulate marketing, control wage rates and prevent profiteering. It was largely motivated by the interests of the landlord class in parliament, its implementation was patchy and its success limited. But it combined with repeated attempts to regulate standards of cloth manufacture and encourage English shipping, motivated by a fairly cogent theory of economic nationalism, to generate a substantial tradition of national economic regulation by the time Henry VII came to the throne. All these themes duly continued in Tudor legislation, intensified at times by the pressures of population growth, price inflation, periodic poor harvests and the cloth export slump of 1551. More than 40 statutes passed between 1509 and 1559 sought to regulate standards of manufacture, or to reinforce the local control of standards which had proved more effective than nationwide prescription in previous centuries. Unsuccessful attempts at price control by statute and proclamation were made in the 1530s and 1550s, statutory wage controls were renewed in 1514 and 1563, and profiteering by middlemen was attacked especially sharply in 1552. Navigation acts continued to be passed to encourage native enterprise in shipbuilding and trade; treaties with foreign powers, especially perhaps under Henry VII, took care to promote the health of trade; and English merchant interests were upheld against those of their Hanseatic rivals, to a greater or lesser extent depending on each regime's need for support in Germany or in London.[19]

With this legacy of economic legislation came a tradition of moral regulation, again running back to the fourteenth century, and combining more specific aims with the prince's general duty to discourage immoral behaviour. The wearing of clothing too extravagant for one's social station was condemned, both to protect English industry from more fashionable foreign imports, and to reassert the value of social hierarchy at a time of rapid social change: thus the sumptuary act of 1463 would allow only a nobleman to wear the height of continental fashion, extremely pointed shoes and a jacket which was not 'of such length that the same may cover his privy members and buttocks'. All Tudor regimes pursued this line of legislation doggedly, though none found a means to enforce such policy effectively. Even the special watchers appointed in London in 1562 to monitor 'monstrous and outrageous greatness of hosen' could not counteract the pressures of fashion and social pretension, which, ironically, may well have been intensified by the minute correlations of dress and rank at all levels of society laid out in successive statutes.[20]

Meanwhile, morally tainted leisure pursuits such as gambling and football were proscribed because they distracted people from archery, and thereby imperilled the kingdom's military preparedness. (The possession of handguns by those below the level of the gentry came to be added to this list of abuses, partly to preserve archery but also, no doubt, to inhibit poaching and rebellion.) This control of unlawful games seems at least to have struck more of a chord with local authorities, where it might usefully coincide with the social control exercised by borough or parish elites over the unruly young or the poor. A concern for such control was already evident from the 1460s in areas where agrarian recovery and the development of the cloth industry stimulated social differentiation and population mobility. Wolsey mounted a particularly aggressive campaign against undesirable pastimes in the 1520s, and there are signs that local elites cooperated in it. As the century went on, however, such concerns were steadily focused on the alehouse as the natural centre of disorderly activity. JPs were equipped by statute in 1495 to suppress alehouses and bind their keepers to good behaviour, but the legislative foundation for early Stuart magistrates' concern with alehouse regulation was laid in 1552, when a licence and a bond for good behaviour were made compulsory for anyone keeping an alehouse. Such licensing had been introduced by individual towns from the 1510s, and by the 1560s worried corporations were initiating much more detailed supervision than that provided for in 1552. Here as elsewhere in social policy, urban self-help in response to underlying change – alehouses seem to have proliferated in the wake of the Black Death and steadily onwards through the fifteenth and sixteenth centuries – ran ahead of government interest.[21]

The campaign against alehouses perhaps represented a change of emphasis rather than a wholly novel enterprise, but in six areas of economic and social policy, early Tudor regimes were markedly more ambitious than their predecessors: the regulation of land use, the management of grain supplies, the stimulation of import substitution, the encouragement of urban regeneration, the control of epidemic disease and the relief of the poor. These were issues brought sharply to the attention of government by the economic climate of the early sixteenth century, as population pressure began to press upon England's ability to feed its inhabitants, many towns faced economic stagnation or disruptive change, the sweating sickness arrived to complement the plague, and the continuing expansion of the cloth industry threatened to make the whole economy alarmingly dependent on sheep-farming and cloth-making.

The enclosure of arable land for pasturing sheep and cattle was perceived in governmental circles as a threat to the livelihood of yeomen and husbandmen from at least 1483, and in 1489 and 1515 statutes were passed with the aim of arresting the process. Wolsey took the issue further with a comprehensive investigation by royal commissioners and a vigorous campaign of prosecutions against enclosing landlords, at least 264 of them. Cromwell preferred to try to limit the size of farms and sheepflocks by statute, but there were loopholes in the act of 1534 and few prosecutions resulted. Protector Somerset resolved to imitate Wolsey's commissions of enquiry, but ineptly raised popular expectations which he proved unable to meet, except by alarming landlords with the prospect of summary local redress. His fall was only the most extreme example of the awkwardness of all such agrarian policy, for most of the preceding statutes had been modified or limited by opposition in the house of commons. Just as many statutes regulating standards of manufacture or fixing prices were the result of successful parliamentary lobbying by economic interest groups, so policies that undermined the ability of the landed classes to exploit their estates in the most profitable manner were bound to meet obstruction in enactment and implementation. Many proponents of legislation for the common weal in the 1530s and 1540s complained all too fairly that private interest among the legislators and magistrates harmed the common good. The final irony is that, as far as we can tell, comparatively little depopulating enclosure was being carried out after 1489: any government wishing to open more land for arable cultivation would have had to undo the entire economic history of England since the

Black Death. What is notable is not the government's inability to control such change, but its ambition to try, and the range of means with which it tried. [22]

Wolsey showed similar enterprise with the grain commissions of 1527–8, ordering commissioners to search out every barnful of grain in the country to prevent hoarding at a time of poor harvests. The initiative was repeated in 1534 with more special commissions, and regularly thereafter using the JPs; it introduced an unprecedented degree of state control over food supplies, coordinated directly by the privy council and implemented efficiently by local authorities. The quarantine measures ordered against the plague in London and Oxford in 1518 were also to be models for the future. The development of industrial stimulation to generate employment and replace expensive imports was less clear-cut. It usually involved the introduction of foreign experts under government patronage, and from the 1550s the use of monopoly patents to give the new industries an assured market. This began, predictably, with military manufactures: gunfounding and other ironworking from the 1490s, armouries staffed by foreign craftsmen from the 1510s, and a boom in the Wealden iron industry from three furnaces to fifty or more during the wars of the 1540s. But by Edward's reign dyestuffs, glass and new types of cloth were being promoted, and from the 1560s a wide range of projects flourished under Cecil's benevolent eye. Such schemes reflected a growing conviction among mid-Tudor commentators and councillors that the most effective economic policies were those which influenced the market but let it take its course, rather than those which sought to buck the market entirely. As Sir John Mason, a privy councillor from 1550 to 1566, put it in 1550, 'Nature will have her course'. [23]

This attitude chimed well with the reality that so much economic legislation was the result of private or local enterprise. Sometimes such initiatives were channelled through official drafting – most notably in Cromwell's office – to produce measures of wider import, glossed with the rhetoric of advancing the common weal, which by the 1530s was becoming *de rigueur* even for measures of a traditional kind. Sometimes a snowball effect was evident, as more and more interested parties secured legislation until some sort of general policy was in place. Thus between 1532 and 1544, 101 towns secured statutes encouraging urban development by granting powers to the corporation to seize and build upon plots of land which tenants or landlords left derelict. What began with single acts for York and Norwich ended

with three statutes each covering more than 20 towns at one go.
Similarly, a run of charters confirming or enhancing the economic
privileges and regulatory powers of individual corporations culminated in Marian statutes granting corporate towns and their residents a
monopoly on retailing and large-scale cloth manufacture. Towns did
not have to enforce these rights, just as they did not have to utilise
their powers of compulsory redevelopment; but they were equipped
to defend and promote their interests if they needed to do so. [24]

Most striking of all was the development of poor relief. English
initiatives ran behind, and indeed imitated, those in the great cities
of the Netherlands, but by 1600 they had produced a more comprehensive secular system of provision for the poor than in any other
European nation-state. This worked in the only practicable way, by
empowering local elites to cope with the local poor as circumstances
demanded; but it was ordered by statute and regulated by the JPs. It
operated in parallel with older and more communitarian forms of
relief such as the help-ale, by which those fallen on hard times
brewed ale for their more fortunate neighbours to buy at charitably
inflated prices; but it also sought to cope with vagrants and others
outside the scope of such neighbourly charity. The system developed
from, rather than replacing, the administration of parochial relief
funds, charitable confraternities and almshouses, by the leading men
of later fifteenth-century communities. However, it was also the
product of sweeping legislative projects such as that proposed by
Christopher St German in 1531, under which a nationwide scheme
combining parochial relief; employment for vagabonds on public
works, and an investigation into the causes of inflation and poverty
was to be coordinated by a 'great standyng counsayll' exercising
delegated parliamentary power. [25]

St German's proposals never became law, but slightly less ambitious schemes did. Legislative concern tended to be concentrated
first on vagrancy, because of the fear that the mobile and apparently
workshy poor might turn to crime or stir up rebellion. A run of acts
ordered that they be sent home, prescribing deterrent penalties
before their departure: three days in the stocks in 1495 (a refinement
of the stocking or imprisonment laid down in 1388, but apparently
rarely applied); then a whipping (quicker to administer) in 1531.
Gradually, as in a short-lived act of 1536, setting the able-bodied poor
to work came to be seen as a constructive complement to this policy,
though the means chosen in the notorious 1547 act – slavery for persistent vagrants – fortunately did not meet with much success.

Meanwhile provision for the impotent poor gradually increased. Begging licences could be issued by JPs under the 1531 act, parochial collections were to be taken under that of 1536, and poor rates could be levied under that of 1552. Such rates, although their payment was still technically voluntary, were given the backing of oversight by the JPs in 1563, and finally in 1572 their payment was made compulsory.

As late as 1660 perhaps two in three English parishes were coping with their poor without the need to levy such rates, but the structure was in place if they needed it. Such room for local initiative matches the way in which local experiments ran ahead of national legislation at every turn. Licensed beggars were given badges at Gloucester as early as 1504, regular parochial collections began in London in 1533, and Norwich and York were levying compulsory poor rates from 1549–50. None the less, many less stressed or less forward-thinking towns and villages did take their cue from the statutes; patchy though the system was, it was far more standardised, recognisably national and centrally coordinated than what had gone before.[26]

Loyalty and Treason

Perhaps the parish constable loomed larger in the mind of the whipped vagrant or the badged beggar than did the king or the parliament. Yet the sanctions available to impose loyalty to the crown on its individual subjects grew in the early Tudor period, and especially in the 1530s. Oaths of loyalty to the succession were demanded of all adult males in 1534. Oaths of loyalty to the royal supremacy were demanded of all clergy in 1534–5, and then of all new office-holders, lay and clerical, from 1536. There were precedents for such oaths in the English campaigns in France, where conquered Frenchmen swore to be Henry's true subjects, and in the dynastic convulsions of 1460 and 1471, when dozens of leading men were sworn to the Yorkist succession. But in scale – and in its implications for those, such as More and Fisher, who refused to swear – the enterprise was entirely new. With it came a dramatic extension of the statutory law of treason. The 1534 act made it treason to call the king a heretic, a schismatic, a tyrant, an infidel or a usurper, whereas the previous statute of 1352 had defined no explicit offence of treason by words. Fifteenth-century regimes, especially that of Henry VI, had mounted dozens of treason trials when the evidence proved only that the accused had spoken or written such seditious words, but they had to argue that the words involved compassing or imagining the king's death, and it was never easy to secure convictions. Henry VIII himself found that the judges would not countenance a prosecution under the 1352 statute against the Nun of Kent, who had threatened the king with divine destruction if he failed to renounce Anne Boleyn. Hence the new act, and a run of statutes for the rest of the reign defining further treasons, mostly related to Henry's ever-changing provisions for the succession.[27]

The implementation of the new treason act under Cromwell's supervision was constrained by legal forms and doubtless by his own sense of the politically acceptable. By the standards of Ivan the Terrible's *oprichnina*, of the St Bartholomew's Day massacres, of the suppression of the German Peasant War or even perhaps of the Marian burnings, it was considerably less bloody than it might have been. There was no formal network of government agents, evidence was sifted carefully, trials were conducted by due process, and juries felt free to acquit when they were not convinced of guilt. Of 883 suspects known to have been accused of treason between 1532 and 1540, 178 were participants in the revolts of 1536 and 20 were the victims of court politics. Amongst these the gallows and the axe were predictably active. But of the remaining 562, only 110 were executed and 98 of those were caught up in conspiracies of one sort or another. Prosecutions were declining in frequency even in Cromwell's last years of power, and people who just happened to say the wrong thing at the wrong time did not feature largely on the list of his executed victims. But all this should not lead us to underestimate the fear and resentment generated by arrests and interrogations. The 1534 act was regarded by 1547 as a draconian measure whose repeal would win popularity for the new regime, and despite partial restoration in 1552 and a similar process of relaxation and re extension under Mary, it was never fully reinstated.

The act's demise did not testify to insouciance on the part of mid Tudor regimes about their ability to secure convictions. Mary took the unprecedented step in 1554 of punishing the jurors who had failed to convict the conspirator Sir Nicholas Throckmorton. And the relaxation of the treason law did not mark any lack of concern for what ordinary people said about the government. The pillory and the prison were used to punish seditious talk that fell short of treason in the 1530s as they had been by Henry V and Henry VII, and such prac

tice was regularised and sharpened by a statute of 1555 which prescribed three months in prison, plus the loss of one's ears or a fine of
£100, for those speaking seditious and slanderous words to the
reproach and dishonour of the king and queen. Martial law, traditional for the despatch of those captured in armed rebellion against
the crown, was used in 1536 and 1549 not only against the rebels but
also against those elsewhere in the country spreading news of their
exploits. The overall impression is that one had to be increasingly
careful what one said, at court or in the country, in the long crisis of
Reformation and Counter-Reformation, as for a while in the briefer
dynastic crises of Henry VII's reign. As one Richard Bishop of Bungay
rather exaggeratedly grumbled in 1537, if two or three people were
spotted walking together, 'the constable come to them and will know
what communication they have, or else they shall be stocked'.[28]

Parliament

Parliament and its statutes formed another means by which the
Tudors' subjects were coopted into a more coherent governmental
enterprise, as Thomas More again found to his cost: much of the discussion between him and his accusers centred on the competence of
parliament, and the conflict between his conscience (aligned with
the consensus of Christendom) and the statutes enacting the break
with Rome. Questions of the constitutional status of parliament
before, during and after the early Tudor period have been almost as
controversial amongst historians, yet certain developments are clear.
The geographical scope of parliamentary representation increased
widely between 1509 and 1558, expanding the membership of the
commons from 296 to 376. The Welsh counties and boroughs,
Cheshire and Calais were added between 1536 and 1542, but the
trend went back before Cromwell's time to the enfranchisement of
Berwick (recaptured from the Scots in 1482), in 1510–12. Together
with the 40 or so English boroughs enfranchised between Henry
VIII's accession and Mary's death, these new constituencies
intensified the degree to which the English parliament exceeded
continental assemblies in the breadth of its representation of the
political nation. There are signs that this was deliberate. Jersey was
asked to send MPs in 1542 but failed to do so; only County Durham,

stymied by its bishop, remained unrepresented until 1673, though its inhabitants tried to secure the franchise by a bill in 1563. Even in the case of individual boroughs, their population and political or administrative significance – as county towns, or the seats of new bishoprics – were taken into account in admitting them to the franchise. Such policy rested on the idea already current in the fourteenth century that, as Chief Justice Thorp put it in 1365, 'parliament represents the body of all the realm'.[29]

For purposes of practical government this had two great consequences. Parliament was the means to make statute, recognised from at least the mid-fifteenth century as new law able to override common law custom, to bind all the king's subjects and all his dominions, even those not represented there, and to be impervious to judicial nullification. And parliament drew together the political nation: prelates, peers, leading townsmen and landed gentry (whose 'invasion of the boroughs' from around 1400 made them account for at least two-thirds of the commons' membership by Edward IV's reign). This made parliament the means to consult national political opinion and secure its backing for royal initiatives. Thus parliament, although not conferring the right to rule as some historians have imagined, had repeatedly legislated to declare or confirm the proper course of the succession to the throne in the fifteenth century. Its unique role in such matters was confirmed by the demise of the more flexible but less authoritative alternative, the great council, from Henry VII's later years.[30]

Such considerations made parliament the only means to enact, and then to reverse, the break with Rome and the attendant changes, and the institution's stature undoubtedly grew in the process. No earlier writer stated as confidently or comprehensively as Sir Thomas Smith that 'The most high and absolute power of the realm of England consisteth in the Parliament'. Smith's account, written in 1565, also enshrined the notion of the king-in-parliament, by which law was made not by the monarch in cooperation with the parliament, but by a parliament consisting of king, lords and commons, three equal partners in the legislative process. There had been hints of this view as early as 1401, when parliament, consisting of king, lords and commons, was likened to the Holy Trinity; it fitted with the increasing use of the phrase 'by authority of parliament' in fifteenth-century acts; and in 1522 Chief Justice Fyneux stated that 'the parliament of the king and the lords and the commons are a corporation'. But the principle was explicitly written into statutes only from 1534, and its most famous enunciation was made by Henry VIII himself: 'we be informed by our judges' he told MPs in 1542, 'that we at no time stand so highly in our estate royal as in the time of Parliament, wherein we as head and you as members are conjoined and knit together into one body politic'. Mid-Tudor writers did not absorb the notion at once, but from Smith's time onwards it became increasingly standard.[31]

However, ambiguities remained in the relationship between king and statute. Edward IV had modified statutes after their enactment, usually just to add provisos exempting individuals from their effects. Henry VII did the same, though to a lesser extent. From the fact that he never had to veto a bill one might guess that he took as close a grip on parliamentary proceedings as on other aspects of government, an impression borne out by the fact that he signed not just every surviving original act from his reign but every single membrane of every act. But it was his reign that witnessed procedural standardisation limiting the king's flexibility in the legislative process. Henry VIII never tampered with completed statutes, though he did veto some. He signed less than a quarter of the original acts surviving from his later parliaments, suggesting a further decline in the value of personal royal initiatives in parliament. He did, however, secure a wide range of acts empowering him to act in important areas without further parliamentary approval: to modify or replace the arrangements for Welsh government enacted in 1536–43 (perhaps on the creation of Edward as prince of Wales); to alter the act of 1543 restricting use of the vernacular bible; to designate his heirs by will or letters patent. Such acts raised the possibility that the consolidation of parliament's powers might result only in a more effective empowerment of royal autocracy. Similarly, parliamentary seating arrangements in the second half of Henry's reign suggested not a king absorbed by parliament, but one more majestically separated out from it.[32]

The relationship between king, parliament and statute was at its most sensitive in the government of the church. Here the common lawyers' instincts ran contrary to Henry's vision of a personal supremacy in the mode of Justinian or King David. A parliamentary supremacy over the church fitted both the lawyers' high view of statute and their prominent role in parliament. The judges and the crown's legal officers attended in the lords to advise on technical points, and a large body of men trained at the inns of court – as high a proportion of MPs in 1422 as in 1584 – secured election to the commons, where the speaker was always a lawyer after 1523 and usually even before that date. Christopher St German laid out the principles of such a parliamentary supremacy in his *New Additions* in 1531, on the grounds that 'the kynge in his parlyament' was 'the hyghe soueraygne ouer the people / whiche hath not onely charge on the bodies, but also on the soules of his subiectes'; he elaborated his case in two further works in 1534–5, using Fortescue's definition of English government as *politicum et regale* to steer Henry away from theocratic kingship. Cromwell turned such ideas into statute, and common lawyer councillors such as Audley stood up for them later in the reign. The result under Henry was a compromise dependent on the king's management of his parliaments and his bishops, but the circumstances of Edward's minority tended to confirm the statutory nature of the state's control over the church, an issue which survived to trouble Elizabeth as those bent on further reformation took to parliamentary agitation as the means to force it upon her.[33]

One must be careful in judging the effects of the increase in parliament's legislative stature on its political standing. On the one hand, crude hindsight suggests that the Tudors were creating a Frankenstein's monster, destined to turn upon their Stuart successors. On the other, comparison with parliaments between 1376 and 1450 suggests that the Tudor assemblies were tame affairs, meeting comparatively irregularly, not daring to remove unpopular royal ministers, rebuke royal misgovernment, or place controls on the use of taxation. At first sight, neither view accords well with the Eltonian image of the Tudor parliament as a well-forged and powerful instrument of royal government. But all three can be reconciled. In record-keeping, in procedure, in the assertion of privileges and in consciousness of parliament's historic constitutional importance, the Tudor epoch (and not just the period from the 1530s on) was a time of consolidation and growth, especially among the commons. This was natural when parliament was engaged on such momentous legislative activity. Much of it also went with the legal training of so many MPs, and it prepared the ground for future confrontations, especially with the rediscovery of the commons' boldness in earlier centuries. For such confrontations to take place, however, there had to be a renewal of the financial and political strain brought on by the Hundred Years War, and the alternately autocratic or incompetent kingship that had accompanied it. By and large the Tudors avoided both the problems and the proclivities of Richard II, Henry VI or Charles I.[34]

The Tudors' success in dealing with parliaments was also a matter of management. From Edward IV to Elizabeth there was a solid core of MPs tied to the crown by household or administrative service, and at awkward moments – as in the subsidy debates of 1523 – they were expected to earn their fees. Leading noblemen, especially those on the privy council, also assisted royal nominees or their own clients to gain election, and may well have expected to influence their activity on controversial issues. From at least 1515, circular letters to the sheriffs requested the return of suitable MPs, and under Mary these were specified to be of 'the wise, grave and Catholic sort'. Such letters may not have had much effect: that of 1586 requesting the return of the same members as in the previous parliament produced a house in which 48 per cent of MPs were novices. But more precise means were available. Cromwell in particular worked hard to discourage opponents of crown policy in both houses from attending, and to chivvy potential supporters. He sought to coordinate elections in the crown's interest, promising the king 'never more tractable parliament' in 1539. His successors enfranchised numerous boroughs under the influence of the Duchy of Cornwall or the Duchy of Lancaster to provide safe seats for crown nominees, and Northumberland and his fellow councillors attempted electoral management on an almost Cromwellian scale in 1551 and 1553.

Once parliament met, constant management was required to keep a legislative programme on track. The clearest sign of this is that the prominence of the two houses in the processing of official business varied with the presence of the crown's leading manager in the commons or the lords: definite shifts towards the lords are evident on the elevation of Cromwell and Cecil to the peerage. Nevertheless, the passage of government measures could prove remarkably troublesome, even in assemblies produced by such well-organised elections as those of 1539. The crown's control of parliament was not as effortless as it looks, and in less competent hands or more adverse circumstances it could readily have broken down.[35]

A clear side-effect of the increasing (or reviving) centrality of parliament in government, and the ever clearer range and power of statute, was an intensification of parliament's role as what Elton dubbed a 'point of contact'. Private bills presented by individuals, towns, trade guilds and other economic interest groups were proliferating at a great rate by the early Elizabethan period, such that the average number of bills considered in each session rose from 68 in 1547–58 to 126 in 1559–81. The earlier history of such measures is

hard to chart in the absence of a commons' journal, though we
know from their own records that some boroughs and the London
livery companies lobbied hard for beneficial legislation in the reigns
of Henry VII, Edward IV and before. Similarly, there seems to have
been a steady increase in the interest shown at local level in what
had gone on at parliament. In the early fourteenth century there
are signs that MPs were called upon to report back to their constituents, and a day-by-day report on the parliament of 1485 was submitted to Colchester by its burgesses. But by the early seventeenth
century things had clearly gone further than this. Events in parliament were a staple topic of discussion amongst the gentry and more
humble voters, and manuscript newsletters about events in parliament, and copies of documents central to parliamentary proceedings, circulated widely.[36]

Statutes and Proclamations

One obvious way in which Englishmen were drawn into an awareness
of parliament was in the printing and circulation of statutes. The
statutes from each session were printed as a set as soon as it ended,
irregularly and as a private enterprise from 1484, by the king's
printer from 1504, and regularly from 1515. From 1510 individual
statutes of more general interest – those for the customs or for subsidies, those for general pardons, the act in restraint of appeals – were
printed in larger numbers. By the 1540s this was done for between a
quarter and a half of all acts, run off 500 at a time for public proclamation and display. This made the art of writing preambles to
statutes a means to communicate not merely with the political nation
gathered at Westminster, but with the nation at large. A print-run of
500 would almost have provided one copy for every market town in
England. The composition of such preambles was another of
Cromwell's specialities, though not one of his innovations. Subsidy
acts in particular already contained brief prefaces under Henry VII,
justifying the need for taxation by the state of international politics;
by 1512 these were becoming much fuller and, as we shall see, more
closely coordinated with a range of royal propaganda.[37]

A more immediate and widespread means of communication
between monarch and people was the royal proclamation. Pro-

clamations had been used since the fourteenth century, but in
Edward IV's reign bald Latin instructions to announce certain information were replaced by carefully crafted English texts. These
sought to explain and justify royal policy, as in the regulation of the
coinage in 1464 when Edward claimed to be acting 'for many grete
and especiall causes and consideracions concernyng the wele and
prosperite of this lond and his subgettes of the same, whos welfare
and increce is unto him the grettest confort that may be'. Richard III
used proclamations for intense denunciations of his rivals and
glorifications of his own regime, and Henry VII, though less manic,
was equally keen to justify himself. Thus he explained at length why
the Anglo-Scottish war of 1496 was due to no fault of his own, but to
James IV's 'wilful headiness'. The average number of proclamations
issued each month increased steadily from 1485 to 1553, standing at
0.24 under Henry VII, 0.99 in 1539–47 and 1.11 in 1549–53;
Somerset's regime, beset by disorder and bent on religious and
economic change, reached a peak of 2.41 per month. By the 1540s
many were printed for public posting in addition to proclamation
by the sheriff, and with print runs as high as 1200 these reached
deep into Tudor society.[38]

Much ink has been spilt over the legislative status of these proliferating proclamations: did they represent an autocratic attempt to
make law without parliament? The answer seems to be no. Contemporaries were uncertain how far proclamations could make new
law, though the Marian judges took the view in 1555 that they could
not, and most Tudor usage conformed to that view. They were used
in flexible combination with statutes, to suspend their operation or
sharpen their enforcement; but only in areas such as the coinage
which were generally taken to be the special concern of the royal prerogative did they consistently make permanent changes to the law,
and from the 1530s many of their functions in modifying statutes
were themselves grounded in acts of parliament. They were used
above all for short-term purposes, to cope with war, rebellion, and
economic dislocation, and as such presented little challenge to the
supremacy of statute. By 1550–1, knowledge of their contents was
sufficiently indispensable to the serious local magistrate that a hand-
book-sized collection of the most important proclamations was
printed, on the model of the widely produced handbooks for JPs. But
such dissemination in more durable form pales into insignificance
compared with the statute-printing industry. In 1539, Henry and
Cromwell equipped themselves with an act of proclamations, after an

obscure but troubled passage through parliament which suggests some concern over their intentions. Under this, proclamations issued by the king with the advice of his council might have equal force with statute and be enforced by a special conciliar tribunal. But only one in nine of the proclamations issued during the act's lifetime – those overriding statute or prescribing uncommonly heavy penalties – cited its authority, and its repeal in 1547 left Mary and Elizabeth to continue with a vigorous but generally traditional usage of proclamations.[39]

Printing and Preaching

The circulation of printed statutes and proclamations was one element in a much wider dissemination of information and argument in print favourable to the purposes of government. We might hesitate to call all such material propaganda, since it is not always clear that its production was directly inspired by the king and his ministers, and much of it merely met the growing demand for news, history and political discussion. Historical material unfavourable to Richard III, for example, cannot all be pigeonholed as 'Tudor propaganda', although it both reflected and reinforced Henry VII's denigration of his predecessor. Similarly, some at least of the laudatory epitaphs published at the deaths of Henry VII, Henry VIII and Edward VI were probably the result of private enterprise by authors and printers. Yet a significant body of published work was conceived and distributed as part of a coherent programme to influence national opinion in favour of the king's proceedings, at first over foreign policy and then over the break with Rome and the royal supremacy. Such initiatives were not new. Verses and painted genealogies had been distributed to publicise Henry VI's claim to the French throne, and in the political crises of 1460–1 and 1469–71 considerable efforts were made using proclamations and manuscript bills to stimulate public support for or against the Yorkists.[40]

Printing allowed the extension of such activity onto a new scale. The first step was the dissemination of single documents. In 1483 the Anglo-French treaties of 1475 and the recent Franco-Burgundian treaty which violated them were produced in print, presumably to justify Edward IV's hostile measures against France early that year. Henry VII spread the details of the pope's confirmation of his title and dispensation for his marriage to Elizabeth of York in the same way, but it was only in his last decade that more elaborate material followed. The plans for Catherine of Aragon's reception were published in 1500, but the betrothal in 1508 of Henry's daughter Mary to Charles of Ghent, ruler of the Netherlands and heir to the Spanish kingdoms and the Holy Roman Empire, raised such efforts to a new level of sophistication. A long description of the diplomatic ceremonial and magnificent festivities was published in Latin and English editions. The Latin version was graced with poems by Henry's Latin secretary Pietro Carmeliano and illustrated with woodcuts; the English was simpler, but made its point that this, 'the most noble aliaunce and gretest Mariage of all Christendome' had been achieved by Henry's 'celestial and incomparable wisdom and providence'.[41]

Henry VIII's first wars with France and Scotland saw a full-blown campaign in 1512–13 combining all these elements and more. For the international and learned market a Latin tract justified war against the French who were oppressing the pope and detaining English lands in France, and the papal bull absolving Louis XII's subjects from their allegiance to him was published separately. Two editions of an allegorical poem in English, *The Gardyners Passetaunce*, rehearsed the tract's arguments for the tax-paying public, and they were briefly recapitulated in the subsidy bill in the 1512 parliament and the royal proclamation ordering the subsidy's collection. Alexander Barclay, one of England's leading poets, contributed *A Figure of Our Mother Holy Church Oppressed by the French King*, and another, John Skelton, joined in after the battle of Flodden with two sets of unpleasantly mocking verses on the dead king of Scots. There seem to have been two other, lost, works against James IV, and there was a detailed account of Flodden, attributing the crushing English victory to 'the grace socour and help of Allmyghtty God'.

The impact of such material is hard to judge, but its scale is striking: even when edition sizes were only of the order of 600–800, there was almost one item here for every parish in England. Presumably they were not spread so thinly, but we know that they were passed around and copied into manuscripts like other early printed books. The rate of exposure to such material might have begun to approach that envisaged by John Rastell when he urged Cromwell in the mid-1530s to distribute at least 10,000 copies of his new anti-papal charge to juries. What their readers made of these works is, sadly, imponderable, and it is hard to say whether even those who issued them wanted to repeat the exercise. The more peaceful diplomacy of 1518–22 generated some publications, but the war of 1522–5 brought nothing except Skelton's inimitably abusive *Howe the Douty Duke of Albany lyke a cowarde knyght, ran awaye shamfully with an hundred thousande tratlande Scottes and faint harted Frenchmen*, which seems to have been commissioned by Wolsey but may well not have been published in print.[42]

The anti-heretical campaign of the 1520s generated work for the king's printers, but this was mostly aimed at the international audience; it was the break with Rome which unleashed the next great domestic wave of official publications, ably coordinated by Thomas Cromwell. Every kind of argument was thrown in to support royal policy. The opinions of European universities favourable to the divorce were printed in 1531, first in Latin, then in English. Fourteenth-century French and Italian attacks on papal power were translated, with suitable alterations to make them fit the contemporary English situation. The leading scholars of the English church were called in, to write treatises in defence of the supremacy as Edward Foxe, Richard Sampson and Stephen Gardiner did in 1534–5, or at least to pen publishable anti-papal sermons such as those of Cuthbert Tunstall and John Longland. Common law precedents for royal control of the clergy were assembled in a volume of 1538, while the Latin-reading humanist public at home and abroad was wooed by Richard Morison's *Apomaxis* of 1537–8, a lively review of the events of the 1530s justifying Henry's actions at every turn. The lower end of the market was not neglected, with two editions of the vigorous *Glasse of Truthe* to popularise the findings of the king's research scholars in 1531–2, and in 1534 *A Little Treatise against the muttering of some papists in corners* to counter the sorts of arguments used by the disaffected. And while the rebellions of 1536 were a blow to the regime, they were a grand opportunity for its propagandists. That autumn's most polished productions, Richard Morison's *Lamentation* and *Remedy for Sedition*, managed to mix Plato, Erasmus and Machiavelli with Chaucer, Wat Tyler and the Wars of the Roses to show Englishmen their duty in obeying the king, and in 1539 Morison developed his patriotic strain of argument further in tracts against the Exeter conspiracy and the threatening continental powers. Henry's subjects certainly did not swallow the contents of such books wholesale – John Wayne, a Colchester clergyman, reportedly shouted at a man who invited him to read such works as the

Glasse of Truthe 'Hence, hence, away with them, they be naught, I say'
– but they did at least provide access to the king's opinions for those
who would listen.[43]

Ensuing regimes all used the printing press for similar purposes.
Even Mary, often seen as outgunned by her exiled protestant
enemies, produced a good deal of material both for the domestic
and for the international market. She publicised Northumberland's
repentant speech from the scaffold in five languages, printed the
terms of her marriage treaty to defuse fears of Spanish domination,
and celebrated her accession, her marriage and the return to Rome
in collaboration with the international Habsburg publishing
network. She also rewarded (and perhaps encouraged) the authors
of English works denouncing rebellion. Her reign also reminds us
that printing was only part of a much wider effort. Its obverse was
censorship, in which the crown began to reinforce the medieval
ecclesiastical machinery from 1530, and to take it over from 1538.
Mary's reign brought the incorporation of the Stationers' Company
in 1557, giving the company a royal monopoly on printing and a
clear interest in not offending the queen by allowing the wrong
things to get printed. Mary also resorted to the rather desperate
expedient of declaring martial law against those possessing heretical
or seditious books, a hint that controlling the press was a long way
from controlling what people actually read.[44]

Much circulated in manuscript, like the prophecies of dire
upheaval populated by symbolic animals which seem to have been
popular in the 1530s, and were often interpreted to refer to contemporary events. Great effort was put into tracing these, and spreading
them was made a felony in 1542; one loyal author even took it upon
himself to explain that Henry VIII could not possibly be the
Mouldwarp, the terrible mole-like monarch who would bring disaster on the realm, because he was too handsome and courageous.
Meanwhile Henrician government penetrated deep into people's
minds and libraries with orders such as that to expunge the title of
the pope from their books. Thus one anonymous owner of a manuscript of John Lydgate's translation of Boccaccio's *Fall of Princes*
noted on the flyleaf, perhaps nervously:

> Who Redith in this booke discretly
> Fyndyng the pope in any place
> put hym owt I besych yow hartely
> For I Refuse hym & all his trace

> Submyttying my sylff to o[ur] king[es] grace
> Who is ow[r] hede & most noble gouerno[r]
> whom god preserue euery tym & how[r].

Such effects provide a remarkable contrast with the failure of late medieval kings from Edward II to Edward IV to eliminate the inconvenient cults of political saints such as Thomas of Lancaster, Archbishop Scrope and Henry VI; they testify to the long, though erratic, reach of the early Tudor state.[45]

In a partially literate society, what people heard was at least as important as what they read. Cromwell was well aware of the need for a preaching campaign in favour of the royal supremacy, and sent out specimen sermons to assist in it, but there were earlier and more secular precedents. Since the early stages of the Hundred Years War, prayers and processions for royal success in war had been encouraged. Sermons had been organised explaining the English case against France, and bell-ringing ordered to celebrate victory. Such martial prayers were repeated in 1492 and 1513, and church bells in London were rung in honour of the French defeat at Pavia in 1525. Henry VII extended the practice to cover peaceful diplomacy, ordering the bishops and town authorities to arrange sermons to explain, and bonfires to celebrate, the great benefits bestowed on the realm by his daughter's betrothal to Charles of Ghent which, he reminded them, had been achieved 'by our greate labor, studie and policitie'.[46]

At least by the start of Henry VIII's reign, such choreographed joy also marked dynastic events. Church bells were rung at Kingston upon Thames when the short-lived Prince Henry was born in 1511, and Newcastle upon Tyne staged a 'trihumphe of the prince'. At Louth in 1537 there was a 'generall p[ro]cession for ioye of the nativitie of prince Edward' with ale, bread and wine. And at Dover there was beer, bread, wine and a bonfire to greet the news that Queen Jane was with child, a mere foretaste of the celebration of Prince Edward's birth: the general procession, Te Deum, 'masse of the holy gost in best man[er] most solempnye don & song', beer, ale and bread, were crowned by a hogshead of wine in the church and the market place and a generous reward of 7s. 6d. to the yeoman of the guard who brought the news, even though he did not know the prince's name.[47]

It is easy to doubt the sincerity of celebrations induced by royal fiat, especially when they were accompanied by harsh repression of inappropriate responses to the same events: one Thomas Hall was put in prison by the king's council for greeting the happy event of 1511 with the words 'the queen is delivered of a knave child'. Yet such doubts might be too hasty. Similarly artificial rejoicing at the defeat of the Spanish Armada under Elizabeth gradually blended with more spontaneous bell-ringing on the anniversary of her accession to produce a durable popular manifestation of protestant patriotism and loyalty. And it is far from clear how much of this celebration was ordered from above: Mary presumably did not command the widespread bell-ringing prompted by the false news that she had had a child in 1555. Likewise, Henry VIII's ambiguous relationship with his subjects was summed up at the end of his reign, when far more parishes arranged prayers for his soul, apparently spontaneously, than on the death of any previous ruler. Were they fond of him, or did they think his soul more in need of help?[48]

Magnificence and Providence

At least such phenomena indicate some popular response to royal efforts: the problem with the wider realms of the monarchy's self-glorification is to detect any effect at all on its subjects. For those who saw them – notably the social elite and the inhabitants of London, two important political constituencies – royal buildings must have had an impact. Certainly contemporaries thought that magnificence befitted a king, and building was an acknowledged way to display magnificence. At Greenwich and Richmond Palaces, at St George's Chapel Windsor and King's College Cambridge, and above all in his spectacular chapel at Westminster, Henry VII fulfilled the brief, at considerable cost. Henry VIII, after a slow start in which his minister Wolsey rather outran him, became a builder of palaces on a scale to rival Francis I, and incurred expenses to match. Each Henry filled his palaces with the splendid products of Burgundian, French and Italian culture. A magnificent court was a token of successful kingship. Even Cromwell, though concerned to balance the books, listed the construction of Hampton Court and Whitehall, and the splendid festivities at Anne Boleyn's coronation and the Anglo-French meeting of 1532, among the king's achievements since he entered royal service.[49]

The king's person was likewise meant to impress, and the Tudors dressed accordingly. Henry VII was highly peripatetic, at least in his insecure early years, and followed his Yorkist predecessors in reviving the twelfth-century practice of holding crown-wearings, occasions on which he would sit enthroned and crowned for all to see his kingly power. At least no one who saw either Henry could comment on his unkingly appearance, as some had done in Henry VI's case. Henry VIII made doubly sure of this by wide dissemination from the later 1530s of Holbein's calculatedly flattering and imposing image. From panel-paintings and palace murals it spread to the plea rolls, the great seal, the coinage, and the frontispiece of the Great Bible placed in every parish church. So effective an icon of power was this depiction of Henry that Edward VI was deliberately painted in the same pose. The key to its impact lay not only in its apparent realism and its boldly assertive posture, but also in the lengthening of Henry's legs by several inches (as comparison with his suits of armour shows), turning him from an overweight ex-sportsman into a colossus.[50]

In the cultivation of royal prestige, competition with other rulers was a powerful force, as the role played by Latin material in printed propaganda suggests. Henry VIII's search for an official title, concluded with the award by the pope of 'Defender of the Faith' in 1521 in reward for his attack on Luther, was stimulated by his envy of the French title of 'Most Christian King' and the Spanish 'Catholic King'. The quest for Henry VI's canonisation sprang partly from the need for a recent English royal saint to compete with Louis IX of France. Henry VII's sovereign of 1489 and large silver coinages with a renaissance portrait in profile, produced from about 1505 on, imitated the impressive coins of his continental neighbours, as did the new designs issued for Edward VI in 1551 at the end of the great debasement. Annual tokens of papal favour such as the golden rose and the blessed sword and hat were also the object of competition amongst princes, and Henry VII acquired exceptional prestige by becoming the only monarch ever to be sent the sword and hat by three popes in succession. Henry VIII scored two golden roses and one or two swords and hats, and Philip and Mary were rewarded for the return to Rome in 1555 with the simultaneous gift of both the golden rose and the sword and hat. Such gifts were received in much splendour and witnessed by as many foreign ambassadors as possible. Papal backing, like these other elements of international prestige, had to be flaunted in order to draw the maximum benefit in respect for England and for the Tudor dynasty, respect which could convert into hard diplomatic profit.[51]

Papal favour blended with a wider providentialism which surely reinforced the loyalty of the Tudors' domestic subjects. At its simplest it was dynastic and heraldic, a constant affirmation that the Tudors represented the true line of succession to the throne. Tudor ancestors such as John of Gaunt were glorified, Henry VI was adopted as a dynastic saint and his canonisation was pushed hard at Rome, at least until Henry VIII lost interest. From Henry VII's reign, Beaufort and Tudor badges appeared everywhere: in stone, wood and stained glass all over the king's buildings (and, by imitation, those of his loyal subjects); on coins and seals; on royal charters, even more intensively than the badges of York and March had done under Edward IV; on the king's barge, which sported a Tudor dragon on its prow as it glided up the Thames from Greenwich to Richmond; even in the songs sung at court. The red and white Tudor rose was especially ubiquitous, encapsulating the message that the Tudors had been raised up by God to bring peace and harmony to England by ending dynastic strife.

On Henry VII's first progress these elements were already to the fore, as several well-prompted towns welcomed the king with references to Henry VI, and York produced a pair of mechanical roses, one red, one white, which intertwined themselves before Henry's eyes. To this mixture was added the British History, the farrago of legend and prophecy surrounding King Arthur and his princely successors which had previously been harnessed to enhance the Yorkists' royal credentials. Its most obvious manifestation was the naming of Prince Arthur, but even in the celebration of his birth it blended with more sophisticatedly classical glorifications of the Tudor golden age and King Henry its conquering Caesar, penned by Henry VII's French and Italian court poets.[52]

Such political messianism had been seen in England before, most notably in the pageants for Henry VI's entry into London in 1432; it went well with the stress on England as the new Israel, its kings and their conquests blessed by God, evident from 1377 and generalised under Henry V. It might be thought to have reached its apogee in the pageants for Arthur's marriage to Catherine in 1501, which likened the prince to Christ and Henry VII to God the Father. But under Henry VIII it took on extra significance from the Reformation, as the conventional visual images of royal piety promulgated by Henry VII were transformed into the biblically informed image of the godly prince with sword and book, bolstered by references to David and Solomon. Edward's ministers maintained this line of representation, and Mary had, as so often, to divert rather than destroy it; she extended traditional models of royal piety by comparisons with Judith and other appropriate Old Testament leaders, as well as with the Virgin Mary.[53]

Such ideas set Tudor monarchy in the context of a divinely blessed present and a divinely ordained future, but the Tudors were also hard at work on the past. It behoved them to be so at a time of great and growing public interest in history, when chronicles, historical poems and popular works like John Rastell's *Pastyme of People* of 1529 enjoyed a wide currency in print and manuscript. Some reinterpretation of history aided the royal cause in the present: thus King John's stock as a doughty anti-papalist rose as Thomas Becket's fell. There were also benefits to be drawn from identification with successful predecessors. Henry VIII was especially keen to associate himself with his glorious namesake Henry V, imitating him slavishly and having him depicted in the register of the Order of the Garter with Henry's own features. Both Henries made much of St George and of his order the Garter, again linking themselves with Edward III, Henry V and the heroic English past. Their providentialism necessitated inserting themselves into a prominent place in the traditions of English kingship: hence Henry VII's plans for an innovative monument to himself in Westminster Abbey. This was to be placed on top of the shrine of Edward the Confessor, and to depict Henry at Bosworth receiving the crown directly from God.[54]

The early Tudor monarchs were also concerned with more contemporary history. Edward IV began to circulate official accounts of political events such as the *Arrival*, the narrative of his recovery of the throne in 1471, both in England and at foreign courts. Henry VII took this a large step further by appointing a recognised court historian, Bernard André, as continental monarchs did, and then in 1506 commissioning a complete history of England from the Italian humanist Polydore Vergil; his work was completed by 1513 and first published, in Latin, in 1534. By and large it contrived with remarkable success to mix critical historical scholarship with glorification of the Tudors. Its greatest problem was its rejection of the historicity of Arthur. This attracted bitter criticism from native antiquarians such as John Leland and John Bale, leaders in the patriotic burgeoning of interest in England's past. The debate was potentially awkward for Henry VIII, since he also sought to identify himself with Leland

and his ilk, not least through patronage of the printing of editions of Chaucer, Gower and Lydgate in an extension of the linguistic nationalism courted by the crown since Henry V's reign and before. Nonetheless, Henry seems to have succeeded in having his Arthurian cake and eating it.[55]

Polydore Vergil's popular counterpart (and great imitator) was Edward Hall. His *Union of the Two Noble and Illustre Famelies of Lancastre and York* was first published in 1548. Although rooted in the traditions of the London chronicles, this went well beyond them in dramatic power. It used the history of the fifteenth century and its dynastic troubles as the backdrop for the glories of Henry VIII: his magnificent court (detailed down to the last velvet doublet and golden spangle), his victorious wars, and his heroic breach with Rome. It is far from clear that it represented official views in any formal sense, but it was a sufficiently potent work to be suppressed by the Marian regime in 1555. Meanwhile at court the visual arts were harnessed to securing the Tudors' place in history. Henry VII commissioned tapestries depicting the events of his reign from Bosworth to Prince Arthur's marriage, and Henry VIII decorated his palaces with murals and panel paintings showing his coronation, the French campaign of 1513 and the Field of Cloth of Gold, stimulating the production of similar works for his courtiers.[56]

We should be careful not to see too coherent a programme in all this. There is little sign that contemporaries thought in terms of a royal marketing campaign, and the proposals generated by the few that did now look distinctly odd, such as Clement Armstrong's suggestion that a talismanic impression of the royal seal should be distributed to all heads of households as a sign of their delegated authority in the royal mission to lead the people into the zone of material and spiritual well-being beyond the sun. The use of royal imagery did not progress in a straight line. Edward IV used the closed imperial crown on his great seal after 1471, but Henry VII did not, nor did Henry VIII until 1532. On the golden *bulla* used to seal the Anglo-French treaties of 1527, Henry sat on an imposing throne with renaissance decoration of a sort introduced into his domestic seals only in the 1540s. The same was true of court pageantry, which declined both in scale and in didactic content under Edward and Mary when one might have thought the monarchy most in need of reinforcement. Coronations and royal funerals, the central occasions when the most profound statements were made about kingship, changed remarkably little during the Tudor period. And royal control over civic pageantry was sufficiently loose for the wrong messages entirely to be conveyed on occasion.

We might also doubt how far anything other than the simplest messages was successfully transmitted. It was thought to be bad for the reputation of Edward VI's government when the king's nose began to turn red on debased silver coins, but it is unlikely that the finer points of imperial crowns or scallop-backed thrones meant much to most of those who handled the Tudor coinage. None of the three otherwise competent eyewitnesses to the pageants of 1501 grasped the central features of their cosmological and christological allegories, which have had to be teased out by scholars able to study the texts in a way no contemporary bar the author and perhaps the king's intimates could have done. Printed descriptions of such occasions as Charles V's entry into London in 1522 or Anne Boleyn's coronation may have helped to disseminate the pageant-makers' masterpieces, but many of their devices aimed more at evoking wonder than at conveying any more detailed lesson. John Rastell's model of England populated by moving mechanical animals and fish and singing birds, and bearing two castles out of which a mechanical Henry VIII and a mechanical Charles V leant to embrace one another, is a good example.[57]

In part, merely putting on a good show was enough. The London chroniclers may not have understood the finer points of political symbolism, but they enthused about the splendour of the king, his courtiers and his foreign visitors on occasions such as those of 1501 and 1522. The most fundamental point of all, that the Tudors were fit to reign, significant on an international scale and powerful enough to be obeyed, was made with some ease. It was made not only to the Londoners – a more significant part of the national population than we might think because of the tendency for youngsters to work in London and return home later in life – but also to the noblemen and gentlemen called in by the king to take part or to grace the crowd.

Court festivals coopted them into the Tudor enterprise in subtler ways. At the tournaments of 1501, the duke of Buckingham, wearing Prince Arthur's ostrich feather badge and Catherine of Aragon's castles, entered the lists in a pageant car shaped like a chapel in Tudor green and white, decorated with Henry VII's personal badge of the red rose; Lord William Courtenay was inside a red dragon led by a green and white leash; and the prizewinner, Thomas marquess of Dorset, was presented with a Tudor rose made of rubies and crowned with a diamond. Such conditioning was no guarantee of docility: Dorset and Courtenay were in prison by the end of the reign and Buckingham was executed for treason in 1521. Yet constant familiarity with these visual symbols, as with the chosen language of government – empire, majesty, common weal and so on – must have affected the way people thought about the Tudor regime and their obligations towards it.[58]

An instance of such assimilation at the aristocratic level is a drawing made for the fifth earl of Northumberland, depicting the young Henry VIII, crowned with flames and holding the sun, within a Tudor rose; from the rose towards the Percy crescent moon stream droplets of light, the sole source, as the explanatory verse states, of the crescent's own radiance. At the opposite end of the social scale from Percy's emblem or Dorset's rose of rubies and diamonds stands an earthenware water bottle for a pilgrim or traveller, dug up in London in the nineteenth century and datable to 1485–c.1525. It is decorated on one side with the royal arms crowned with an imperial crown, and inscribed in Latin 'God save the king, queen and kingdom', on the other with the monogram of the name of Jesus, the single word 'leal' (loyal) and two, probably royal, badges. What it meant to its bearer we cannot guess; but that he or she carried it in preference to any other says something, however tentative, for the degree to which loyalties to the crown were entrenching themselves in the minds and hearts of the subjects of the early Tudors.[59]

Such loyalties were reinforced by the real achievements of early Tudor government, and in turn facilitated those achievements. The growing availability of royal justice, and effective political control over the nobility and gentry, made more credible the claim of the red and white rose that peace and justice accompanied the Tudors' providential rule. Increasing statutory provision for poor relief and executive intervention in economic life made more credible the notion that Tudor monarchs felt especially bound 'to advance, set forth and increase their commonwealths committed to their cure and charges', as a proclamation of 1539 put it.[60] The closer assimilation of the church to the state, without any visitation of divine judgement on Henry VIII, lent credence to the idea of a king directly entrusted by God with the care of his subjects' souls as well as their bodies. The construction of a more effective taxation system exploited readier submission to royal initiatives, and helped to fund the magnificence at home and abroad that inspired such submission. The growth of parliament increased the sense that this was all a national, rather than merely a personal or dynastic exercise. Treason laws curbed dissent, but relied on the loyalty of those local governors and ordinary citizens prepared to report on offenders. Statutes, proclamations and printed propaganda gave more and more of those outside the charmed circle in regular contact with the king the sense that he was in communication with them. Many of these trends reached back into the fourteenth and fifteenth centuries, by their nature few ever reached any sort of satisfactory closure, and most brought some side-effect or reaction to trouble Elizabethan or early Stuart regimes. But the density of their interaction in the early Tudor period made it an unquestionably important episode in the intensification of the English state.

CONCLUSION

The most important force for change in early Tudor government is the most complex to analyse: the dynamic by which developments in different areas of governmental activity reinforced and amplified one another. Royal political control and the ability to provide effective justice interacted so closely that much of the time they blended into each other. Financial strength, whether derived from an enlarged crown estate or from intensified direct taxation, was made possible by tighter supervision of local elites, but in turn it facilitated expenditure – on magnificence, war, patronage and the suppression of rebellion – to make such supervision more palatable or less resistible. The growth of the state in the minds of its subjects, albeit fragmentary, encouraged the loyalty that submitted to political control, cooperated in the king's judicial enterprise, and paid taxes.

Many of the institutions and devices central to these changes were in existence by 1400 or well before: conciliar jurisdiction and the writ subpoena, JPs, a royal household acting as a royal affinity in the provinces, laws against retaining, directly assessed personal taxation and parliament itself, to name but a few. However, they had never been applied in the same way as they were by the kings from Edward IV on, nor in the same social and political context. Throughout, society interacted with the state: the ambitions of monarchs and the projects of their ministers were at times welcomed, at times obstructed or diverted, according to the perceived self-interest or duty of those who held power locally, from the greatest nobleman to the constables, churchwardens and jurymen who held sway in village life. By their appropriation of governmental initiatives for their own purposes, selective cooperation, evasion, and at times outright revolt, they played their part in the development of the Tudor state.

Perhaps we should not expect such complex processes to produce clear-cut and readily observable results, at least not in a span as short as that covered by the first four Tudor reigns. Yet their interaction does seem to have made significant alterations in the way England was governed by the time Elizabeth came to the throne. The expansion of the crown estates and the court gave monarchs the means to a more interventionist style of government, less respectful of the natural political order in the localities generated by the distribution of landed wealth and noble lordship. Henry VII and Henry VIII, at times with reckless overconfidence, at times at the behest of their self-interested courtiers, pursued such interventionism so consistently that they remodelled the structures of local politics, placing local control increasingly in the hands of a widening gentry elite with closer links to the crown. Similar trends consolidated the power of urban oligarchs, but also extended the king's power over them. Royal ambitions seem to have been the same even in the regions least amenable to central control, though there, in Ireland and the far north, they produced unhappy swings between under-resourced attempts at direct rule and unrealistic notions of the terms on which the local lords might be expected to govern for the king. Meanwhile the need to coordinate such activity stimulated the rise of a more active and clearly defined king's council, of the king's secretaries and of increasingly influential bureaucratic ministers, from Bray and Dudley to Cromwell and Cecil.

Military and judicial developments accompanied and reinforced these changes. Sharp restrictions on retaining were succeeded by a shift towards the county militia; both reduced the influence of individual lords over the nation's military resources, yet left open the opportunity for loyal noblemen to win honour in the king's wars. The rise of the equity courts began to substitute royal arbitration for that provided by noblemen or gentlemen, and in turn stimulated reforms in the common law courts which improved the general availability and quality of royal justice. Measures against violent disputes over land and perversions of justice seem, albeit gradually, to have changed the context of local political conflict and facilitated the king's control of local elites. Judicial change also reinforced political change in its centralising effects, turning eyes to Westminster; perhaps also turning hearts to a more homogeneous England, just as parliament, proclamations and propaganda tended to do.

Financial strength was not the primary key to governmental recovery, but it was an important manifestation of political strength and an enabling factor in other policies. Here the early Tudors' success lay less in the niceties of administrative change than in the range of sources of income they tapped, and the intensity with which they succeeded in exploiting some of them without provoking insuperable opposition. At times they had to draw back: over Henry VII's judicial fiscalism in 1509, over non-parliamentary taxation in 1525, over debasement in 1551. Nevertheless they succeeded in funding ambitious activity at home and abroad without undue cost in political disruption or long-term debt. Their sales of land closed some doors for those who ruled after them, but their refurbishment of the tax system and their annexation of the resources of the church opened others. The break with Rome and its consequences also served to intrude the king's power more visibly into the lives of his subjects than ever before. Here it ran in parallel with trends towards the standardisation of local judicial and administrative systems and the intensification of governmental regulation of the economy and social change.

Few of these changes were smooth, rapid or complete in their outworking, and many had unforeseen and even counter-productive effects. Efficient lawcourts rapidly became clogged with suitors and lost their efficiency. Financial institutions with less cumbersome administrative processes proved more open to peculation than their slower predecessors. Local assessment of subsidies turned into local underassessment of subsidies. In the long run, gentry oligarchies proved in some ways less amenable to royal management as governors of their counties than individual peers had been. The royal supremacy in the church made more likely opposition to the ruler inspired by disagreement with his or her policy in religion, and the legal and parliamentary route taken in the expansion of the Tudors' power constrained the options of their Stuart successors when parliaments began to seem more a hindrance than a help.

Among the forces steering change, royal personality was doubtless important, and another Henry VI could probably have undone much of what Edward IV and his Tudor successors achieved. Yet that is not the whole story. Kings changed in the course of their reigns, as they took different advice or learned to do things differently, and as their circumstances altered. Edward IV's second reign was far more settled than his first, and many policies characteristic of the early Tudors, most notably the expansion of the demesne, were in evidence only after 1471. Henry VII's idiosyncratic blend of fiscal and political manipulation of his leading subjects only came into its own in his last dozen years, and to have attempted it in the queasy 1480s would probably have been suicidal. A minority or the rule of a queen, it is true, threatened trouble: the reign of Edward VI was politically unstable, as to a lesser extent were those of Mary and

Elizabeth, in her early years. There was mismanagement and corruption in mid-Tudor government. But there was also much solid achievement in financial, judicial, social and military policy, continuing the efforts of Henry VII and Henry VIII and coping with the consequences of the latter's spendthrift warmongering. To a large degree, the governmental system established between 1461 and 1547 survived the crises of 1547–69.

Likewise, political change around the monarch certainly influenced the development of government and the rhythms of administration. To take a simple example, Wolsey and Cromwell both used their relationship with Henry VIII to bypass the proper course of the seals in the validation of royal grants, such that the signet and privy seal were largely replaced by the king's signature; in the intervals before, after and between their ministries, however, the administrative proprieties always revived. As this suggests, politics mattered but it was not all-important: underlying structures or patterns of development did as much to shape the Tudor state as the waves of political change at court. And that political change was as much about issues of policy as about personal advancement or rivalry.[1]

The continuities of mid-Tudor government are a particular reminder that much of the underlying steadiness of governmental development was attributable neither to royal enthusiasm nor to the vision of the leading ministers, but to the attitudes and experience of their more anonymous colleagues. The sets of assumptions we examined in the introduction played a consistent part in shaping the Tudor state precisely because they were not the property of any individual. Those of the common lawyers, above all, permeated the system of government at every level, from a Dudley or a Cromwell at the king's elbow, through a Fortescue or Fyneux presiding in the Westminster courts, to the neophyte JP trying out his inns of court learning on the intricacies of a local quarrel.

Meanwhile the experience gained over long careers by individual councillors and lesser royal servants was invaluable in maintaining the consistent functioning of individual institutions and the system as a whole. William Paulet's career in financial administration already stretched to 24 years dealing with wardships, woods and the royal household when he began his 22-year stint as lord treasurer in 1550; and when in 1554 William, Lord Paget thought Sir William Petre might want to resign as secretary of state, he argued that he should not be allowed to do so, because 'he has been there so long that he is as good as a Council register and reminds the members of everything that has occurred in the past'.[2]

It was fortunate that such survivors were a feature of the period, as much across the dynastic caesura of 1485 as later, for the record-keeping of government remained unimpressive. There is some encouragement for those who would see a growth in bureaucratic practice from the 1530s in the state paper office, where by 1547 documents were being filed in a study, in bags by subject or by country: 'A litle bagge of mattiers of venyce', 'A great bagge of Mattiers of Calays', and so on. Even this system broke down under Somerset. Elsewhere material for an archivist's nightmare abounded. The repository for common pleas records had to be repaired in 1520 because 'by the moysture of the Flore of the seid howse and for rottyng of the Cofyrs stondyng in the Flore of erth in the same they have be and yett doo reste gretly broken by Rattis and myse and some of them be rottyn and distroyed'. In 1558 the battle with Westminster wildlife was still going on in the exchequer, where some of the records were 'so evell loked after that they have bene vtterlie perished with pigeons donge'. In parliament there is no sign that any coherent archive passed from one clerk to the next until James I's reign, though from 1515 the journals of the house of lords did settle into a standard form as the various records of proceedings kept since at least 1449 were, amid 'mild confusion', combined into one. Even the augmentations archives were allowed to 'lye very confusedly dispersed'. All this gives little comfort to the thesis of a decisive shift into modern bureaucratic government in the era of Thomas Cromwell.[3]

We should probably expect as much, given what we know of the development of government in continental Europe. The demographic collapse of the fourteenth century and the ensuing economic contraction were common to most of Europe. So was the crisis in state finance which was their most direct impact on government: a Venetian estimate suggested that the revenues of twelve out of fifteen western European states had declined drastically in the first quarter of the fifteenth century, often by a half or more. Equally general in the fifteenth century, at least in the major monarchies, was serious political crisis which impeded, if it did not neutralise, the effectiveness of kingship. This in turn demanded some kind of reassertion of royal power from the middle of the century. Rulers such as Charles VI of France (1380–1422), Joanna II of Naples (1414–35), and Henry IV of Castile (1454–74) left their successors a considerable task.

Charles VII (1422–61) in France, Alfonso the Magnanimous (1435–58) in Naples, and Ferdinand and Isabella (1474–1516) in Castile each had to fight civil wars before they could begin to reign effectively. But in the end they each had considerable success in reconstructing royal authority. They utilised broadly parallel means: exaltation of the ruler's theoretical position (often reinforced by the arguments for papal monarchy generated by the church's own constitutional crisis), some renegotiation of the relationship between king, nobility and urban elites, fiscal and bureaucratic intensification, a strong assertion of royal judicial supremacy, often facilitated by new institutions, and a tightening control over the church within their domains. Statebuilders such as Frederick the Victorious of the Rhine Palatinate (1449–76) or Charles the Bold of Burgundy (1467–77), though necessarily more bent on territorial consolidation, followed a roughly similar path.[4]

In this sense the 'new monarchy' was a European phenomenon. Yet these rulers' achievements were often brittle and ambiguous. Most of the conquests and even some of the inherited territories of Charles the Bold and Frederick the Victorious were soon lost, and the revolts of 1520–1 suggested that Ferdinand and Isabella had in some ways inflamed rather than tamed Castilian politics. By the later sixteenth century France and the former Burgundian lands had collapsed into civil war, and the Spanish kingdoms and their Neapolitan satellite were eviscerating their economies and enervating their governmental apparatus in the effort to maintain international conflict. And when monarchical power did reassert itself in the next century, the 'absolutist' regimes it produced are increasingly seen to have been animated by clientage systems, negotiated compromise with social elites and a practical stress on the king as a doer of justice not so very different from that prevailing in the 'new monarchies'.[5]

In this context the achievements of early Tudor government look substantial but not, perhaps, surprising. The successors of Henry VI broadly resembled the successors of Charles VI, Henry IV and so on in their aims and their methods. They were 'new monarchs' in that they were reasserting royal power and making it in some ways more effective than it had ever been before, but not in the sense that their ambitions, their instruments or the kind of states they forged were radically new. Their governments were probably more effective on an absolute scale than those of earlier rulers such as Philip the Fair (1285–1314) in France and Edward I (1272–1307) in England. But they were no more comprehensively enterprising and innovative than these earlier kings had been in the context of their day.

To my mind the pattern of change in early Tudor government does not properly fit the Eltonian model, with its stress on the individual contribution of Cromwell, the centrality of bureaucratic development, and the uniquely revolutionary character of the 1530s. Cromwell's ministry was certainly important in some areas of administration and in some of the wider processes of state formation, but in other spheres equally central to governmental development, above all justice, taxation, social policy and the balance of power in the localities, earlier changes were more vital. In the very long term, moreover, other periods probably produced more decisive changes. The judicial developments of the Angevin era were qualitatively more significant than those of this period. The fiscal achievement of the later seventeenth century was quantitatively far more striking, and probably reflected an important change in the way local elites related to central authority and its demands. Genuinely bureaucratic government – if it exists at all – arguably had to await the reforms of the nineteenth century, and by the canons of historical sociology so did the creation of a recognisably modern state.[6]

These qualifications should not make us overlook the importance of Elton's underlying themes of the breadth and intensity of the state's development in the early Tudor period. Although many of the developments set in motion or accelerated then may have had to await the more propitious social and intellectual context of Stone's or James's chosen decades around 1600 to achieve their fullest (and their most geographically widespread) outworking, that should not detract from the importance of the trends set under Henry VII and Henry VIII. James Harrington is the favourite seventeenth-century commentator of those historians who stress the social changes of the century after 1540 as the driving force behind the turbulent history of the Stuart age. Yet even he made a special place for the 'natural subtlety' of Henry VII's dealings with the nobility and with social problems, in the change from the 'Gothic balance' of medieval English politics to the different world he knew. Similarly, the fact that the Ireland of Harrington's day was so dramatically different from England was due in no small part to the accelerating political integration and state growth which in most of England and Wales succeeded the initial reconstruction of royal power. Ireland, it has been persuasively argued, knew the new monarchy, but from the

1540s, unable to keep pace with English developments and thus with the expectations of Westminster, was forced onto a different and ultimately tragic course.[7]

Throughout, England's past shaped in two respects the ways in which it shared in the general European development of state power. In the short term, the special features of the crisis of Henry VI's reign focused the attention of his successors on the areas of government which had broken down most significantly in his day, notably justice, finance and the king's relationship with the nobility. In the longer term, the legacy of centralised but consultative government which had grown up over the generations since the Conquest was fulfilled in the 'monarchical republic' of Elizabeth, as Patrick Collinson has dubbed it. Cromwell's work lay not in the creation of something entirely new, but in the codification and application of principles already important in the development of the medieval English state.[8]

English political development was by no means wholly insular, but when Englishmen read foreign authors they transmuted their ideas as well as translating their language. Fortescue cited Ptolemy of Lucca, Giles of Rome, Poggio Bracciolini and Leonardo Bruni, but seemed little influenced by them. His *Governance of England* survives in ten fifteenth- and sixteenth-century manuscripts, Thomas Starkey's much more European *Dialogue between Pole and Lupset* in one. William Marshall's translation of Marsilius of Padua's *Defensor Pacis*, published in 1535, omitted Marsilius' arguments for elective monarchy but retained those for hereditary monarchy, and left out the section on the correction of a ruler who transgresses the law since it was 'nothynge appertaynynge to this realme of Englande'. However, Marshall's version was by no means an apology for despotism, for he assimilated Marsilius' legislative will of the people to the institution of parliament.[9]

It was not only common lawyers such as Fortescue and Marshall who sought to maintain the idiosyncrasies of English political and constitutional developments. Sir Thomas Smith, the humanist professor of civil law, placed parliament at the heart of his analysis of the *Republica Anglorum*, and heartily praised the jury system, that legacy from 'our auncient Princes and legislators'. One foreigner commented in Henry VII's reign that 'if the King should propose to change any old established rule, it would seem to every Englishman as if his life were taken from him'. He went on to predict that 'the present King Henry will do away with a great many, should he live ten years longer', but in practice such idiosyncrasies were refined and reinforced by the track taken towards the increase of royal power, often as the line of least resistance, under the Tudor monarchs. Embedded in the Tudor state by the studied cautiousness of Elizabeth's reign, they survived to haunt the Stuarts with constitutional uncertainties amidst a legacy of religious division, financial frailty and administrative corruption. Early Tudor government was a creation of considerable strength, but also of serious inflexibilities and dangerous limitations.[10]

ABBREVIATIONS USED IN THE NOTES

AHR	*American Historical Review*
AJLH	*American Journal of Legal History*
BBCS	*Bulletin of the Board of Celtic Studies*
BIHR	*Bulletin of the Institute of Historical Research*
EETS	Early English Text Society
EcHR	*Economic History Review*
EHR	*English Historical Review*
HJ	*Historical Journal*
HLQ	*Huntington Library Quarterly*
HR	*Historical Research*
JBS	*Journal of British Studies*
JEH	*Journal of Ecclesiastical History*
LP	*Letters and Papers, Foreign and Domestic, of the Reign of Henry VIII*, ed. J. S. Brewer, J. Gairdner and R. H. Brodie (22 vols in 35, London, 1862–1932)
NH	*Northern History*
PP	*Past and Present*
PRO	Public Record Office
SCH	Studies in Church History
SS	Selden Society
STC²	A. W. Pollard and G. R. Redgrave, *A Short-Title Catalogue of Books printed in England, Scotland and Ireland, and of English Books printed abroad, 1475–1640*, 2nd edn, ed. W. A. Jackson, F. S. Ferguson and K. F. Pantzer (3 vols, London, 1976–91)
TRHS	*Transactions of the Royal Historical Society*
WHR	*Welsh History Review*

Statutes are cited from *Statutes of the Realm*, ed. A. Luders et al. (11 vols, London, 1810–28)

NOTES AND REFERENCES

Introduction

1. A. Fletcher, *Tudor Rebellions* (3rd edn, Harlow, 1983), pp. 105–12; M. L. Bush,'The Richmondshire uprising of October 1536 and the Pilgrimage of Grace', *NH*, 29 (1993), 74–5.
2. K. B. McFarlane, *The Nobility of Later Medieval England* (Oxford, 1973), pp. xviii, 280.
3. Ibid., pp. xxxi, 119, 141, 179, 283.
4. W. H. Coates in *AHR*, 59 (1954), 361; G. R. Elton, *The Tudor Revolution in Government: Administrative Changes in the Reign of Henry VIII* (Cambridge, 1953), pp. 415, 416, 425, 426; J. R. Lander, *Crown and Nobility, 1450–1509* (London, 1976): Elton used Lander's unpublished thesis; B. P. Wolffe, *The Royal Demesne in English History: The Crown Estate in the Governance of the Realm from the Conquest to 1509* (London, 1971).
5. Elton, *Tudor Revolution*, p. 8.
6. G. R. Elton, 'Henry VII: rapacity and remorse' and 'Henry VII: a restatement', in his *Studies in Tudor and Stuart Politics and Government* (4 vols to date, Cambridge, 1974–92), i, pp. 45–65, 66–99; J. P. Cooper, 'Henry VII's last years reconsidered', *HJ*, 2 (1959), 103–29; G. R. Elton, 'The Tudor revolution: a reply', *PP*, 29 (1964), 48.
7. G. L. Harriss, 'Medieval government and statecraft', *PP*, 24 (1963), 8–39; Harriss, 'Medieval doctrines in the debates on supply, 1610–1629', in *Faction and Parliament: Essays on Early Stuart History*, ed. K. V. Sharpe (Oxford, 1978), pp. 73–103.
8. D. R. Starkey, 'After the "revolution"', in *Revolution Reassessed: Revisions in the History of Tudor Government and Administration*, ed. C. Coleman and D. R. Starkey (Oxford, 1986), pp. 199–201; Starkey, 'Introduction: court history in perspective', in *The English Court from the Wars of the Roses to the Civil War*, ed. Starkey (London, 1987), pp. 1–24; C. Carpenter, *Locality and Polity: a study of Warwickshire Landed Society, 1401–1499* (Cambridge, 1992), pp. 3–9; M. A. Hicks, 'Idealism in late medieval English politics', in his *Richard III and His Rivals: Magnates and their Motives in the Wars of the Roses* (London, 1991), pp. 41–59; S. J. Gunn, 'The act of resumption of 1515', in *Early Tudor England: Proceedings of the 1987 Harlaxton Symposium*, ed. D. T. Williams (Woodbridge, 1989), pp. 87–106.
9. L. Stone, *The Crisis of the Aristocracy 1558–1641* (Oxford, 1965), p. 15; M. E. James, *Family, Lineage and Civil Society: a study of Society, Politics and Mentality in the Durham Region, 1500–1640* (Oxford, 1974), p. 178; James, *Society, Politics and Culture: Studies in Early Modern England* (Cambridge, 1986); M. Weiss, 'A power in the North? The Percies in the fifteenth century', *HJ*, 19 (1976), 501–9; R. W. Hoyle, 'The first earl of Cumberland: a reputation reassessed', *NH*, 22 (1986), 63–94; Hoyle, 'Henry Percy, sixth earl of Northumberland, and the fall of the house of Percy', in *The Tudor Nobility*, ed. G. W. Bernard (Manchester, 1992), pp. 180–211; S. J. Gunn, 'Peers, commons and gentry in the Lincolnshire revolt of 1536', *PP*, 123 (1989), 52–79. For an introduction to some of these themes in the fourteenth

213

and fifteenth centuries, see G. L. Harriss, 'Political society and the growth of government in late medieval England', *PP*, 138 (1993), 28–57.

10. P. Corrigan and D. Sayer, *The Great Arch: English State Formation as Cultural Revolution* (Oxford, 1985), pp. 45–54.

11. P. Williams, 'The Tudor state', *PP*, 25 (1963), 39–58; Williams, *The Tudor Regime* (Oxford, 1979), pp. 52–3, 107, 215, 251, 291–2, 350, 351–405, 420, 457–67.

12. Elton, 'Tudor government', *HJ*, 31 (1988), 428; Starkey, 'After the revolution', pp. 201–5; Williams, *Tudor Regime*, pp. 459, 463–4.

13. S. B. Chrimes, *Henry VII* (London, 1972), p. 68.

14. J. Fortescue, *De Laudibus Legum Anglie*, ed. S. B. Chrimes (Cambridge, 1942), pp. 81–9; Fortescue, *The Governance of England*, ed. C. Plummer (Oxford, 1885), passim; *De Republica Anglorum by Sir Thomas Smith*, ed. M. Dewar (Cambridge, 1982), passim; W. R. D. Jones, *The Tudor Commonwealth 1529–1559* (London, 1970), pp. 55, 116–17; E. Dudley, *The Tree of Commonwealth*, ed. D. M. Brodie (Cambridge, 1948), pp. 51–2; G. R. Elton, *Reform and Renewal: Thomas Cromwell and the Common Weal* (Cambridge, 1973), pp. 13–17; A. B. Ferguson, *The Articulate Citizen in the English Renaissance* (Durham, NC, 1965), p. 391; F. Raab, *The English Face of Machiavelli: A Changing Interpretation 1500–1700* (London, 1965), pp. 40–5.

15. *The Reports of Sir John Spelman*, ed. J. H. Baker (2 vols, SS 93–4, 1976–7), ii, pp. *24–8*; A. M. Kleimola, 'Ivan the Terrible and his "go-fers": aspects of state security in the 1560s', *Russian History*, 14 (1987), 283–92.

16. Elton, 'The Tudor revolution: a reply', pp. 27, 39.

17. A. L. Brown, 'The king's councillors in fifteenth-century England', *TRHS*, 5th series 19 (1969), 115; M. H. Mills, 'The medieval shire house', in *Studies presented to Sir Hilary Jenkinson*, ed. J. Conway Davies (London, 1957), pp. 254–71.

18. Carpenter, *Locality and Polity*, pp. 281–91, 347–60; John Watts' forthcoming book on the reign of Henry VI will explore these themes extensively, and I have learnt much from discussing them with him.

19. *The Household of Edward IV: The Black Book and the Ordinance of 1478*, ed. A. R. Myers (Manchester, 1959), p. 129; C. L. Scofield, *The Life and Reign of Edward IV* (2 vols, London, 1923), i, p. 106; *George Ashby's Poems*, ed. M. Bateson (EETS extra series 76, 1899), pp. 12–41 (quotation ll. 204, 209–10); M. Dowling, *Humanism in the Age of Henry VIII* (London, 1986), p. 186.

20. A. B. Ferguson, *The Indian Summer of English Chivalry: Studies in the Decline and Transformation of Chivalric Idealism* (Durham, NC, 1960); M. E. James, 'English politics and the concept of honour, 1485–1642', and 'At a crossroads of the political culture: the Essex revolt, 1601', in *Society, Politics and Culture*, pp. 308–465; S. J. Gunn, 'Chivalry and the politics of the early Tudor court', in *Chivalry in the Renaissance*, ed. S. Anglo (Woodbridge, 1990), pp. 107–28; R. C. McCoy, *The Rites of Knighthood: The Literature and Politics of Elizabethan Chivalry* (Berkeley, CA, 1989).

21. E. W. Ives, *The Common Lawyers of Pre-Reformation England. Thomas Kebell: a Case Study* (Cambridge, 1983), pp. 36–59, 362–7; *Spelman's Reports*, ii, pp. *123–37, 178*; C. St German, *Doctor and Student*, ed. T. F. T. Plucknett and J. L. Barton (SS 91, 1974).

22. Ives, *Common Lawyers*, pp. 222–36, 247–62; Fortescue, *Governance*, pp. 127, 133, 145–9, 152; Dudley, *Tree of Commonwealth*, pp. 24–5, 32, 35–6, 41–5, 53–4, 56–7, 60–7; *Christopher St German on Chancery and Statute*, ed. J. A. Guy (SS supplementary series 6, 1985), pp. 20–5, 34–44.

23. PRO, SC1/44/83; J. A. F. Thomson, *The Early Tudor Church and Society, 1485–1529* (London, 1993), p. 47; T. A. R. Evans, 'The number, origins and careers of scholars', in *The History of the University of Oxford, volume II, Late Medieval Oxford*, ed. J. I. Catto and R. Evans (Oxford, 1992), pp. 496–7.

24. C. T. Allmand, 'The civil lawyers', in *Profession, Vocation and Culture in Later Medieval England: Essays dedicated to the Memory of A. R. Myers*, ed. C. H. Clough

(Liverpool, 1982), pp. 155–80; R. J. Mitchell, 'English students at Padua, 1460–75', *TRHS*, 4th series 19 (1936), 106–7; J. H. Burns, *Lordship, Kingship and Empire: The Idea of Monarchy, 1400–1525* (Oxford, 1992), pp. 100–9; R. J. Mitchell, *John Tiptoft (1427–1470)* (London, 1938), pp. 85–90, 131–5, 143, 165; F. D. Logan, 'Doctors' Commons in the early sixteenth century: a society of many talents', *HR*, 61 (1988), 151–65; D. R. Kelley, *Foundations of Modern Historical Scholarship: Language, Law and History in the French Renaissance* (New York and London, 1970), pp. 55–100; Dowling, *Humanism*, pp. 165–8; C. Sturge, *Cuthbert Tunstal* (London, 1938), p. 394.

25. T. Starkey, *A Dialogue between Pole and Lupset*, ed. T. F. Mayer (Camden Soc. 4th series 37, 1989); T. Smith?, *A Discourse of the Common Weal of this Realm of England*, ed. E. Lamond (Cambridge, 1893); T. F. Mayer, *Thomas Starkey and the Commonweal: Humanist Politics and Religion in the Reign of Henry VIII* (Cambridge, 1989), p. 203; M. Dewar, *Sir Thomas Smith: A Tudor Intellectual in Office* (London, 1964), p. 21; *The Crowland Chronicle Continuations: 1459–1486*, ed. N. Pronay and J. Cox (London, 1986), pp. 66–7, 78–95, 100–1, 125, 151, 191–3.

26. Q. Skinner, *The Foundations of Modern Political Thought* (2 vols, Cambridge, 1978), ii, pp. 259–67, 284–301; G. Redworth, *In Defence of the Church Catholic: The Life of Stephen Gardiner* (Oxford, 1990), pp. 10–11, 66–7, 94.

27. S. R. Gammon, *Statesman and Schemer: William, First Lord Paget – Tudor Minister* (Newton Abbot, 1973), pp. 119, 206; Dewar, *Smith*, pp. 5, 39–44.

28. Dowling, *Humanism*, pp. 112–36; R. Weiss, *Humanism in England during the Fifteenth Century* (2nd edn, Oxford, 1957); D. R. Starkey, 'England', in *The Renaissance in National Context*, ed. R. Porter and M. Teich (Cambridge, 1992), pp. 146–63; Elton, *Reform and Renewal*, p. 1; J. K. McConica, *English Humanists and Reformation Politics under Henry VIII and Edward VI* (Oxford, 1965), p. 89; M. Todd, *Christian Humanism and the Puritan Social Order* (Cambridge, 1987), pp. 22–93.

29. Ferguson, *Articulate Citizen*, pp. 11–129, 162–71, 315–40; Mayer, *Starkey*, pp. 24–5, 49–63, 97; F. Caspari, *Humanism and the Social Order in Tudor England* (Chicago, 1954), passim (Elyot quotation p. 94); Starkey, 'England', p. 150; *Humanist Scholarship and Public Order: Two Tracts against the Pilgrimage of Grace by Sir Richard Morison*, ed. D. S. Berkowitz (Washington, DC, 1984), p. 116, 136.

30. A. Fox and J. A. Guy, *Reassessing the Henrician Age: Humanism, Politics and Reform 1500–1550* (Oxford, 1986), pp. 9–73; Mayer, *Starkey*, pp. 112–26; Starkey, 'England', pp. 154–5; T. F. Mayer, 'Tournai and tyranny: imperial kingship and critical humanism', *HJ*, 34 (1991), 270–6; C. Lloyd and S. Thurley, *Henry VIII: Images of a Tudor King* (Oxford, 1990), pp. 40, 67; P. Collinson, 'Sir Nicholas Bacon and the Elizabethan via Media', *HJ*, 23 (1980), 257–61; Dowling, *Humanism*, pp. 211–14, 224–9.

31. Ives, *Common Lawyers*, pp. 189–93, 285–6, 308–29; Ferguson, *Articulate Citizen*, p. 152; Ferguson, *Indian Summer*, pp. 92–4; D. Baker-Smith, ' "Inglorious glory": 1513 and the humanist attack on chivalry', in *Chivalry in the Renaissance*, pp. 129–44; Dewar, *Smith*, p. 110; Gammon, *Statesman and Schemer*, p. 127.

32. Dowling, *Humanism*, pp. 112–13, 201–5; G. E. Hodnett, *English Woodcuts 1480–1535* (2nd edn, Oxford, 1973), no. 1507.

33. S. J. Gunn, 'The French wars of Henry VIII', in *The Origins of War in Early Modern Europe*, ed. J. Black (Edinburgh, 1987), pp. 35–6; J. J. Scarisbrick, *Henry VIII* (Harmondsworth, 1971 edn), pp. 32, 218–62, 521–43; J. A. Guy, 'Thomas Cromwell and the intellectual origins of the Henrician revolution', in *Reassessing the Henrician Age*, pp. 165–8; E. W. Ives, 'The genesis of the Statute of Uses', *EHR*, 82 (1967), 691; G. R. Elton, 'Thomas Cromwell redivivus', in *Studies*, iii, pp. 373–90; P. J. Gwyn, *The King's Cardinal: The Rise and Fall of Thomas Wolsey* (London, 1990); *Cardinal Wolsey: Church, State and Art*, ed. S. J. Gunn and P. G. Lindley (Cambridge, 1991).

1 Lordship

1. M. M. Condon, 'Ruling elites in the reign of Henry VII', in *Patronage, Pedigree and Power in Later Medieval England*, ed. C. D. Ross (Gloucester, 1979), p. 130; J. A. Guy, *The Cardinal's Court: The Impact of Thomas Wolsey in Star Chamber* (Hassocks, 1977), pp. 23–5.

2. D. A. L. Morgan, 'The king's affinity in the polity of Yorkist England', *TRHS*, 5th series 23 (1973), 18–21; A. J. Pollard, *North-Eastern England during the Wars of the Roses: Lay Society, War and Politics 1450–1500* (Oxford, 1990), pp. 118–19, 124, 141, 285–341; R. Horrox, *Richard III: A Study of Service* (Cambridge, 1989), pp. 27–88, 132–5; D. E. Lowe, 'The council of the Prince of Wales and the decline of the Herbert family during the second reign of Edward IV (1471–1483)', *BBCS*, 27 (1977), 278–97; Lowe, 'Patronage and politics: Edward IV, the Wydevills, and the council of the Prince of Wales, 1471–83', ibid., 29 (1981), 545–73; C. Carpenter, *Locality and Polity: A Study of Warwickshire Landed Society, 1401–1499* (Cambridge, 1992), pp. 518–28; M. K. Jones, 'Richard III and the Stanleys', in *Richard III and the North*, ed. R. Horrox (Hull, 1986), p. 29; D. J. Clayton, *The Administration of the County Palatine of Chester, 1442–85* (Chetham Society 3rd series 35, 1990), pp. 154–5, 169; S. M. Wright, *The Derbyshire Gentry in the Fifteenth Century* (Derbyshire Record Society 8, 1983), pp. 78–81, 87–9, 105–7, 111–12, 138–40; E. Acheson, *A Gentry Community: Leicestershire in the Fifteenth Century, c.1422–c.1485* (Cambridge, 1992), pp. 24–7, 101, 104–5; I. Rowney, 'Resources and retaining in Yorkist England: William, Lord Hastings and the Honour of Tutbury', in *Property and Politics: Essays in Later Medieval English History*, ed. A. J. Pollard (Gloucester, 1984), pp. 139–55; Hastings may be the odd man out: M. A. Hicks, 'Lord Hastings' indentured retainers?', in his *Richard III and his Rivals: Magnates and their Motives in the Wars of the Roses* (London, 1991), pp. 229–46.

3. See Table 3. 1.

4. S. J. Payling, *Political Society in Lancastrian England: The Greater Gentry of Nottinghamshire* (Oxford, 1991), pp. 1–18; Pollard, *North-Eastern England*, p. 84; J. C. K. Cornwall, *Wealth and Society in Early Sixteenth Century England* (London, 1988), pp. 123, 127–8, 141; R. B. Smith, *Land and Politics in the England of Henry VIII: The West Riding of Yorkshire 1530–1546* (Oxford, 1970), p. 214.

5. J. H. Hexter, 'Storm over the gentry', in his *Reappraisals in History* (London, 1961), pp. 117–62; Wright, *Derbyshire Gentry*; Payling, *Political Society*; Acheson, *Gentry Community*; M. J. Bennett, *Community, Class and Careerism: Cheshire and Lancashire Society in the Age of Sir Gawain and the Green Knight* (Cambridge, 1983); Carpenter, *Locality and Polity*, pp. 523–96; Pollard, *North-Eastern England*, pp. 100, 353–61, 383–92, 619–20.

6. Carpenter, *Locality and Polity*, pp. 314–21, 360–98; Smith, *Land and Politics*, pp. 144–50; R. Virgoe, 'The recovery of the Howards in East Anglia, 1485–1529', in *Wealth and Power in Tudor England: Essays presented to S. T. Bindoff*, ed. E. W. Ives, R. J. Knecht and J. J. Scarisbrick (London, 1978), pp. 19–20; B. Coward, *The Stanleys Lords Stanley and Earls of Derby, 1385–1672: The Origins, Wealth and Power of a Landowning Family* (Chetham Society, 3rd series 30, 1983), pp. 24–5, 162–3.

7. D. A. S. Luckett, 'Crown patronage and local administration in Berkshire, Dorset, Hampshire, Oxfordshire, Somerset and Wiltshire, 1485–1509' (University of Oxford DPhil thesis, 1992), pp. 61–72; W. R. B. Robinson, 'Early Tudor policy towards Wales: the acquisition of lands and offices in Wales by Charles Somerset, earl of Worcester', *BBCS*, 20 (1962–4), 421–7; Robinson, 'Early Tudor policy towards Wales, part 2: the Welsh offices held by Henry Earl of Worcester (1526–1549)', ibid., 21 (1964–6), 45–7; Carpenter, *Locality and Polity*, p. 288.

8. Carpenter, *Locality and Polity*, pp. 636–7; C. Arnold, 'The commission of the peace for the West Riding of Yorkshire, 1437–1509', in *Property and Politics: Essays in Later Medieval English History*, ed. A. J. Pollard (Gloucester, 1984), pp. 116–38; Smith, *Land and Politics*, p. 154; M. L. Zell, 'Early Tudor JPs at work', *Archaeologia Cantiana*, 93 (1977), 125–43; P. Clark, *English Provincial Society from the Reformation to the Revolution: Religion, Politics and Society in Kent 1500–1640* (Hassocks, 1977), pp. 17–19; Wright, *Derbyshire Gentry*, pp. 93–109; R. Virgoe, 'The crown, magnates, and local government in fifteenth-century East Anglia', in *The Crown and Local Communities in England and France in the Fifteenth Century*, ed. J. R. L. Highfield and R. Jeffs (Gloucester, 1981), pp. 72–87; Virgoe, 'Recovery of the Howards', pp. 1–20; S. J. Gunn, *Charles Brandon, Duke of Suffolk c.1484–1545* (Oxford, 1988), pp. 158, 166, 210–12, 217–18; A. H. Smith, *County and Court: Government and Politics in Norfolk, 1558–1603* (Oxford, 1974), pp. 31–5, 61–70.

9. J. R. Lander, *English Justices of the Peace, 1461–1509* (Gloucester, 1989); Smith, *Land and Politics*, pp. 144–56; Condon, 'Ruling elites', p. 121; S. J. Gunn, 'Henry Bourchier, earl of Essex (1472–1540)', in *The Tudor Nobility*, pp. 162–4.

10. J. A. Guy, *Tudor England* (Oxford, 1988), pp. 165–73; C. Given-Wilson, *The Royal Household and the King's Affinity: Service, Politics and Finance in England 1360–1413* (New Haven, CT, and London, 1986); M. A. Hicks, 'The 1468 statute of livery', *HR*, 64 (1991), 28; S. K. Walker, *The Lancastrian Affinity, 1361–1399* (Oxford, 1990); T. B. Pugh, 'Henry VII and the English nobility', in *The Tudor Nobility*, pp. 87–8; Pugh, 'The magnates, knights and gentry', in *Fifteenth-Century England 1399–1509*, ed. S. B. Chrimes, C. D. Ross and R. A. Griffiths (Manchester, 1972), pp. 115, 128; Bush, 'Problem of the far North', p. 45.

11. J. M. W. Bean, *From Lord to Patron: Lordship in Late Medieval England* (Manchester, 1989), pp. 210, 220–1; C. D. Ross, *Richard III* (London, 1981), p. 177; Harris, *Buckingham*, p. 167; Carpenter, *Locality and Polity*, pp. 101–4, 123–8, 145–7, 396, 406, 429–31; Gunn, *Charles Brandon*, p. 125.

12. R. L. Storey, 'Gentlemen-bureaucrats', in *Profession, Vocation and Culture in Later Medieval England: Essays dedicated to the memory of A. R. Myers*, ed. C. H. Clough (Liverpool, 1982), pp. 97–109; F. G. Emmison, *Tudor Secretary: Sir William Petre at Court and at Home* (London, 1961); A. L. Rowse, *Tudor Cornwall* (2nd edn, London, 1969), pp. 187–93; R. H. Fritze, 'Faith and Faction: Religious Changes, National Politics, and the Development of Local Factionalism in Hampshire, 1485–1570', Cambridge University PhD thesis, 1981, pp. 60–72; F. M. Heal, *Of Prelates and Princes: A Study of the Economic and Social Position of the Tudor Episcopate* (Cambridge, 1980), pp. 35–42; M. J. Kelly, 'Canterbury Jurisdiction and Influence during the Episcopate of William Warham, 1503–1532', Cambridge PhD thesis 1963, pp. 27–32.

13. M. M. Condon, 'From caitiff and villain to pater patriae: Reynold Bray and the profits of office', in *Profit, Piety and the Professions in Later Medieval England*, ed. M. A. Hicks (Gloucester, 1990), pp. 137–68; Dudley, *Tree of Commonwealth*, p. 10; Smith, *Land and Politics*, pp. 224–5.

14. John Skelton, *The Complete English Poems*, ed. J. Scattergood (Harmondsworth, 1983), p. 289; J. J. Scarisbrick, 'Cardinal Wolsey and the common weal', in *Wealth and Power*, pp. 57–8; J. A. Guy, 'Wolsey and the Tudor polity', in *Cardinal Wolsey: Church, State and Art*, ed. S. J. Gunn and P. G. Lindley (Cambridge, 1991), p. 70; M. L. Robertson, ' "The art of the possible: Thomas Cromwell's management of West Country government', *HJ*, 32 (1989), 797–806.

15. S. J. Gunn, 'The courtiers of Henry VII', *EHR*, 108 (1993), 23–49; Bernard, *Power of the Early Tudor Nobility*, pp. 146–9, 156–62; H. Miller, *Henry VIII and the English Nobility* (Oxford, 1986), pp. 84–5, 172–3.

16. D. A. L. Morgan, 'The house of policy: the political role of the late Plantagenet household, 1422–1485', in *The English Court from the Wars of the Roses to the Civil*

War, ed. D. R. Starkey (London, 1987), pp. 34–54; Morgan, 'King's affinity', pp. 19–21; Horrox, *Richard III*, pp. 15, 152–77, 227–72; Guy, 'Wolsey and the Tudor polity', pp. 65–73.

17. Horrox, *Richard III*, p. 7; A. J. Fletcher, 'Honour, reputation and local officehold-ing in Elizabethan and Stuart England', in *Order and Disorder in Early Modern England*, ed. A. J. Fletcher and J. Stevenson (Cambridge, 1985), pp. 97–9; *Plumpton Correspondence*, ed. T. Stapleton (Camden Society 4, 1839), pp. cii–cxvii, 120–96; G. W. Bernard, 'The rise of Sir William Compton, early Tudor courtier', *EHR*, 96 (1981), 754–77.

18. Condon, 'Ruling elites', pp. 125–7; Morgan, 'House of policy', p. 62; Luckett, 'Crown patronage', p. 210.

19. S. G. Ellis, *Tudor Ireland: Crown, Community and the Conflict of Cultures 1470–1603* (Harlow, 1985), p. 101; E. W. Ives, 'Court and county palatine in the reign of Henry VIII: the career of William Brereton of Malpas', *Transactions of the Historic Society of Lancashire and Cheshire*, 123 (1971), 1–38; *Letters and Accounts of William Brereton of Malpas*, ed. E. W. Ives (Record Society of Lancashire and Cheshire 116, 1976).

20. Carpenter, *Locality and Polity*, pp. 560–96; Luckett, 'Crown patronage', pp. 97–100; Gunn, 'Courtiers of Henry VII', pp. 32–3, 45–6.

21. D. R. Starkey, 'Intimacy and innovation: the rise of the privy chamber, 1485–1547', in *The English Court*, pp. 71–118; Starkey, *The Reign of Henry VIII: Personalities and Politics* (London, 1985).

22. A. Wall, 'Patterns of politics in England, 1558–1628', *HJ*, 31 (1988), 947–63; Fritze, 'Faith and Faction', pp. 80–251; Clark, *English Provincial Society*, pp. 49–82; Gunn, *Charles Brandon*, pp. 159–64, 198–201, 214–15; Lander, *English Justices of the Peace*, pp. 129–39; Zell, 'Early Tudor JPs', pp. 126–7; S. J. Gunn, 'The accession of Henry VIII', *HR*, 64 (1991), 286; D. N. J. MacCulloch, *Suffolk and the Tudors: Politics and Religion in an English County 1500–1600* (Oxford, 1986), pp. 228–33, 239; Luckett, 'Crown patronage', pp. 131–68; W. B. Robison, 'The national and local significance of Wyatt's rebellion in Surrey', *HJ*, 30 (1987), 787–90.

23. Carpenter, *Locality and Polity*, pp. 283–4; Miller, *English Nobility*, pp. 140–1; Starkey, 'Intimacy and innovation', pp. 87–8.

24. Bean, *From Lord to Patron*, pp. 121–9, 146–8, 200–25; J. G. Bellamy, *Bastard Feudalism and the Law* (London, 1989), pp. 80–5.

25. M. A. Hicks, 'The 1468 statute of livery', *HR*, 64 (1991), 15–28; A. Cameron, 'The giving of livery and retaining in Henry VII's reign', *Renaissance and Modern Studies*, 18 (1974), 17–35.

26. A. Goodman, *The Wars of the Roses: Military Activity and English Society, 1452–97* (London, 1981), p. 134; W. H. Dunham, *Lord Hastings' Indentured Retainers 1461–83* (Transactions of the Connecticut Academy of Arts and Sciences, 39, 1955), pp. 84–116; PRO, SC1/58/53, SC1/60/88; Arnold, 'Commission of the peace', pp. 130–1; Luckett, 'Crown patronage', pp. 207–27; M. J. Bennett, *Lambert Simnel and the Battle of Stoke* (Gloucester, 1987), p. 83; Bennett, 'Henry VII and the northern rising of 1489', *EHR*, 105 (1990), 42–5; M. K. Jones and M. G. Underwood, *The King's Mother: Lady Margaret Beaufort, Countess of Richmond and Derby* (Cambridge, 1992), p. 81; *Collection des Voyages des Souverains des Pays-Bas*, ed. L. P. Gachard (4 vols, Brussels, 1876–82), i, p. 477; *A Relation, or rather a True Account, of the Island of England*, ed. C. A. Sneyd (Camden Society Old Series 37, 1847), p. 39; Ellis, *Tudor Ireland*, p. 79.

27. Cooper, 'Retainers', pp. 83–93; Haigh, *Reformation and Resistance*, pp. 95–6; Bernard, *Power of the Early Tudor Nobility*, pp. 31–2; Miller, *English Nobility*, pp. 64–5; S. L. Adams, 'A puritan crusade? The composition of the earl of Leicester's expedition to the Netherlands, 1585–1586', in *The Dutch in Crisis, 1585–1588: People and Politics in Leicester's Time*, ed. P. Hoftijzer (Leiden, 1988), pp. 17–23.

28. J. J. Goring, 'The general proscription of 1522', *EHR*, 86 (1971), 681–705; Goring, 'Social change and military decline in Mid-Tudor England', *History*, 60 (1975), 185–97; Goodman, *Wars of the Roses*, pp. 139–45; A. H. Smith, 'Militia rates and militia statutes 1558–1663', in the *English Commonwealth 1547–1640*, ed. P. Clark, A. G. R. Smith and N. Tyacke (Leicester, 1979), pp. 93–110; L. Boynton, *The Elizabethan Militia, 1558–1638* (London, 1967).

29. G. W. Bernard, *The Power of the Early Tudor Nobility: A Study of the Fourth and Fifth Earls of Shrewsbury* (Brighton, 1985), pp. 173–208; Bernard, 'Introduction: The Tudor nobility in perspective', in *The Tudor Nobility*, ed. Bernard (Manchester, 1992), pp. 1–39.

30. M. E. James, 'English politics and the concept of honour, 1485–1642', in *Society, Politics and Culture*, pp. 308–415; S. J. Gunn, 'Chivalry and the politics of the early Tudor court', in *Chivalry in the Renaissance*, ed. S. Anglo (Woodbridge, 1990), pp. 107–28; C. F. Richmond, '1485 and all that, or what was going on at the battle of Bosworth', in *Richard III: Loyalty, Lordship and Law*, ed. P. W. Hammond (London, 1986), pp. 187–8; S. J. Gunn, 'The French wars of Henry VIII', in *The Origins of War in Early Modern Europe*, ed. J. Black (Edinburgh, 1987), p. 40; Miller, *English Nobility*, pp. 133–61; C. S. L. Davies, 'England and the French war, 1557–9', in *The Mid-Tudor Polity c.1540–1560*, ed. J. Loach and R. Tittler (London, 1980), pp. 162–6.

31. Bernard, *Power*, pp. 146, 162; Wright, *Derbyshire Gentry*, p. 124; E. W. Ives, *The Common Lawyers of Pre-Reformation England. Thomas Kebell: a Case Study* (Cambridge, 1983), p. 129; Coward, *Stanleys*, pp. 13–14, 116–17, 142–4; MacCulloch, *Suffolk*, pp. 55–72, 226–7; D. Willen, *John Russell, First Earl of Bedford: One of the King's Men* (London, 1981), p. 30; Gunn, *Charles Brandon*, pp. 39–54, 167–7.

32. Carpenter, *Locality and Polity*, pp. 560–96; Ellis, *Tudor Ireland*, p. 118; *State Papers, King Henry the Eighth* (11 vols, London, 1830–52), ii, p. 140n; M. L. Bush, 'The problem of the far North: a study of the crisis of 1537 and its consequences', *NH*, 6 (1971), 40–9; E. Dudley, *The Tree of Commonwealth*, ed. D. M. Brodie (Cambridge, 1948), p. 57; J. Fortescue, *The Governance of England*, ed. C. Plummer (Oxford, 1885), p. 152.

33. J. P. Cooper, 'Retainers in Tudor England', in his *Land, Men and Beliefs: Studies in Early Modern History* (London, 1983), p. 79; L. Stone, *The Crisis of the Aristocracy, 1558–1641* (Oxford, 1965), p. 237; S. B. Chrimes, *English Constitutional Ideas in the Fifteenth Century* (Cambridge, 1936), pp. 171–2; J. R. Lander, 'Bonds, coercion and fear: Henry VII and the peerage', in his *Crown and Nobility, 1450–1509* (London, 1976), p. 271n.

34. Pugh, 'Henry VII', p. 95; Stone, *Crisis*, p. 236; M. A. Shaaber, *Some Forerunners of the Newspaper in England, 1476–1622* (Philadelphia, 1929), p. 141; Gunn, 'Henry Bourchier', pp. 166–8.

35. Gunn, *Charles Brandon*, pp. 215–17; Smith, *County and Court*, pp. 21–44; Gunn, 'Henry Bourchier', pp. 152–66; C. E. Moreton, *The Townshends and their World: Gentry, Law and Land in Norfolk c.1450–1551* (Oxford, 1992), pp. 27–81; C. A. Haigh, *Reformation and Resistance in Tudor Lancashire* (Cambridge, 1975), pp. 87, 104–7.

36. K. Mertes, *The English Noble Household, 1250–1600: Good Governance and Politic Rule* (Oxford, 1988), pp. 59–64, 187–8, 213; F. M. Heal, *Hospitality in Early Modern England* (Oxford, 1990), pp. 44–7, 56–9; B. J. Harris, *Edward Stafford, Third Duke of Buckingham, 1478–1521* (Stanford, 1986), pp. 77–8, 92–3; S. E. Vokes, 'The early career of Thomas, Lord Howard, earl of Surrey and third duke of Norfolk, 1474–c.1525', University of Hull PhD thesis 1988, pp. 310–15; Smith, *Land and Politics*, pp. 137–8; R. W. Hoyle, 'The first earl of Cumberland: a reputation reassessed', *NH*, 22 (1986), 63–7.

37. Harris, *Buckingham*, pp. 78–82, 96–135, 143–4; C. Rawcliffe, *The Staffords, Earls of Stafford and Dukes of Buckingham 1394–1521* (Cambridge, 1978), pp. 89, 165–77.

38. Stone, *Crisis*, pp. 208–14; Heal, *Hospitality*, pp. 88–191; Gunn, *Charles Brandon*, pp. 50, 63, 128, 164, 203.

39. Bernard, *Power*, pp. 158–62; Vokes, 'Thomas, Lord Howard', pp. 307–9; Coward, *Stanleys*, pp. 86–7, 115–22; Harris, *Buckingham*, p. 95; Gunn, *Charles Brandon*, pp. 45–53, 64, 126–30, 154–8, 205–6, 210–14; Hoyle, 'Cumberland', 67–71; Gunn, 'Henry Bourchier', pp. 158–66; G. W. Bernard, 'The downfall of Sir Thomas Seymour', in *The Tudor Nobility*, p. 221; MacCulloch, *Suffolk*, pp. 286–337; W. C. MacCaffrey, 'Talbot and Stanhope: an episode in Elizabethan politics', *BIHR*, 33 (1960), 76–7, 80–2.

40. G. S. Thomson, *Lords Lieutenants in the Sixteenth Century* (London, 1923); Smith, *County and Court*, p. 50; Wall, 'Patterns of politics', pp. 955–8.

41. P. Williams, *The Tudor Regime* (Oxford, 1979), p. 456; A. L. Brown, 'The king's councillors in fifteenth-century England', *TRHS*, 5th series 19 (1969), 95–118; J. L. Watts, 'The counsels of King Henry VI, c.1435–1445', *EHR*, 106 (1991), 279–98; J. R. Lander, 'The Yorkist council and administration, 1461–85' and 'Council, administration and councillors, 1461–85', in *Crown and Nobility*, pp. 171–90, 191–219; P. J. Holmes, 'The great council in the reign of Henry VII', *EHR*, 101 (1986), 840–62; Holmes, 'The last Tudor great councils', *HJ*, 33 (1990), 1–22; Miller, *English Nobility*, pp. 102–5.

42. Condon, 'Ruling elites', pp. 128–33; Condon, 'An anachronism with intent? Henry VII's council ordinance of 1491/2', in *Kings and Nobles in the Later Middle Ages: A Tribute to Charles Derek Ross*, ed. R. A. Griffiths and J. Sherborne (Gloucester, 1986), pp. 228–53; Ives, *Common Lawyers*, p. 229; Luckett, 'Crown patronage', pp. 229–89; C. Rawcliffe, 'Baronial councils in the later middle ages', in *Patronage, Pedigree and Power*, pp. 87–108; C. Rawcliffe and S. Flower, 'English noblemen and their advisers: consultation and collaboration in the later middle ages', *JBS*, 25 (1986), 157–77; Pollard, *North-Eastern England*, pp. 355–8; Lowe, 'Council of the Prince of Wales', pp. 288–9.

43. Guy, 'Wolsey and the Tudor polity', pp. 56–65; Guy, 'The privy council: revolution or evolution', in *Revolution Reassessed: Revisions in the History of Tudor Government and Administration*, ed. C. Coleman and D. R. Starkey (Oxford, 1986), pp. 59–85; D. R. Starkey, 'Court, council, and nobility in Tudor England', in *Princes, Patronage and the Nobility: The Court at the Beginning of the Modern Age c.1450–1650*, ed. R. G. Asch and A. M. Birke (Oxford, 1991), pp. 175–203.

44. J. A. Guy, 'The king's council and political participation', in A. Fox and J. A. Guy, *Reassessing the Henrician Age: Humanism, Politics and Reform 1500–1550* (Oxford, 1986), pp. 121–47; T. F. Mayer, *Thomas Starkey and the Commonweal: Humanist Politics and Religion in the Reign of Henry VIII* (Cambridge, 1989), pp. 133–7; Miller, *English Nobility*, pp. 54–62, 103–12, 126, 164–7; Starkey, 'Court, council and nobility', pp. 194–202.

45. D. E. Hoak, *The King's Council in the Reign of Edward VI* (Cambridge, 1976); Hoak, 'Two revolutions in Tudor government: the formation and organization of Mary I's privy council', in *Revolution Reassessed*, pp. 87–115; N. P. Tanner, *The Church in Late Medieval Norwich, 1370–1532* (Toronto, 1984), p. 70.

46. Condon, 'Ruling elites', pp. 123–5; Condon, 'From caitiff and villain to pater patriae', pp. 145–6; G. R. Elton, 'How corrupt was Thomas Cromwell?', *HJ*, 36 (1993), 908; M. A. Hicks, 'Dynastic change and northern society: the career of the fourth earl of Northumberland, 1470–89', *NH*, 14 (1978), 93.

47. J. Otway-Ruthven, *The King's Secretary and the Signet Office in the XV Century* (Cambridge, 1939); *British Library Harleian Manuscript 433*, ed. R. Horrox and P. W. Hammond (4 vols, Gloucester, 1979–83), I, pp. xvii–xix; S. B. Chrimes, *Henry VII* (London, 1972), pp. 115–18; G. R. Elton, *The Tudor Revolution in Government: Administrative Changes in the Reign of Henry VIII* (Cambridge, 1953), pp. 261–315; D. R. Starkey, 'Court and government', in *Revolution Reassessed*, pp. 98–100; Robertson, 'The art of the possible', pp. 798–816.

48. C. S. Knighton, 'The principal secretaries in the reign of Edward VI: reflections on their office and archive', in *Law and Government under the Tudors: Essays presented to Sir Geoffrey Elton*, ed. C. Cross, D. M. Loades and J. J. Scarisbrick (Cambridge, 1988), pp. 163–75; A. J. Slavin, *Politics and Profit: A Study of Sir Ralph Sadler, 1507–1547* (Cambridge, 1966), pp. 46–67, 172–211; Emmison, *Tudor Secretary*, p. 268; S. R. Gammon, *Statesman and Schemer: William, First Lord Paget – Tudor Minister* (Newton Abbot, 1973), pp. 55–88, 111–15, 249; Stone, *Crisis*, p. 760.

49. Hoak, *King's Council*, pp. 127–9; Miller, *English Nobility*, pp. 164–253; Harris, *Buckingham*, p. 171; Gunn, 'Chivalry', p. 126; Gunn, 'Courtiers of Henry VII', pp. 33–4; Virgoe, 'Recovery of the Howards', pp. 12–16.

50. J. R. Lander, 'Attainder and forfeiture, 1453 to 1509', in *Crown and Nobility*, pp. 127–58, 308; M. A. Hicks, 'Attainder, resumption and coercion 1461–1529', *Parliamentary History*, 3 (1984), 15–31; G. R. Elton, *Policy and Police: The Enforcement of the Reformation in the Age of Thomas Cromwell* (Cambridge, 1972), pp. 239–40.

51. C. J. Harrison, 'The petition of Edmund Dudley', *EHR*, 87 (1972), 86.

52. J. R. Lander, 'Bonds, coercion and fear', pp. 267–300; Pugh, 'Henry VII and the English nobility', pp. 57–91; Ross, *Richard III*, pp. 180–1; Bennett, *Lambert Simnel*, p. 116; Condon, 'Ruling elites', pp. 119–21, 129.

53. Gunn, *Charles Brandon*, pp. 60–2; D. M. Loades, *The Reign of Mary Tudor* (2nd edn, London, 1991), p. 224; S. E. Lehmberg, 'Parliamentary attainder in the reign of Henry VIII', *HJ*, 18 (1975), 675–702.

54. Miller, *English Nobility*, pp. 35, 38–40; Miller, 'Henry VIII's unwritten will: grants of lands and honours in 1547', in *Wealth and Power*, p. 88; Stone, *Crisis*, p. 759; K. B. McFarlane, *The Nobility of Later Medieval England* (Oxford, 1973), pp. 146–8; B. W. Beckingsale, *Thomas Cromwell: Tudor Minister* (London, 1978), p. 141; Gammon, *Statesman and Schemer*, pp. 127, 181.

55. P. Clark and P. Slack, *English Towns in Transition 1500–1700* (Oxford, 1976), pp. 7, 11, 29, 56; D. M. Palliser, *The Age of Elizabeth: England under the Later Tudors 1547–1603* (2nd edn, London, 1992), p. 236; A. L. Brown, *The Governance of Late Medieval England 1272–1461* (London, 1989), p. 154; R. Horrox, 'Urban patronage and patrons in the fifteenth century', in *Patronage, the Crown and the Provinces in Later Medieval England*, ed. R. A. Griffiths (Gloucester, 1981), pp. 145–66; Dunham, *Lord Hastings' Indentured Retainers*, pp. 98–9.

56. Horrox, 'Urban patronage', pp. 157–60; Gunn, *Charles Brandon*, p. 218; D. M. Palliser, *Tudor York* (Oxford, 1979), pp. 15–16; J. Loach, *Parliament under the Tudors* (Oxford, 1991), pp. 28–32, 37–9.

57. Palliser, *Tudor York*, p. 45; S. Rigby, 'Urban "oligarchy" in late medieval England', in *Towns and Townspeople in the Fifteenth Century*, ed. J. A. F. Thomson (Gloucester, 1988), pp. 62–86; J. I. Kermode, 'Obvious observations on the formation of oligarchies in late medieval English towns', ibid., pp. 86–106; Clark and Slack, *English Towns*, pp. 55–6; C. Phythian-Adams, *Desolation of a City: Coventry and the Urban Crisis of the Late Middle Ages* (Cambridge, 1979).

58. Clark and Slack, *English Towns*, pp. 126–35; R. Tittler, 'The incorporation of boroughs, 1540–1558', *History*, 62 (1977), 24–42; Tittler, 'The emergence of urban policy, 1536–58', in *The Mid-Tudor Polity*, pp. 80–9.

59. S. Rappaport, *Worlds Within Worlds: Structures of Life in Sixteenth-Century London* (Cambridge, 1989); I. W. Archer, *The Pursuit of Stability: Social Relations in Elizabethan London* (Cambridge, 1991), pp. 21–34, 58–148; C. M. Barron, 'London and the crown, 1451–61', in *The Crown and Local Communities in England and France in the Fifteenth Century*, ed. J. R. L. Highfield and R. Jeffs (Gloucester, 1981), pp. 90–2, 99–100; S. E. Brigden, *London and the Reformation* (Oxford, 1989), pp. 133, 164–5, 240–1.

60. Barron, 'London and the crown', pp. 96–9; Archer, *Pursuit of Stability*, pp. 24–7; G. Walker, *John Skelton and the Politics of the 1520s* (Cambridge, 1988), pp. 103–16; Gunn, 'Accession of Henry VIII', pp. 280–1.

61. H. Miller, 'London and parliament in the reign of Henry VIII', *BIHR*, 35 (1962), 128–49; I. W. Archer, 'The London lobbies in the later sixteenth century', *HJ*, 31 (1988), 17–44; Archer, *Pursuit of Stability*, pp. 32–9; Brigden, *London and the Reformation*, pp. 238–9; G. D. Ramsay, *The City of London in International Politics at the Accession of Elizabeth Tudor* (Manchester, 1975), pp. 51–9.

62. M. W. Thompson, *The Decline of the Castle* (Cambridge, 1987), pp. 21–6; S. G. Ellis, 'Crown, community and government in the English territories, 1450–1575', *History*, 71 (1986), 187–204; S. B. Chrimes, *Henry VII* (London, 1972), p. 257; Pollard, *North-Eastern England*, pp. 371–2, 382; J. J. Scarisbrick, *Henry VIII* (Harmondsworth, 1971 edn), pp. 552–4.

63. S. G. Ellis, 'A border baron and the Tudor state: the rise and fall of Lord Dacre of the North', *HJ*, 35 (1992), 253–77; Hicks, 'Dynastic change', pp. 94, 98–100.

64. M. Weiss, 'A power in the North? The Percies in the fifteenth century', *HJ*, 19 (1976), 501–9; R. Robson, *The English Highland Clans: Tudor Responses to a Medieval Problem* (Edinburgh, 1989), p. 149.

65. Ellis, 'Border baron', pp. 267, 270–1; M. E. James, 'A Tudor magnate and the Tudor state: Henry fifth earl of Northumberland', in *Society, Politics and Culture*, pp. 48–90; Guy, *Cardinal's Court*, pp. 27, 122; R. W. Hoyle, 'Henry Percy, sixth earl of Northumberland, and the fall of the house of Percy', in *The Tudor Nobility*, pp. 180–211.

66. Ellis, *Tudor Ireland*, pp. 61–148.

67. Loades, *Reign of Mary Tudor*, pp. 52, 54; Hoak, *King's Council*, pp. 63–5, 202; M. E. James, *Family, Lineage and Civil Society: A Study of Society, Politics and Mentality in the Durham Region, 1500–1640* (Oxford, 1974), pp. 30–6, 49–51; S. M. Harrison, *The Pilgrimage of Grace in the Lake Counties, 1536–7* (London, 1981), pp. 30–41; M. E. James, 'Change and continuity in the Tudor North: Thomas first Lord Wharton', in *Society, Politics and Culture*, pp. 131–5.

68. Hicks, 'Dynastic change', pp. 89–92; James, 'Tudor magnate', pp. 66–8; James, 'The concept of order and the Northern Rising, 1569', in *Society, Politics and Culture*, pp. 282–3, 292, 297; Pollard, *North-Eastern England*, pp. 344–58, 384–92; Hoyle, 'Cumberland', pp. 67–9.

69. James, 'Change and continuity', pp. 91–147; Bush, 'Problem of the far North', pp. 40–63.

70. Pollard, *North-Eastern England*, pp. 356–8, 386–9, 393–6; M. J. Tucker, *The Life of Thomas Howard, Earl of Surrey and Second Duke of Norfolk, 1443–1524* (The Hague, 1964), pp. 54–72 (he was technically deputy warden to the king himself, then to Prince Arthur); James, 'Change and continuity', pp. 123–4; B. L. Beer, *Northumberland: The Political Career of John Dudley, Earl of Warwick and Duke of Northumberland* (Kent, Ohio, 1973), pp. 181–2; Gunn, *Charles Brandon*, pp. 184–91, 205–6; Bernard, *Power of the Early Tudor Nobility*, pp. 157–8.

71. R. R. Reid, *The King's Council in the North* (London, 1921), pp. 92–190, 490, 492; Robson, *Highland Clans*, pp. 90–2; University of Durham Department of Palaeography, Durham Priory Reg. Parv. iv, fos. 171v–2r; Guy, 'Wolsey and the Tudor polity', p. 69; M. E. James, 'Two Tudor funerals', in *Society, Politics and Culture*, p. 186.

72. Reid, *Council in the North*, pp. 95, 107n; C. A. J. Skeel, *The Council in the Marches of Wales* (London, 1904), p. 50.

73. Lowe, 'Council of the Prince of Wales', pp. 278–97; Lowe, 'Patronage and politics', pp. 545–73; M. K. Jones, 'Sir William Stanley of Holt: politics and family allegiance in the late fifteenth century', *WHR*, 14 (1988), 1–22; J. B. Smith, 'Crown and community in the principality of North Wales in the reign of Henry Tudor', *WHR*, 3 (1966), 145–71; Robinson, 'Early Tudor policy towards Wales', pp. 421–38; Robinson, 'Early Tudor policy towards Wales, part 3: Henry, earl of Worcester and Henry VIII's legislation for Wales', *BBCS*, 21 (1964–6), 338–42; S. J. Gunn, 'The regime of Charles, duke of Suffolk, in North Wales and the

reform of Welsh government, 1509–25', *WHR*, 12 (1985), 461–94; *Glamorgan County History, iii*, ed. T. B. Pugh (Cardiff, 1971), pp. 555–67; G. Williams, *Recovery, Reorientation and Reformation: Wales, c.1415–1642* (Oxford, 1987), pp. 241–56.

74. Williams, *Recovery, Reorientation and Reformation*, pp. 257–75; W. R. B. Robinson, 'The Tudor revolution in Welsh government 1536–1543: its effects on gentry participation', *EHR*, 103 (1988), 1–20; P. Williams, *The Council in the Marches of Wales under Elizabeth I* (Cardiff, 1958).

75. J. J. Scarisbrick, *The Reformation and the English People* (Oxford, 1984), pp. 70–4, 125–31; J. Youings, *The Dissolution of the Monasteries* (London, 1971), pp. 47, 54, 74–5, 88, 187; R. Hutton, 'The local impact of the Tudor reformations', in *The English Reformation Revised*, ed. C. A. Haigh (Cambridge, 1987), pp. 120–2, 126; Elton, *Policy and Police*, pp. 79, 230–43, 253–4, 259–60, 329–36, 340–5; Reid, *Council in the North*, p. 158; J. A. Youings, 'The council of the West', *TRHS*, 5th series 10 (1960), 41–59; Miller, *English Nobility*, pp. 64–8, 149–54, 234–8.

2 Justice

1. E. W. Ives, *The Common Lawyers of Pre-Reformation England. Thomas Kebell: a case study* (Cambridge, 1983), p. 222; J. H. Baker, 'Readings in Gray's Inn, their decline and disappearance', in his *The Legal Profession and the Common Law: Historical Essays* (London, 1986), p. 34; M. Hastings, *The Court of Common Pleas in Fifteenth-Century England: A Study of Legal Administration and Procedure* (Ithaca, NY, 1947), p. 5.

2. J. H. Baker, *The Order of Serjeants at Law* (SS supplementary series 5, 1984), p. 280; Ives, *Common Lawyers*, p. 261.

3. W. J. Jones, *The Elizabethan Court of Chancery* (Oxford, 1967), pp. 27–36.

4. M. E. Avery, 'The history of the equitable jurisdiction of chancery before 1460', *BIHR*, 42 (1969), 129–44; N. Pronay, 'The chancellor, the chancery, and the council at the end of the fifteenth century', in *British Government and Administration. Studies presented to S. B. Chrimes*, ed. H. Hearder and H. R. Loyn (Cardiff, 1974), pp. 87–103; J. A. Guy, 'The development of equitable jurisdictions, 1450–1550', in *Law, Litigants and the Legal Profession*, ed. E. W. Ives and A. H. Manchester (London, 1983), pp. 80–6; Guy, *The Public Career of Sir Thomas More* (Brighton, 1980), p. 66 n. 8; F. Metzger, 'The last phase of the medieval chancery', in *Law-Making and Law-Makers in British History*, ed. A. Harding (London, 1980), p. 88; *Christopher St German on Chancery and Statute*, ed. J. A. Guy (SS supplementary series 6, 1985), p. 68n.

5. E. G. Henderson, 'Legal rights to land in the early chancery', *AJLH*, 26 (1982), 97–122; Metzger, 'Last phase', pp. 81, 84–7; Jones, *Chancery*, pp. 177–81, 225–35, 306.

6. *The Reports of Sir John Spelman*, ed. J. H. Baker (2 vols, SS 93–4, 1976–7), ii, pp. 24–43, 70–83; Ives, *Common Lawyers*, pp. 189–221; J. A. Guy, *The Cardinal's Court: The Impact of Thomas Wolsey in Star Chamber* (Hassocks, 1977), pp. 44–5.

7. A. J. Slavin, 'The fall of Lord Chancellor Wriothesley; a study in the politics of conspiracy', *Albion*, 7 (1975), 265–86; Guy, *More*, pp. 37–49, 80–93; L. A. Knafla, *Law and Politics in Jacobean England: The Tracts of Lord Chancellor Ellesmere* (Cambridge, 1977), pp. 123–81.

8. *Select Cases before … the Court of Star Chamber AD 1477–1509*, ed. I. S. Leadam (SS 16, 1903), p. lx; R. A. Griffiths, *The Reign of King Henry VI: The Exercise of Royal Authority 1422–1461* (London, 1981), pp. 128–48, 562–97; C. D. Ross, *Edward IV*

(London, 1974), pp. 395–404; Ross, *Richard III* (London, 1981), pp. 173–5; M. C. Carpenter, *Locality and Polity: A Study of Warwickshire Landed Society, 1401–1499* (Cambridge, 1992), pp. 502, 708–9; J. R. Lander, 'The Yorkist council, justice and public order: the case of Straunge versus Kynaston', *Albion*, 12 (1980), 1–22.

9. *Original Letters illustrative of English History*, ed. H. Ellis, 1st series, 2nd edn (3 vols, London, 1825), i, p. 40; Guy, *Cardinal's Court*, pp. 9–21; *Select Cases in the Council of Henry VII*, ed. C. G. Bayne and W. H. Dunham (SS 75, 1956), pp. xxxvii–xl, lxxv–cx; J. A. Guy, *The Court of Star Chamber and its Records to the reign of Elizabeth I* (PRO handbooks 21, 1985), pp. 38–43.

10. M. M. Condon, 'An anachronism with intent? Henry VII's council ordinance of 1491/2', in *Kings and Nobles in the Later Middle Ages: A Tribute to Charles Derek Ross*, ed. R. A. Griffiths and J. Sherborne (Gloucester, 1986), p. 237; Guy, *Cardinal's Court*, pp. 32, 34.

11. S. E. Lehmberg, 'Star chamber: 1485–1509', *HLQ*, 24 (1960–1), 189–214; Guy, *Cardinal's Court*, pp. 36–72, 80–2; Guy, *Court of Star Chamber*, pp. 9–10, 23, 51–60.

12. Condon, 'Anachronism with intent?', pp. 236–7; J. A. Guy, 'Privy Council: revolution or evolution', in *Revolution Reassessed: Revisions in the History of Tudor Government and Administration*, ed. C. Coleman and D. R. Starkey (Oxford, 1986), pp. 66–7, 71, 82–4; *The Ancient State, Authoritie, and Proceedings of the Court of Requests by Sir Julius Caesar*, ed. L. M. Hill (Cambridge, 1975), pp. ix–xxi, xxviii–xxxviii; *Select Cases in the Court of Requests AD 1497–1569*, ed. I. S. Leadam (SS 12, 1898), pp. liv–lxxii; W. H. Bryson, *The Equity Side of the Exchequer: Its Jurisdiction, Administration, Procedures and Records* (Cambridge, 1975), pp. 10–11; *Spelman's Reports*, ii, pp. 184–7.

13. J. B. Post, 'Equitable resorts before 1450', in *Law, Litigants and the Legal Profession*, ed. E. W. Ives and A. H. Manchester (London, 1983), pp. 68–79; E. Powell, 'Arbitration and the law in England in the late middle ages', *TRHS*, 5th series 33 (1983), 49–67; I. Rowney, 'Arbitration in gentry disputes of the later middle ages', *History*, 67 (1982), 367–76; C. Rawcliffe, 'The great lord as peacekeeper: arbitration by English noblemen and their councils in the later middle ages', in *Law and Social Change in British History*, ed. J. A. Guy and H. G. Beale (London, 1984), pp. 34–54; S. J. Gunn, *Charles Brandon, Duke of Suffolk c.1484–1545* (Oxford, 1988), p. 133.

14. M. K. Jones and M. G. Underwood, *The King's Mother: Lady Margaret Beaufort, Countess of Richmond and Derby* (Cambridge, 1992), pp. 85–90; M. A. Hicks, 'Restraint, mediation and private justice: George, duke of Clarence as "good lord" ', *Journal of Legal History*, 4 (1983), 56–71; Guy, *Cardinal's Court*, pp. 47–9, 97–105; Jones, *Chancery*, pp. 269–80.

15. Metzger, 'Last phase', p. 82; Guy, *Court of Star Chamber*, pp. 43–5; *Ancient State*, pp. xxxv–vii; Jones, *Chancery*, pp. 239–48; Carpenter, *Locality and Polity*, pp. 354–9, 396–7, 431–3, 622–5; P. C. Maddern, *Violence and Social Order: East Anglia 1422–1442* (Oxford, 1992), pp. 154–66.

16. P. M. Barnes, 'The chancery corpus cum causa file, 10–11 Edward IV', in *Medieval Legal Records edited in memory of C. A. F. Meekings*, ed. R. F. Hunnisett and J. B. Post (London, 1978), pp. 435–41; Metzger, 'Last phase', pp. 80–1; Guy, *Court of Star Chamber*, pp. 38, 41, 47, 50; Guy, *Cardinal's Court*, pp. 137–8; M. L. Bush, 'Protector Somerset and requests', *HJ*, 17 (1974), 451–64.

17. *Council of Henry VII*, pp. clxi–ii, 22, 24; Rawcliffe, 'Great lord', p. 53; Jones, *Chancery*, pp. 274–6; Guy, *Court of Star Chamber*, pp. 44–5.

18. *Select Pleas in the Court of Admiralty, i*, ed. R. G. Marsden (SS 6, 1894), pp. lvii–lx; Pronay, 'The chancellor', pp. 96–100; R. W. Heinze, 'The enforcement of royal proclamations under the provisions of the statute of proclamations, 1539–1547', in *Tudor Men and Institutions*, ed. A. J. Slavin (Baton Rouge, LA, 1972),

pp. 205–31; R. Somerville, 'Henry VII's "Council learned in the law"', *EHR*, 54 (1939), 427–42; Somerville, 'The duchy of Lancaster council and court of duchy chamber', *TRHS*, 4th series 23 (1941), 159–77; B. P. Wolffe, *The Crown Lands, 1461–1536* (London, 1970), pp. 74.

19. W. C. Richardson, *History of the Court of Augmentations, 1536–1554* (Baton Rouge, LA, 1961), pp. 128, 149, 371–435, 492; H. E. Bell, *An Introduction to the History and Records of the Court of Wards and Liveries* (Cambridge, 1953), pp. 87–111; Guy, 'Privy council', pp. 79–81; M. R. Horowitz, 'Richard Empson, minister of Henry VII', *BIHR*, 55 (1982), 40–4; Wolffe, *Crown Lands*, pp. 147–61.

20. R. Somerville, 'The palatinate courts in Lancashire', in *Law-Making and Law-Makers in British History*, ed. A. Harding (London, 1980), pp. 57–61; K. M. E. Murray, *The Constitutional History of the Cinque Ports* (Manchester, 1935), pp. 91, 105–19; C. J. Kitching, 'The Durham palatinate and the courts of Westminster under the Tudors', in *The Last Principality: Politics, Religion and Society in the Bishopric of Durham, 1494–1660*, ed. D. Marcombe (Nottingham, 1987), pp. 52–9.

21. P. Williams, *The Council in the Marches of Wales under Elizabeth I* (Cardiff, 1958), pp. 4–43, 64; R. R. Reid, *The King's Council in the North* (London, 1921), pp. 142, 274, 344; S. G. Ellis, *Reform and Revival: English Government in Ireland, 1470–1534* (Woodbridge, 1986), pp. 154–63.

22. Blatcher, *King's Bench*, pp. 63–100; Hastings, *Common Pleas*, pp. 169–83; M. M. Condon, 'A Wiltshire sheriff's notebook, 1464–5', in *Medieval Legal Records*, pp. 412–13.

23. Blatcher, *King's Bench*, pp. 138–66; C. W. Brooks, *Pettyfoggers and Vipers of the Commonwealth: The 'Lower Branch' of the Legal Profession in Early Modern England* (Cambridge, 1986), pp. 79–84; Ives, *Common Lawyers*, pp. 211, 276–81; *Spelman's Reports*, ii, pp. 53–61, 220–98.

24. Blatcher, *King's Bench*, pp. 111–37; C. A. F. Meekings, 'A king's bench bill formulary', *Journal of Legal History*, 6 (1985), 86–104.

25. R. H. Helmholz, 'Writs of prohibition and ecclesiastical sanctions in the English courts christian' and 'Assumpsit and *fidei laesio*', in his *Canon Law and the Law of England* (London, 1987), pp. 77–99, 263–89; *Spelman's Reports*, ii, pp. 65–6; S. Lander, 'Church courts and the Reformation in the diocese of Chichester, 1500–1558', in *The English Reformation Revised*, ed. C. A. Haigh (Cambridge, 1987), pp. 34–46; R. A. Houlbrooke, *Church Courts and the People during the English Reformation, 1520–1570* (Oxford, 1979), pp. 16, 77–83, 146–50.

26. B. L. Woodcock, *Medieval Ecclesiastical Courts in the Diocese of Canterbury* (Oxford, 1952), pp. 89–92, 109–10; R. M. Wunderli, *London Church Courts and Society on the eve of the Reformation* (Cambridge, Mass., 1981), pp. 66–9, 92–102, 104–8.

27. *Spelman's Reports*, ii, p. 48; J. H. Baker, 'The law merchant and the common law before 1700', in his *The Legal Profession and the Common Law*, pp. 341–68; R. H. Britnell, 'Colchester courts and court records, 1310–1525', *Essex Archaeology and History*, 17 (1986), 133–40; Brooks, *Pettyfoggers*, pp. 31–2, 96–101, 112–18.

28. Brooks, *Pettyfoggers*, pp. 34–6; D. N. J. MacCulloch, 'Bondmen under the Tudors', in *Law and Government under the Tudors: Essays presented to Sir Geoffrey Elton on his retirement*, ed. C. Cross, D. M. Loades and J. J. Scarisbrick (Cambridge, 1988), pp. 91–109; S. J. Gunn, 'Peers, commons and gentry in the Lincolnshire revolt of 1536', *PP*, 123 (1989), 60–3; Gunn, *Charles Brandon*, p. 216; Gunn, 'Henry Bourchier, earl of Essex (1472–1540)', in *The Tudor Nobility*, ed. G. W. Bernard (Manchester, 1992), pp. 167–8; Ellis, *Reform and Revival*, pp. 141–2; C. C. Dyer, *Lords and Peasants in a Changing Society: The Estates of the Bishopric of Worcester, 680–1540* (Cambridge, 1980), pp. 266–9; J. P. Dawson, *A History of Lay Judges* (Cambridge, Mass., 1960), pp. 208–33; M. K. McIntosh, 'Central court supervision of the ancient demesne manor of Havering, 1200–1625', in *Law, Litigants and the Legal Profession*, pp. 87–93.

29. M. K. McIntosh, 'Social change and Tudor manorial leets', in *Law and Social Change*, pp. 73–85; G. Rosser, *Medieval Westminster, 1200–1540* (Oxford, 1989), pp. 243–4.

30. M. J. Ingram, 'Communities and courts: law and disorder in early seventeenth-century Wiltshire', in *Crime in England, 1550–1800*, ed. J. S. Cockburn (London, 1977), p. 113; Dawson, *Lay Judges*, pp. 244–55; D. J. Guth, 'Enforcing late-medieval law: patterns in litigation during Henry VII's reign', in *Legal Records and the Historian*, ed. J. H. Baker (London, 1978), pp. 91–3; R. H. Britnell, *Growth and Decline in Colchester, 1300–1525* (Cambridge, 1986), pp. 236–45; L. A. Knafla, ' "Sin of all sorts swarmeth": criminal litigation in an English county in the early seventeenth century', in *Law, Litigants and the Legal Profession*, pp. 57–62.

31. R. S. Gottfried, *Bury St Edmunds and the Urban Crisis, 1290–1539* (Princeton, NJ, 1982), pp. 170–1; E. Searle, *Lordship and Community: Battle Abbey and its Banlieu 1066–1538* (Toronto, 1974), pp. 387–99, 411–17, 431–7; M. K. McIntosh, *Autonomy and Community: The Royal Manor of Havering, 1200–1500* (Cambridge, 1986), pp. 244–61; A. R. DeWindt, 'Local government in a small town: a medieval leet jury and its constituents', *Albion*, 23 (1991), 627–54.

32. C. B. Herrup, *The Common Peace: Participation and the Criminal Law in Seventeenth-Century England* (Cambridge, 1987), pp. 67–92, 136–92; Maddern, *Violence and Social Order*, pp. 111–34; R. B. Goheen, 'Peasant politics? Village community and the crown in fifteenth-century England', *AHR*, 96 (1991), 46–9.

33. C. Whittick, 'The role of the criminal appeal in the fifteenth century', in *Law and Social Change*, pp. 55–72; Guth, 'Enforcing late-medieval law', p. 87; J. Samaha, *Law and Order in Historical Perspective: The case of Elizabethan Essex* (New York, 1974), p. 48.

34. G. R. Elton, *Star Chamber Stories* (Cambridge, 1958), pp. 78–113; M. W. Beresford, 'The common informer, the penal statutes and economic regulation', *EcHR*, 2nd series 10 (1957–8), 221–38; J. G. Bellamy, *Criminal Law and Society in Late Medieval and Tudor England* (Gloucester, 1984), pp. 90–112; *The Tudor Constitution: Documents and Commentary*, ed. G. R. Elton (2nd edn, Cambridge, 1982), p. 334.

35. Wunderli, *London Church Courts*, pp. 31–40, 43–9, 51–2, 94–5; Guy, *Court of Star Chamber*, p. 46.

36. *Spelman's Reports*, ii, pp. 104–14, 118–19; J. G. Bellamy, *Bastard Feudalism and the Law* (London, 1989), pp. 25–33, 65–73; Griffiths, *Henry VI*, pp. 145–6; Ross, *Edward IV*, p. 395; S. B. Chrimes, *Henry VII* (London, 1972), p. 64.

37. Bellamy, *Bastard Feudalism*, pp. 16, 29–31, 125, 129–30, 139–41; Bellamy, *Criminal Law*, pp. 15–19; *Council of Henry VII*, pp. xlix–lxxii; Guy, *Court of Star Chamber*, p. 60.

38. Bellamy, *Bastard Feudalism*, pp. 10–17; *Council of Henry VII*, p. cxxviii; *Spelman's Reports*, ii, p. 49; R. B. Pugh, *Imprisonment in Medieval England* (Cambridge, 1968), pp. 151, 236–7; Guy, *Cardinal's Court*, pp. 32–3, 72–4, 85, 121–3; Guy, 'Wolsey and the Tudor polity', in *Cardinal Wolsey: Church, State and Art*, ed. S. J. Gunn and P. G. Lindley (Cambridge, 1991), pp. 70–3; Guy, *Court of Star Chamber*, p. 60.

39. J. R. Lander, *English Justices of the Peace, 1461–1509* (Gloucester, 1989), passim; M. L. Zell, 'Early Tudor JPs at work', *Archaeologia Cantiana*, 93 (1977), 125–43; J. H. Langbein, *Prosecuting Crime in the Renaissance: England, Germany, France* (Cambridge, Mass., 1974), pp. 5–125; Samaha, *Law and Order*, pp. 76–84; T. A. Green, *Verdict According to Conscience: Perspectives on the English Criminal Jury Trial 1200–1800* (Chicago, 1985), p. 122; *Early Treatises on the Practice of the Justices of the Peace in the Fifteenth and Sixteenth Centuries*, ed. B. H. Putnam (Oxford, 1924), pp. 7–107, 225–37.

40. Samaha, *Law and Order*, p. 81; Lander, *Justices of the Peace*, pp. 93–102, 109–44; 4 Henry VII c. 12; R. B. Smith, *Land and Politics in the England of Henry VIII: The West Riding of Yorkshire, 1530–1546* (Oxford, 1970), pp. 153–9; D. N. J. MacCulloch, *Suffolk and the Tudors: Politics and Religion in an English County 1500–1600* (Oxford,

1986), pp. 108, 338–9, 414–15; F. A. Youngs, 'Towards petty sessions: Tudor JPs and divisions of counties', in *Tudor Rule and Revolution: Essays for G. R. Elton from his American Friends*, ed. D. J. Guth and J. W. McKenna (Cambridge, 1982), pp. 201–16; Guy, *Cardinal's Court*, pp. 120, 137; Reid, *Council in the North*, pp. 159–60; Williams, *Council in the Marches*, pp. 107–9, 195–7; J. S. Cockburn, *A History of English Assizes from 1558 to 1714* (Cambridge, 1972), pp. 153–87.

41. G. Williams, *Recovery, Reorientation and Reformation: Wales, c.1415–1642* (Oxford, 1987), p. 263; S. M. Wright, *The Derbyshire Gentry in the Fifteenth Century* (Derbyshire Record Society, 8, 1983), p. 142; Ellis, *Reform and Revival*, pp. 134–41.

42. Bellamy, *Criminal Law*, pp. 54–73; Maddern, *Violence*, pp. 4–6, 72–3; Samaha, *Law and Order*, p. 21.

43. Bellamy, *Criminal Law*, pp. 73–8; Reid, *Council in the North*, p. 62; R. Somerville, *A History of the Duchy of Lancaster, i, 1265–1603* (London, 1953), pp. 278–81; Guy, *Cardinal's Court*, pp. 58–9; Bellamy, *Bastard Feudalism*, pp. 123–44.

44. Chrimes, *Henry VII*, pp. 177–84; S. E. Lehmberg, *The Reformation Parliament 1529–1536* (Cambridge, 1970), pp. 97–8, 125–6, 154–5, 235–9; Lehmberg, *The Later Parliaments of Henry VIII 1536–1547* (Cambridge, 1977), pp. 64, 95–101, 154, 176, 181, 196, 224–6; G. R. Elton, *Reform and Renewal: Thomas Cromwell and the Common Weal* (Cambridge, 1973), pp. 142–57.

45. E. W. Ives, ' "Agaynst taking awaye of women": the inception and operation of the abduction act of 1487', in *Wealth and Power in Tudor England: Essays presented to S. T. Bindoff*, ed. E. W. Ives, R. J. Knecht and J. J. Scarisbrick (London, 1978), pp. 21–30; A. Cameron, 'Complaint and reform in Henry VII's reign: the origins of the statute of 3 Henry VII, c. 2?', *BIHR*, 51 (1978), 83–9; Cameron, 'A Nottinghamshire quarrel in the reign of Henry VII', *BIHR*, 45 (1972), 27–37.

46. *Spelman's Reports*, ii, pp. *68, 391*; Ross, *Edward IV*, pp. 321–2; Ellis, *Reform and Revival*, p. 161; Guy, *More*, pp. 5–6, 26–9; S. E. Lehmberg, 'Sir Thomas Audley: a soul as black as marble?', in *Tudor Men and Institutions*, p. 6; Ives, *Common Lawyers*, pp. 259–62.

47. Baker, *Order of Serjeants at Law*, p. 294; *Council of Henry VII*, p. xxxiv; Woodcock, *Ecclesiastical Courts*, pp. 106–7; Ives, *Common Lawyers*, pp. 308–18; Condon, 'Anachronism with intent?', p. 241; J. P. Cooper, 'Henry VII's last years reconsidered', *HJ*, 2 (1959), 119–20; *Spelman's Reports*, ii, pp. *76–7*; Lehmberg, 'Audley', pp. 25–6; W. K. Jordan, *Edward VI: The Threshold of Power* (London, 1970), pp. 442–4.

48. Pronay, 'The chancellor', pp. 94–6; Guy, *Court of Star Chamber*, pp. 61–2; Brooks, *Pettyfoggers*, pp. 58–63, 71, 101–7.

49. Brooks, *Pettyfoggers*, pp. 77–9; H. Garrett-Goodyear, 'The Tudor revival of Quo Warranto and local contributions to state building', in *On the Laws and Customs of England: Essays in Honor of Samuel E. Thorne*, ed. M. S. Arnold, T. A. Green, S. A. Scully and S. D. White (Chapel Hill, NC, 1981), p. 246.

50. *Council of Henry VII*, pp. 1–169; *Ancient State*, pp. 39–84; *List of Proceedings in the Court of Star Chamber, preserved in the Public Record Office, vol. I AD 1485–1558* (PRO Lists and Indexes 13, 1901), pp. 1–7; Guy, *Cardinal's Court*, pp. 121–4; Lehmberg, *Later Parliaments*, p. 142.

3 Livelihood

1. B. P. Wolffe, *The Royal Demesne in English History: The Crown Estate in the Governance of the Realm from the Conquest to 1509* (London, 1971), p. 115; J. Fortescue, *The Governance of England*, ed. C. Plummer (Oxford, 1885), pp. 119, 125, 133.

2. Fortescue, *Governance*, pp. 119, 133; M. Le Mené, 'La conjoncture économique Angevine sous le règne de Louis XI', in *La France de la fin du xve siècle*, ed. B. Chevalier and P. Contamine (Paris, 1985), pp. 58–9; W. Prevenier and W. Blockmans, *The Burgundian Netherlands* (Cambridge, 1986), p. 193.

3. Fortescue, *Governance*, p. 152; *George Ashby's Poems*, ed. M. Bateson (EETS extra series 76, 1899), pp. 12–41; *The Reign of Henry VII from Contemporary Sources*, ed. A. F. Pollard (3 vols, London, 1914), ii, p. 21; M. L. Bush, 'Up for the common-weal: the significance of tax grievances in the English rebellions of 1536', *EHR*, 106 (1991), 312 (quoting Sir Thomas Tempest).

4. *Reign of Henry VII*, ii, p. 4; F. C. Dietz, *English Government Finance 1485–1558* (Urbana, Ill., 1921), pp. 91, 94, 147; Wolffe, *Royal Demesne*, pp. 223–4.

5. M. L. Bush, *The Government Policy of Protector Somerset* (London, 1975), pp. 7–39; J. Youings, *The Dissolution of the Monasteries* (London, 1971), p. 78; D. M. Loades, *The Tudor Navy: An Administrative, Political and Military History* (Aldershot, 1992), p. 155; Fortescue, *Governance*, pp. 122–6.

6. W. K. Jordan, *Edward VI: The Young King* (London, 1968), p. 393; J. D. Alsop, 'The theory and practice of Tudor taxation', *EHR*, 97 (1982), 18.

7. R. A. Griffiths, *The Reign of King Henry VI* (London, 1981), pp. 108, 376; D. M. Loades, *The Tudor Court* (London, 1986), pp. 74–9; G. R. Elton, *The Tudor Revolution in Government: Administrative Changes in the Reign of Henry VIII* (Cambridge, 1953), pp. 370–414; *The Household of Edward IV: The Black Book and the Ordinance of 1478*, ed. A. R. Myers (Manchester, 1959), pp. 21–49; D. M. Loades, *The Reign of Mary Tudor* (2nd edn, London, 1991), p. 136; *The History of the King's Works*, iv, ed. H. M. Colvin (London, 1982), pp. 6–7; S. G. Ellis, *Tudor Ireland: Crown, Community, and the Conflict of Cultures, 1470–1603* (London, 1985), p. 176.

8. Wolffe, *Royal Demesne*, pp. 143–225; S. J. Gunn, 'The act of resumption of 1515', in *Early Tudor England: Proceedings of the 1987 Harlaxton Symposium*, ed. D. T. Williams (Woodbridge, 1989), pp. 87–106.

9. M. Aston, 'Caim's castles: poverty, politics and disendowment', in *The Church, Politics and Patronage in the Fifteenth Century*, ed. R. B. Dobson (Gloucester, 1984), pp. 45–81; W. C. Richardson, *History of the Court of Augmentations 1536–1554* (Baton Rouge, LA, 1961), p. 178; P. A. Cunich, 'The monastic spoils: reinterpreting the accounts of the first court of augmentations', forthcoming (I am very grateful to Dr Cunich for a copy of this important article); Youings, *Dissolution*, pp. 32–45, 106; B. Bradshaw, *The Dissolution of the Religious Orders in Ireland under Henry VIII* (Cambridge, 1974), pp. 47–65.

10. J. D. Alsop, 'The revenue commission of 1552', *HJ*, 22 (1979), 529; Richardson, *Augmentations*, p. 200n; Loades, *Mary Tudor*, p. 239; Wolffe, *Royal Demesne*, p. 204; R. W. Hoyle, 'Introduction: aspects of the crown's estate, c.1558–1640', in *The Estates of the English Crown, 1558–1640*, ed. R. W. Hoyle (Cambridge, 1992), p. 5; J. J. Scarisbrick, 'Henry VIII and the dissolution of the secular colleges', in *Law and Government under the Tudors: Essays presented to Sir Geoffrey Elton on his retirement*, ed. M. C. Cross, D. M. Loades and J. J. Scarisbrick (Cambridge, 1988), pp. 51–66; W. K. Jordan, *Edward VI: The Threshold of Power* (London, 1970), pp. 181–203; F. Heal, *Of Prelates and Princes: A Study of the Economic and Social Position of the Tudor Episcopate* (Cambridge, 1980), pp. 101–50; Cunich, 'Monastic spoils'; K. S. Wyndham, 'The royal estate in mid sixteenth-century Somerset', *BIHR*, 52 (1979), 129–37.

11. R. Somerville, *A History of the Duchy of Lancaster, i, 1265–1603* (London, 1953), pp. 173–5, 185–9, 242–55, 263–77; Wolffe, *Royal Demesne*, p. 222.

12. D. R. Starkey, 'After the revolution', in *Revolution Reassessed: Revisions in the History of Tudor Government and Administration*, ed. C. Coleman and D. R. Starkey (Oxford, 1986), p. 203; M. K. McIntosh, *Autonomy and Community: The Royal Manor of Havering, 1200–1500* (Cambridge, 1986), pp. 65–6; *The Duchy of*

Lancaster's Estates in Derbyshire 1485–1540, ed. I. W. S. Blanchard (Derbyshire Archaeological Society Record Series 3, 1971), pp. 11–13.

13. B. P. Wolffe, *The Crown Lands 1461 to 1536: An Aspect of Yorkist and Early Tudor Government* (London, 1970), pp. 142–6; H. Miller, *Henry VIII and the English Nobility* (Oxford, 1986), p. 218; Youings, *Dissolution*, pp. 92–4; Richardson, *Augmentations*, pp. 3–6, 131–4; D. Thomas, 'The Elizabethan crown lands: their purposes and problems', in *Estates of the English Crown*, pp. 64–75.

14. Somerville, *Duchy of Lancaster*, pp. 305–6; Hoyle, 'Aspects of the crown's estate', pp. 13, 33–44; D. N. J. MacCulloch, 'Bondmen under the Tudors', in *Law and Government under the Tudors*, pp. 91–109; Richardson, *Augmentations*, pp. 33–4, 79–85, 108–10, 142, 239–40, 302–15; S. E. Lehmberg, *The Later Parliaments of Henry VIII, 1536–1547* (Cambridge, 1977), p. 201; Jordan, *Threshold*, pp. 386–401.

15. W. C. Richardson, 'Some financial expedients of Henry VIII', *EcHR*, 2nd series 7 (1954–5), 33–48; Richardson, *Augmentations*, pp. 208, 242–5, 315–24; S. J. Gunn, 'The regime of Charles, duke of Suffolk, in North Wales and the reform of Welsh government, 1509–25', *WHR*, 12 (1985), 486–7; Gunn, 'Henry Bourchier, earl of Essex (1472–1540)', in *The Tudor Nobility*, ed. G. W. Bernard (Manchester, 1992), p. 139; J. Loach, *Parliament and the Crown in the Reign of Mary Tudor* (Oxford, 1986), pp. 164–6.

16. Youings, *Dissolution*, pp. 117–31; Loades, *Mary*, p. 340; Richardson, *Augmentations*, pp. 233–5; K. S. H. Wyndham, 'Crown land and royal patronage in mid-sixteenth century England', *JBS*, 19 (1980), 18–34.

17. A. L. Brown, *The Governance of Late Medieval England 1272–1461* (London, 1989), p. 69; P. Ramsey, 'Overseas trade in the reign of Henry VII: the evidence of customs accounts', *EcHR*, 2nd series 6 (1953–4), 173–9.

18. G. Schanz, *Englische Handelspolitik gegen Ende des Mittelalters* (2 vols, Leipzig, 1881), i, pp. 14–37, 130–42, 182–201, 237–41, 269–77, 301–3; S. B. Chrimes, *Henry VII* (London, 1972), p. 217; C. M. Barron, 'London and the crown, 1451–61', in *The Crown and Local Communities in England and France in the Fifteenth Century*, ed. J. R. L. Highfield and R. M. Jeffs (Gloucester, 1981), pp. 91–100; C. D. Ross, *Edward IV* (London, 1974), pp. 351–2, 384; D. J. Guth, 'Enforcing late-medieval law: patterns in litigation during Henry VII's reign', in *Legal Records and the Historian*, ed. J. H. Baker (London, 1978), pp. 85–6; E. Dudley, *The Tree of Commonwealth*, ed. D. M. Brodie (Cambridge, 1948), pp. 5–7; G. R. Elton, 'Henry VII: a restatement', in his *Studies in Tudor and Stuart Politics and Government*, i (Cambridge, 1974), pp. 82–6.

19. N. S. B. Gras, *The Early English Customs System* (Cambridge, Mass., 1918), pp. 84–5, 91–3, 123–9; W. G. Hoskins, *The Age of Plunder: King Henry's England 1500–1547* (London, 1976), p. 179; G. D. Ramsay, *The City of London in International Politics at the Accession of Elizabeth Tudor* (Manchester, 1975), pp. 50, 150–7.

20. J. M. W. Bean, *The Decline of English Feudalism, 1215–1540* (Manchester, 1968); S. L. Waugh, *The Lordship of England: Royal Wardships and Marriages in English Society and Politics, 1217–1327* (Princeton, NJ, 1988); G. L. Harriss, 'Financial policy', in *Henry V: The Practice of Kingship*, ed. G. L. Harriss (Oxford, 1985), pp. 171–2.

21. *Prerogativa Regis, Tertia Lectura Roberti Constable de Lyncolnis Inne Anno 11 H. 7*, ed. S. E. Thorne (New Haven, CT, 1949); E. W. Ives, *The Common Lawyers of Pre-Reformation England. Thomas Kebell: a Case Study* (Cambridge, 1983), pp. 239–42, 247–57.

22. J. P. Cooper, 'Henry VII's last years reconsidered', HJ, 2 (1959), 110–11; H. E. Bell, *An Introduction to the History and Records of the Court of Wards and Liveries* (Cambridge, 1953), pp. 2–8; W. C. Richardson, 'The surveyor of the king's prerogative', *EHR*, 56 (1941), 52–75.

23. Chrimes, *Henry VII*, p. 216; Richardson, 'Surveyor', p. 60n; B. J. Harris, *Edward Stafford, Third Duke of Buckingham* (Stanford, 1986), pp. 41–3; C. J. Harrison, 'The

petition of Edmund Dudley', *EHR*, 87 (1972), 82–99; W. C. Richardson, *Tudor Chamber Administration 1485–1547* (Baton Rouge, LA, 1952), pp. 13, 260–4; C. Carpenter, *Locality and Polity: A Study of Warwickshire Landed Society, 1401–1499* (Cambridge, 1992), pp. 91–2; Dietz, *Finance*, p. 27n; Elton, *Tudor Revolution*, pp. 145–7; Richardson, *Augmentations*, p. 183; Loades, *Mary*, p. 132.

24. E. W. Ives, 'The genesis of the statute of uses', *EHR*, 82 (1967), 673–97; *The Reports of Sir John Spelman*, ed. J. H. Baker (Selden Society 93–4, 1976–7), ii, pp. 192–203.

25. J. Hurstfield, *The Queen's Wards: Wardship and Marriage under Elizabeth I* (London, 1958).

26. J. G. Russell, *The Field of Cloth of Gold* (London, 1969), pp. 89–90; D. R. Starkey, 'Court and government', in *Revolution Reassessed*, p. 44; D. L. Potter, 'The treaty of Boulogne and European diplomacy, 1549–50', *BIHR*, 55 (1982), 50–65.

27. Ross, *Edward IV*, pp. 377–8; C. E. Challis, *The Tudor Coinage* (Manchester, 1978); ~~J. D. Gould, *The Great Debasement: Currency and the Economy in Mid-Tudor England*~~ (Oxford, 1970).

28. J. J. N. McGurk, 'Royal purveyance in the shire of Kent, 1590–1614', *BIHR*, 50 (1977), 58–68; C. S. L. Davies, 'Provisions for armies, 1509–50; a study in the effectiveness of early Tudor government', *EcHR*, 2nd series 17 (1964–5), 234–48; H. Brinklow, *Complaynt of Roderyck Mors*, ed. J. M. Cowper (EETS extra series 22, 1874), p. 19; A. Woodward, *Purveyance for the Royal Household in the Reign of Queen Elizabeth* (Transactions of the American Philosophical Society, new series 35, 1945); *The Report of the Royal Commission of 1552*, ed. W. C. Richardson (Morgantown, VA, 1974), p. 219; Loades, *Tudor Court*, pp. 69–72; *Statutys for the orderi[n]ge of purueyours or achatours for the kynges housholde* (London, R. Pynson, 1505?), STC² 9337.

29. Griffiths, *Henry VI*, pp. 108–10, 381; Ross, *Edward IV*, pp. 214–16, 248–50; Harriss, 'The management of Parliament', in *Henry V*, pp. 142–51.

30. R. Schofield, 'Taxation and the political limits of the Tudor state', in *Law and Government*, pp. 227–56; M. A. Hicks, 'The Yorkshire rebellion of 1489 reconsidered', *NH*, 22 (1986), 39–62; M. L. Bush, 'Tax reform and rebellion in early Tudor England', *History*, 76 (1991), 379–400; Hoskins, *Age of Plunder*, p. 25; Gunn, 'Act of resumption', pp. 89–98; *Early Tudor Craven: Subsidies and Assessments 1510–1547*, ed. R. W. Hoyle (Yorkshire Archaeological Society Record Series 145, 1987), pp. xxv–xxx; R. W. Hoyle, 'Resistance and manipulation in early Tudor taxation: some evidence from the North', *Archives*, 20 (1993), 158–67; J. A. Guy, 'Wolsey and the parliament of 1523', in *Law and Government*, pp. 1–18; R. H. Britnell, *The Commercialization of English Society 1000–1500* (Cambridge, 1993), p. 180; Challis, *Tudor Coinage*, pp. 238, 242; I. W. Archer, *The Pursuit of Stability: Social Relations in Elizabethan London* (Cambridge, 1991), p. 12.

31. P. K. O'Brien and P. A. Hunt, 'The rise of a fiscal state in England, 1485–1815', *HR*, 66 (1993), 165–9.

32. H. Miller, 'Subsidy assessments of the peerage in the sixteenth century', *BIHR*, 28 (1955), 15–34; *Craven*, pp. xix–xxxi; Hoyle, 'Resistance', pp. 167–76; Schofield, 'Taxation', pp. 234–55; J. D. Alsop, 'Parliament and taxation', in *The Parliaments of Elizabethan England*, ed. D. M. Dean and N. L. Jones (Oxford, 1990), pp. 91–116; F. C. Dietz, *English Public Finance 1558–1641* (London, 1932), pp. 380–93.

33. G. L. Harriss, 'Aids, loans and benevolences', *HJ*, 6 (1963), 1–19; Harriss, 'Financial policy', pp. 165–6; Bush, 'Tax reform', p. 392–4; P. Holmes, 'The great council in the reign of Henry VII', *EHR*, 101 (1986), 855–6; H. L. Gray, 'The first benevolence', in *Facts and Factors in Economic History: Articles by former students of Edwin Francis Gay*, ed. A. H. Cole, A. L. Dunham and N. S. B. Gras (Cambridge, Mass., 1932), pp. 90–113; R. Virgoe, 'The benevolence of 1481', *EHR*, 104 (1989), 25–45.

34. J. J. Goring, 'The general proscription of 1522', *EHR*, 86 (1971), 681–705; G. Walker, *John Skelton and the Politics of the 1520s* (Cambridge, 1988), pp. 102–15;

G. W. Bernard, *War, Taxation and Rebellion in Early Tudor England* (Brighton, 1986); now also Bernard and Hoyle, *HR*, 67 (1994), 190–202.

35. Bush, 'Tax reform', pp. 392–4; Hoskins, *Age of Plunder*, p. 87; D. R. Starkey, 'England', in *The Renaissance in National Context*, ed. R. Porter and M. Teich (Cambridge, 1992), pp. 159–60; Loades, *Mary*, pp. 341–3.

36. S. G. Ellis, *Reform and Renewal: English Government in Ireland, 1470–1534* (Woodbridge, 1986), pp. 70–1; G. L. Harriss, 'Thomas Cromwell's "new principle" of taxation', *EHR*, 93 (1978), 721–38; J. D. Alsop, 'The theory and practice of Tudor taxation', *EHR*, 97 (1982), 1–30; G. L. Harriss, 'Theory and practice in royal taxation: some observations', ibid., 811–19; J. D. Alsop, 'Innovation in Tudor taxation', *EHR*, 99 (1984), 83–93; Fortescue, *Governance*, p. 139; Statute 19 Henry VII c. 32; S. E. Lehmberg, *The Reformation Parliament, 1529–1536* (Cambridge, 1970), pp. 89–91, 133, 207–9; Lehmberg, *Later Parliaments*, pp. 92–5, 178–9, 195–6, 219–20; M. L. Bush, ' "Enhancements and importunate charges": an analysis of the tax complaints of October 1536', *Albion*, 22 (1990), 403–7; Loach, *Parliament*, pp. 134–44; W. T. MacCaffrey, 'Parliament and foreign policy', in *Parliaments of Elizabethan England*, pp. 77–90.

37. A. K. McHardy, 'Clerical taxation in fifteenth-century England: the clergy as agents of the crown', in *The Church, Politics and Patronage in the Fifteenth Century*, ed. R. B. Dobson (Gloucester, 1984), pp. 168–92; F. M. Heal, 'Clerical tax collection under the Tudors: the influence of the Reformation', in *Continuity and Change: Personnel and Administration of the Church in England 1500–1642*, ed. R. O'Day and F. M. Heal (Leicester, 1976), pp. 97–122; Bernard, *War*, p. 123; Harrison, 'Petition', pp. 87–98; J. J. Scarisbrick, 'Clerical taxation in England, 1485 to 1547', *JEH*, 11 (1960), 41–54.

38. Dietz, *Finance 1485–1558*, pp. 51–2; A. Steel, *The Receipt of the Exchequer, 1377–1485* (Cambridge, 1954), pp. 344–8; S. E. Brigden, *London and the Reformation* (Oxford, 1989), pp. 357, 496; Loades, *Mary*, pp. 147–54, 232–9, 345–50; R. B. Outhwaite, 'The trials of foreign borrowing: the English crown and the Antwerp money market in the mid-sixteenth century', *EcHR*, 2nd series 19 (1966), 289–305; Ramsay, *City of London*, pp. 50–3, 60–70.

39. Wolffe, *Royal Demesne*, pp. 69–71.

40. R. Jeffs, 'The Later Medieval Sheriff and the Royal Household', Oxford University DPhil thesis 1960, pp. 98–112; *This is a true copy of thordinau[n]ce to be obseruyd in the kynges Eschequier for takynge of fees of the kynges accomptau[n]t[es]* (London, J. Rastell, 1526?) and subsequent editions, STC² 7695.5–7704.

41. Wolffe, *Royal Demesne*, pp. 158–212; Griffiths, *Henry VI*, pp. 772–90; Starkey, 'After the revolution', p. 203; 'Financial memoranda of the reign of Edward V', ed. R. Horrox, in *Camden Miscellany XXIX* (Camden Society 4th series 34, 1987), pp. 212–13; Wolffe, *Crown Lands*, p. 68.

42. J. D. Alsop, 'The Exchequer in late medieval government, c.1485–1530', in *Aspects of Late Medieval Government and Society: Essays presented to J. R. Lander*, ed. J. G. Rowe (Toronto, 1986), p. 196; Wolffe, *Crown Lands*, pp. 73–85, 162–3; J. A. Guy, 'A conciliar court of audit at work in the last months of the reign of Henry VII', *BIHR*, 49 (1976), 289–95.

43. Alsop, 'Exchequer', pp. 179–200; M. R. Horowitz, 'An early-Tudor teller's book', *EHR*, 96 (1981), 103–16; J. L. Kirby, 'The rise of the under-treasurer of the Exchequer', *EHR*, 72 (1957), 666–77; J. D. Alsop, 'The structure of early Tudor finance, c.1509–1558', in *Revolution Reassessed*, pp. 140–6; S. Jack and R. S. Schofield, 'Four early Tudor financial memoranda', *BIHR*, 36 (1963), 189–206.

44. G. L. Harriss, 'Fictitious loans', *EcHR*, 2nd series 8 (1955–6), 187–99; Harriss, 'Marmaduke Lumley and the Exchequer crisis of 1446–9', in *Aspects of Late Medieval Government*, p. 161.

45. Alsop, 'Exchequer', p. 195; PRO, E404/82/2, unnumbered warrants; Cunich, 'Monastic spoils'; C. Coleman, 'Artifice or accident? The reorganization of the Exchequer of Receipt c.1554–1572', in *Revolution Reassessed*, pp. 166–7.
46. Elton, *Tudor Revolution*, pp. 169–73, 203–23; Richardson, *Augmentations*, passim; Richardson, *Chamber Administration*, p. 242.
47. Elton, *Tudor Revolution*, pp. 98–119, 139–57, 189–203; Coleman, 'Reorganization', pp. 169, 171–2, 178, 186; Richardson, *Augmentations*, pp. 44n, 90–2, 94, 235, 249; D. Hoak, 'The secret history of the Tudor court: the king's coffers and the king's purse, 1542–1553', *JBS*, 26 (1987), 221–9; Challis, *Tudor Coinage*, p. 28; J. D. Alsop, 'Government, finance and the community of the Exchequer', in *The Reign of Elizabeth I*, ed. C. A. Haigh (Basingstoke, 1984), pp. 110–14; G. R. Elton, *Star Chamber Stories* (London, 1958), pp. 114–46; Ramsay, *City of London*, p. 151.
48. Richardson, *Chamber Administration*, pp. 71–7; Harriss, 'Financial policy', pp. 176–7; Alsop, 'Structure', pp. 158–60; Starkey, 'After the revolution', p. 205; S. M. Jack, 'Northumberland, Queen Jane and the financing of the 1553 coup', *Parergon*, new series 6 (1988), 147; J. Murphy, 'The illusion of decline: the privy chamber, 1547–1558', in *The English Court from the Wars of the Roses to the Civil War*, ed. D. R. Starkey (London, 1987), pp. 138–9; Richardson, *Augmentations*, p. 119; LP, XXI, i. 437; J. D. Alsop, 'Protector Somerset and warrants for payment', *BIHR*, 55 (1982), 102–8; Coleman, 'Reorganization', p. 172.
49. Harriss, 'Marmaduke Lumley', pp. 143–78; L. Clark, 'The benefits and burdens of office: Henry Bourgchier (1408–83), Viscount Bourgchier and earl of Essex, and the treasurership of the exchequer', in *Profit, Piety and the Professions in Later Medieval England*, ed. M. A. Hicks (Gloucester, 1990), pp. 119–36; S. E. Vokes, 'The Early Career of Thomas, Lord Howard, Earl of Surrey and Third Duke of Norfolk, 1474–c.1525', University of Hull PhD thesis 1988, pp. 25–6, 152–3, 281–3.
50. Coleman, 'Reorganization', pp. 166–98; A. J. Slavin, 'Lord Chancellor Wriothesley and reform of Augmentations: new light on an old court', in *Tudor Men and Institutions*, ed. A. J. Slavin (Baton Rouge, LA, 1972), pp. 49–69; Elton, *Tudor Revolution*, pp. 243–4; D. N. J. MacCulloch, *Suffolk and the Tudors: Politics and Religion in an English County 1500–1600* (Oxford, 1986), pp. 235–7.
51. Starkey, 'Court and government', pp. 37–46; Hoak, 'Secret history', pp. 209–16; Wolffe, *Royal Demesne*, pp. 210–12; Cunich, 'Monastic spoils'; Richardson, *Chamber Administration*, pp. 94–5.
52. Alsop, 'Structure', pp. 149–50, 156–7; Elton, *Tudor Revolution*, pp. 38–9; Loades, *Tudor Navy*, pp. 81–4; Gunn, 'Act of resumption', p. 92; Wolffe, *Crown Lands*, p. 81; Richardson, *Chamber Administration*, pp. 235–7, 253; Richardson, *Augmentations*, pp. 122–3, 144–50, 188–9, 205–6; S. E. Lehmberg, *Sir Walter Mildmay and Tudor Government* (Austin, TX, 1964), pp. 11–66, 111–28; *Royal Commission of 1552*, p. xxiin.
53. Alsop, 'Structure', pp. 148–62; Coleman, 'Reorganization', pp. 163–98; Elton, *Tudor Revolution*, pp. 224–58.
54. G. L. Harriss, 'Preference at the medieval Exchequer', *BIHR*, 30 (1957), 17–40; Richardson, *Augmentations*, pp. 35, 68–9, 86–90, 96–8; Brinklow, *Complaynt*, p. 24; Hurstfield, *Queen's Wards*, pp. 266–8.
55. Richardson, *Augmentations*, pp. 232–3, 266–8; Hurstfield, *Queen's Wards*, pp. 199–204; Challis, *Tudor Coinage*, pp. 100–3; 'The *Vita Mariae Angliae Reginae* of Robert Wingfield of Brantham', ed. D. N. J. MacCulloch, in *Camden Miscellany XXVIII* (Camden Society 4th series 29, 1984), p. 261.
56. Coleman, 'Reorganization', pp. 171, 191–2; M. M. Condon, 'Ruling elites in the reign of Henry VII', in *Patronage, Pedigree and Power in Later Medieval England*, ed. C. Ross (Gloucester, 1979), pp. 121, 128; Richardson, 'Surveyor', pp. 62–3, 65; S. J. Gunn, 'The courtiers of Henry VII', *EHR*, 108 (1993), 30, 32–3.

57. Alsop, 'Community of the Exchequer', p. 108; Gunn, 'Act of resumption', pp. 93–4; Alsop, 'Revenue commission', pp. 512, 515, 527–8; Loades, *Mary*, pp. 243–5; L. Stone, *The Crisis of the Aristocracy, 1558–1641* (Oxford, 1965), p. 542; S. Doran, 'The finances of an Elizabethan nobleman and royal servant: a case study of Thomas Radcliffe, 3rd earl of Sussex', *HR*, 61 (1988), 286–300.

58. Richardson, 'Expedients', pp. 35–6; Harriss, 'Financial policy', pp. 162–3; I. Arthurson, 'The king's voyage into Scotland: the war that never was', in *England in the Fifteenth Century: proceedings of the 1986 Harlaxton Symposium*, ed. D. T. Williams (Woodbridge, 1987), p. 5; Bush, *Somerset*, pp. 33–4; Jordan, *Threshold*, pp. 457–62.

59. Bush, 'Tax reform', p. 399; J. B. Collins, *Fiscal Limits of Absolutism: Direct Taxation in Early Seventeenth-Century France* (Berkeley, CA, 1988), p. 218; A. W. Lovett, *Early Habsburg Spain, 1516–1598* (Oxford, 1986), pp. 234, 248–54; R. Crummey, *The Formation of Muscovy, 1304–1613* (London, 1987), pp. 174–6, 206–7, 215.

60. R. J. Knecht, *Francis I*, pp. 117–31, 195–8, 240–2, 318, 352–6, 377–89; Lovett, *Early Habsburg Spain*, pp. 219–30; N. Macdougall, *James IV* (Edinburgh, 1989) pp. 146–66, 215–17, 228; J. Wormald, *Court, Kirk and Community: Scotland 1470–1625* (London, 1981), pp. 15–16, 161; O'Brien, Hunt, 'Fiscal state', pp. 149–50, 152–4, 159–60; R. Davis, *The Rise of the Atlantic Economies* (London, 1973), p. 211; Fortescue, *Governance*, p. 114.

4 Empire

1. G. R. Elton, *The Tudor Constitution: Documents and Commentary* (2nd edn, Cambridge, 1982), p. 353; S. Lockwood, 'Marsilius of Padua and the case for the royal ecclesiastical supremacy', *TRHS*, 6th series 1 (1991), 105; A. J. Slavin, 'The Tudor state, Reformation and understanding change: through the looking glass', in *Political Thought and the Tudor Commonwealth: Deep Structure, Discourse and Disguise*, ed. P. A. Fideler and T. F. Mayer (London, 1992), pp. 223–53.

2. J. R. Lander, *The Limitations of English Monarchy in the Later Middle Ages* (Toronto, 1989), pp. 42–3; C. A. J. Armstrong, 'The inauguration ceremonies of the Yorkist kings and their title to the throne', *TRHS*, 4th series 30 (1948), 66–7, 70; D. M. Loades, *The Tudor Navy: An Administrative, Political and Military History* (Aldershot, 1992), pp. 39–41; C. E. Challis, *The Tudor Coinage* (Manchester, 1978), pp. 47–52; T. F. Mayer, 'Tournai and tyranny: imperial kingship and critical humanism', *HJ*, 34 (1991), 258–69; R. Koebner, ' "The imperial crown of this realm": Henry VIII, Constantine the Great and Polydore Vergil', *BIHR*, 26 (1953), 30; *Tudor Royal Proclamations*, ed. P. L. Hughes and J. F. Larkin (3 vols, New Haven, CT, 1964–9), i, passim; *Statutes of the Realm*, ed. A. Luders *et al.* (11 vols, London, 1810–28), ii, passim.

3. C. T. Allmand, *Henry V* (London, 1992), p. 181, plate 7; W. Ullmann, 'This realm of England is an empire', *JEH*, 30 (1979), 177; G. L. Harriss, 'Thomas Cromwell's "new principle" of taxation', *EHR*, 93 (1978), 725; J. W. McKenna, 'How God became an Englishman', in *Tudor Rule and Revolution: Essays for G. R. Elton from his American Friends*, ed. D. J. Guth and J. W. McKenna (Cambridge, 1982), pp. 25–43; S. H. Cuttler, *The Law of Treason and Treason Trials in Later Medieval France* (Cambridge, 1981), pp. 9–17; S. B. Chrimes, *English Constitutional Ideas in the Fifteenth Century* (Cambridge, 1936), p. 38.

4. B. Guenée, *States and Rulers in Later Medieval Europe* (Oxford, 1985), p. 77; N. Macdougall, *James III: A Political Study* (Edinburgh, 1982), p. 98; Koebner,

'Imperial crown', pp. 31–6, 45–7; J. A. Guy, 'Thomas Cromwell and the intellectual origins of the Henrician revolution', in A. Fox and J. A. Guy, *Reassessing the Henrician Age: Humanism, Politics and Reform, 1500–1550* (Oxford, 1986), pp. 159, 165–70, 177; Chrimes, *English Constitutional Ideas*, pp. 324–8; J. Fortescue, *De Laudibus Legum Angliae*, ed. S. B. Chrimes (Cambridge, 1942), pp. ix, xlix, lxxxv, App. 2; *The Reports of Sir John Spelman*, ed. J. H. Baker (SS 93–4, 1976–7), ii, p. 33.

5. L. F. Solt, *Church and State in Early Modern England, 1509–1640* (Oxford, 1990), pp. 46–60; F. M. Heal, *Of Prelates and Princes: A Study of the Economic and Social Position of the Tudor Episcopate* (Cambridge, 1980), pp. 126–47; W. K. Jordan, *Edward VI: The Threshold of Power* (London, 1970), pp. 240–7; R. Hutton, 'The local impact of the Tudor reformations', in *The English Reformation Revised*, ed. C. A. Haigh (Cambridge, 1987), pp. 127–8; G. Alexander, 'Bishop Bonner and the Marian persecutions', ibid., pp. 159–65; D. M. Loades, *The Reign of Mary Tudor* (2nd edn, London, 1991), pp. 362–72.

6. J. I. Catto, 'Religious change under Henry V', in *Henry V: The Practice of Kingship*, ed. G. L. Harriss (Oxford, 1985), pp. 97–115; R. N. Swanson, *Church and Society in Late Medieval England* (Oxford, 1989), pp. 6–15, 70–9, 110–18; Ullmann, 'This realm of England', pp. 188–91, 198–9; H. Chadwick, 'Royal ecclesiastical supremacy', in *Humanism, Reform and the Reformation: The Career of Bishop John Fisher*, ed. B. Bradshaw and E. Duffy (Cambridge, 1989), pp. 177–80, 183.

7. J. A. Guy, *The Public Career of Sir Thomas More* (New Haven, CT, and London, 1980), pp. 131, 149–50; J. D. Alsop, 'Cromwell and the church in 1531: the case of Waltham Abbey', *JEH*, 31 (1980), 328–30; Guy, 'Intellectual origins', pp. 153–61; S. W. Haas, 'Henry VIII's *Glasse of Truthe*', *History*, 64 (1979), 353–62; Haas, 'Martin Luther's "divine right" kingship and the royal supremacy: two tracts from the 1531 parliament and convocation of the clergy', *JEH*, 31 (1980), 317–25; P. Tudor-Craig, 'Henry VIII and King David', *Early Tudor England: Proceedings of the 1987 Harlaxton Symposium*, ed. D. T. Williams (Woodbridge, 1989), pp. 191–8; R. Rex, *Henry VIII and the English Reformation* (Basingstoke, 1993), pp. 29, 103, 105, 173–5.

8. A. Goodman, 'Henry VII and christian renewal', in *Religion and Humanism*, ed. K. Robbins (SCH 17, 1981), pp. 115–25; C. Harrison, 'The petition of Edmund Dudley', *EHR*, 87 (1972), 82–99; M. J. Kelly, 'Canterbury Jurisdiction and Influence during the Episcopate of William Warham, 1503–1532' (Cambridge University PhD thesis, 1963), pp. 105–10; J. P. Cooper, 'Henry VII's last years reconsidered', *HJ*, 2 (1959), 110; R. B. Pugh, *Imprisonment in Medieval England* (Cambridge, 1968), p. 237; A. Kreider, *English Chantries: The Road to Dissolution* (Cambridge, Mass., 1979), pp. 81–5.

9. R. L. Storey, 'University and government 1430–1500', in *The History of the University of Oxford, Volume II, Late Medieval Oxford* (Oxford, 1992), p. 744; J. G. Bellamy, *Criminal Law and Society in Late Medieval and Tudor England* (Gloucester, 1984), pp. 124–32; I. D. Thornley, 'The destruction of sanctuary', in *Tudor Studies presented … to Albert Frederick Pollard*, ed. R. W. Seton-Watson (London, 1924), pp. 190–200; P. I. Kaufman, *The 'Polityque Churche': Religion and Early Tudor Political Culture, 1485–1516* (Macon, GA, 1986), pp. 141–53.

10. J. A. F. Thomson, *The Early Tudor Church and Society, 1485–1529* (London, 1993), pp. 80–105; Cooper, 'Henry VII's last years', p. 110; Kaufman, *The 'Polityque Churche'*, pp. 25–9; Guy, 'Intellectual origins', pp. 165–8; E. W. Ives, 'Crime, sanctuary and royal authority under Henry VIII: the exemplary sufferings of the Savage family', in *On the Laws and Customs of England: Essays in Honor of Samuel E. Thorne*, ed. M. S. Arnold, T. A. Green, S. A. Scully and S. A. White (Chapel Hill, NC, 1981), pp. 297–303; *Spelman's Reports*, ii, pp. 326–46.

11. Bellamy, *Criminal Law and Society*, pp. 132–64; Thornley, 'Sanctuary', pp. 200–7; F. D. Logan, 'The Henrician canons', *BIHR*, 47 (1974), 99–103.

12. P. J. Gwyn, *The King's Cardinal: The Rise and Fall of Thomas Wolsey* (London, 1990), pp. 265–353, 464–500; Kelly, 'Canterbury Jurisdiction', pp. 176–207; J. A. Youings, *The Dissolution of the Monasteries* (London, 1971), pp. 28–34; C. J. Kitching, 'The probate jurisdiction of Thomas Cromwell as vicegerent', *BIHR*, 46 (1973), 102–6; *Faculty Office Registers 1534–1549*, ed. D. S. Chambers (Oxford, 1966), pp. xviii–xxvi.

13. M. Bowker, *The Henrician Reformation: The Diocese of Lincoln under John Longland, 1521–1547* (Cambridge, 1981), pp. 72–8; C. Harper-Bill, 'Dean Colet's convocation sermon and the pre-Reformation church in England', *History*, 73 (1988), 207–9.

14. R. Hutton, 'The local impact of the Tudor reformations', in *The English Reformation Revised*, ed. C. A. Haigh (Cambridge, 1987), pp. 116–18; G. R. Elton, *Policy and Police: the Enforcement of the Reformation in the Age of Thomas Cromwell* (Cambridge, 1972), pp. 68, 80, 259–60, 320; E. Duffy, *The Stripping of the Altars: Traditional Religion in England 1400–1580* (New Haven, CT, and London, 1992), pp. 445–7; J. C. Cox and A. Harvey, *English Church Furniture* (London, 1907), pp. 351–2; *Certain Sermons or Homilies (1547) and A Homily against Disobedience and Wilful Rebellion (1570)*, ed. R. B. Bond (Toronto, 1987), pp. 161–70; D. R. Woolf, 'The power of the past: history, ritual and political authority in Tudor England', in *Political Thought and the Tudor Commonwealth*, pp. 24–5; D. R. Starkey, 'England', in *The Renaissance in National Context*, ed. R. Porter and M. Teich (Cambridge, 1992), pp. 159–60.

15. H. Garrett-Goodyear, 'The Tudor revival of Quo Warranto and local contributions to state building', in *On the Laws and Customs of England*, pp. 231–95; R. Stewart-Brown, 'The Cheshire writs of Quo Warranto in 1499', *EHR*, 49 (1934), 676–84; Thornley, 'Sanctuary', p. 203; S. G. Ellis, 'The destruction of the liberties: some further evidence', *BIHR*, 54 (1981), 150–61.

16. See above, p. 69.

17. H. M. Cam, 'The king's government, as administered by the greater abbots of East Anglia', in her *Liberties and Communities in Medieval England* (London, 1963), pp. 183–204; D. N. J. MacCulloch, *Suffolk and the Tudors: Politics and Religion in an English County 1500–1600* (Oxford, 1986), pp. 19–23, 34–8; C. J. Kitching, 'The Durham palatinate and the courts of Westminster under the Tudors', in *The Last Principality: Politics, Religion, and Society in the Bishopric of Durham, 1494–1660*, ed. D. Marcombe (Nottingham, 1987), pp. 49–70; T. Thornton, 'The integration of Cheshire into the Tudor nation state in the sixteenth century', *NH*, 29 (1993), 54–63; R. Somerville, 'The palatinate courts in Lancashire', in *Law-Making and Law-Makers in British History*, ed. A. Harding (London, 1980), pp. 54–6; E. W. Ives, *The Common Lawyers of Pre-Reformation England. Thomas Kebell: a Case Study* (Cambridge, 1983), pp. 76–7, 452–80.

18. *Spelman's Reports*, ii, p. 346; R. J. Knecht, *Francis I* (Cambridge, 1982), pp. 350, 358–9.

19. R. W. Heinze, *The Proclamations of the Tudor Kings* (Cambridge, 1976), p. 56; S. B. Chrimes, *Henry VII* (London, 1972), pp. 177, 220; S. E. Lehmberg, *The Reformation Parliament 1529–1536* (Cambridge, 1970), pp. 250–2; G. R. Elton, *The Parliament of England, 1559–1581* (Cambridge, 1986), p. 223; R. H. Britnell, *The Commercialization of English Society 1000–1500* (Cambridge, 1993), pp. 25, 90–7, 173–8, 218–23; J. L. Bolton, *The Medieval English Economy 1150–1500* (London, 1980), pp. 327–31; W. R. D. Jones, *The Tudor Commonwealth 1529–1559* (London, 1970), pp. 168–82; C. G. A. Clay, *Economic Expansion and Social Change: England 1500–1700* (2 vols, Cambridge, 1984), ii, pp. 219, 226–7, 229–31, 234; T. H. Lloyd, *England and the German Hanse, 1157–1611: A Study of their Trade and Commercial Diplomacy* (Cambridge, 1991), p. 238–302.

20. W. Hooper, 'The Tudor sumptuary laws', *EHR*, 30 (1915), 433–49; F. E. Baldwin, *Sumptuary Legislation and Personal Regulation in England* (Baltimore, MD, 1926);

N. B. Harte, 'State control of dress and social change in pre-industrial England', in *Trade, Government and Economy in Pre-Industrial England: Essays presented to F. J. Fisher*, ed. D. C. Coleman and A. H. John (London, 1976), pp. 132–65.

21. M. K. McIntosh, 'Local change and community control in England, 1465–1500', *Huntington Library Quarterly*, 49 (1986), 219–42; Heinze, *Proclamations*, pp. 89–94; P. Clark, *The English Alehouse: A Social History 1200–1830* (London, 1983), pp. 29–34, 41–3, 145–71.

22. J. J. Scarisbrick, 'Cardinal Wolsey and the common weal', in *Wealth and Power in Tudor England: Essays presented to S. T. Bindoff*, ed. E. W. Ives, R. J. Knecht and J. J. Scarisbrick (London, 1978), pp. 45–67; Gwyn, *King's Cardinal*, pp. 411–35; G. R. Elton, *Reform and Renewal: Thomas Cromwell and the Common Weal* (Cambridge, 1973), pp. 100–6; C. E. Moreton, *The Townshends and their World: Gentry, Law and Land in Norfolk c.1450–1551* (Oxford, 1992), pp. 168–9, 178–83; M. L. Bush, *The Government Policy of Protector Somerset* (London, 1975), pp. 43–8; Jones, *Tudor Commonwealth*, pp. 202–6.

23. Gwyn, *King's Cardinal*, pp. 440–2, 456–9; Heinze, *Proclamations*, pp. 259–61; P. A. Slack, *Poverty and Policy in Tudor and Stuart England* (London, 1988), pp. 116–17, 138–9; Clay, *Economic Expansion*, ii, pp. 214–16; K. Watts, 'Henry VIII and the founding of the Greenwich armouries', in *Henry VIII: A European Court in England*, ed. D. R. Starkey (London, 1991), pp. 42–6; J. Thirsk, *Economic Policy and Projects: The Development of a Consumer Society in Early Modern England* (Oxford, 1978), pp. 24–56; Jones, *Tudor Commonwealth*, pp. 151, 194–201.

24. Elton, *Reform and Renewal*, pp. 77–94, 121; R. Tittler, 'For the "re-edification of townes": the rebuilding statutes of Henry VIII', *Albion*, 22 (1990), 591–605; Tittler, 'The emergence of urban policy, 1536–58', in *The Mid-Tudor Polity c.1540–1560*, ed. J. Loach and R. Tittler (London, 1980), pp. 81–5.

25. J. M. Bennett, 'Conviviality and charity in medieval and early modern England', *PP*, 134 (1992), 19–41; M. K. McIntosh, 'Local responses to the poor in late medieval and Tudor England', *Continuity and Change*, 3 (1988), 209–30; J. A. Guy, *Christopher St German on Chancery and Statute* (SS supplementary series 6, 1985), pp. 25–33, 127–8, 134–5.

26. Slack, *Poverty and Policy*, pp. 113–24, 170; McIntosh, 'Local responses', pp. 229–34.

27. Elton, *Policy and Police*, pp. 222–30, 401–3; Mayer, 'Tournai', p. 260; S. J. Gunn, 'The duke of Suffolk's march on Paris in 1523', *EHR*, 101 (1986), 616; R. A. Griffiths, *The Reign of Henry VI: The Exercise of Royal Authority, 1422–1461* (London, 1981); *Calendar of Close Rolls, 1468–1476* (London, 1953), no. 858; J. G. Bellamy, *The Law of Treason in England in the Later Middle Ages* (Cambridge, 1970), pp. 116–22; Bellamy, *The Tudor Law of Treason: An Introduction* (London, 1979), pp. 22–39; I. M. W. Harvey, *Jack Cade's Rebellion of 1450* (Oxford, 1991), pp. 31–2; C. A. F. Meekings, 'Thomas Kerver's case, 1444', *EHR*, 90 (1975), 331–46.

28. Elton, *Policy and Police*, pp. 142, 293–326, 384–5, 385–96; Bellamy, *Tudor Law of Treason*, pp. 45–61, 172–3, 228–33; Allmand, *Henry V*, p. 129; *Select Cases in the Council of Henry VII*, ed. C. G. Bayne and W. H. Dunham (SS 75, 1956), p. clxxiii; R. B. Manning, 'The origins of the doctrine of sedition', *Albion*, 12 (1980), 104–7.

29. Elton, *Policy and Police*, pp. 411–18; A. D. K. Hawkyard, 'The enfranchisement of constituencies 1509–1558', *Parliamentary History*, 10 (1991), 1–26; Chrimes, *English Constitutional Ideas*, p. 76.

30. Chrimes, *English Constitutional Ideas*, pp. 24–33, 76–9, 130–3, 212–14, 252–99; J. W. McKenna, 'The myth of parliamentary sovereignty in late-medieval England', *EHR*, 94 (1979), 481–506; M. A. R. Graves, *The Tudor Parliaments: Crown, Lords and Commons, 1485–1603* (London, 1985), pp. 65–6; P. J. Holmes, 'The great council in the reign of Henry VII', *EHR*, 101 (1986), 840–62; Holmes, 'The last Tudor great councils', *HJ*, 33 (1990), 1–22.

31. Elton, *Tudor Constitution*, pp. 240–1, 277; Elton, ' "The body of the whole realm": parliament and representation in medieval and Tudor England', in his *Studies in Tudor and Stuart Politics and Government* (4 vols, Cambridge, 1974–92), ii, pp. 19–61; Chrimes, *English Constitutional Ideas*, p. 69; Bellamy, *Law of Treason in England in the Later Middle Ages*, p. xii.

32. Elton, 'The rolls of parliament, 1449–1547', *Studies*, iii, pp. 123–32; J. I. Miklovich, 'The significance of the royal sign manual in early Tudor legislative procedure', *BIHR*, 52 (1979), 23–36; J. Loach, *Parliament under the Tudors* (Oxford, 1991), p. 54; G. R. Elton, 'The rolls of parliament, 1449–1547', *Studies*, iii, pp. 123–4, 127, 131–2; Graves, *Tudor Parliaments*, p. 80; P. R. Roberts, 'The "Henry VIII clause": delegated legislation and the Tudor principality of Wales', in *Legal Record and Historical Reality: Proceedings of the Eighth British Legal History Conference, Cardiff 1987*, ed. T. G. Watkin (London, 1989), pp. 37–49; C. Lloyd and S. Thurley, *Henry VIII: Images of a Tudor King* (Oxford, 1990), p. 36.

33. Loach, *Parliament under the Tudors*, pp. 20, 45; A. R. Myers, 'Parliament, 1422–1509', in *The English Parliament in the Middle Ages*, ed. R. G. Davies and J. H. Denton (Manchester, 1981), p. 166; Guy, *Christopher St German*, pp. 21–5, 38–44; Chadwick, 'Royal ecclesiastical supremacy', pp. 185–9.

34. J. S. Roskell, 'Perspectives in English parliamentary history', in his *Parliament and Politics in late Medieval England* (2 vols, London, 1981), pp. 448–75; A. L. Brown, 'Parliament, c.1377–1422', in *The English Parliament in the Middle Ages*, pp. 109–40; Loach, *Parliament under the Tudors*, pp. 146–7, 151–2; Graves, *Tudor Parliaments*, pp. 19–36; G. R. Elton, 'The early journals of the House of Lords' and 'The rolls of parliament, 1449–1547', *Studies*, iii, pp. 58–92, 110–42; G. L. Harriss, 'Medieval doctrines in the debates on supply, 1610–1629', in *Faction and Parliament: Essays on Early Stuart History*, ed. K. Sharpe (Oxford, 1978), pp. 73–103.

35. Myers, 'Parliament, 1422–1509', p. 163; H. Miller, 'Lords and Commons: relations between the two houses of parliament, 1509–1558', *Parliamentary History*, 1 (1982), 16–23; Lehmberg, *Reformation Parliament*, pp. 169–70, 254; Lehmberg, *The Later Parliaments of Henry VIII, 1536–1547* (Cambridge, 1977), pp. 3–7, 41–6, 83–4; Loach, *Parliament under the Tudors*, pp. 33–4, 58, 92–3; Graves, *Tudor Parliaments*, pp. 87–8, 74–5, 130–48; Hawkyard, 'Enfranchisement', pp. 19–20.

36. G. R. Elton, 'Tudor government: the points of contact. I. Parliament', *Studies*, iii, pp. 3–21; D. M. Dean, 'Parliament and locality', in *The Parliaments of Elizabethan England*, ed. D. M. Dean and N. L. Jones (Oxford, 1990), pp. 139–62; Loach, *Parliament under the Tudors*, p. 139; Myers, 'Parliament, 1422–1509', pp. 171–3; J. R. Maddicott, 'Parliament and the constituencies, 1272–1377', in *The English Parliament in the Middle Ages*, pp. 81–4; *Parliamentary Texts of the Later Middle Ages*, ed. N. Pronay and J. Taylor (Oxford, 1980), pp. 177–93; D. Hirst, *The Representative of the People? Voters and Voting in England under the Early Stuarts* (Cambridge, 1975), pp. 178–81; R. Cust, 'Politics and the electorate in the 1620s', in *Conflict in Early Stuart England: Studies in Religion and Politics 1603–1642*, ed. R. Cust and A. Hughes (London, 1989), pp. 134–62.

37. G. R. Elton, 'The sessional printing of statutes, 1484–1547', *Studies*, iii, pp. 92–109; Elton, *Policy and Police*, p. 134; Statutes 7 Hen VII c. 11, 12 Hen VII c. 12, 4 Hen VIII c. 19.

38. A. Allan, 'Royal propaganda and the proclamations of Edward IV', *BIHR*, 59 (1986), 146–54; C. Ross, 'Rumour, propaganda and public opinion during the Wars of the Roses', in *Patronage, the Crown and the Provinces in later Medieval England*, ed. R. A. Griffiths (Gloucester, 1981), pp. 25–9; Heinze, *Proclamations*, pp. 5, 20–9, 68.

39. Heinze, *Proclamations*, passim; Elton, 'Sessional printing', pp. 92–3; M. L. Bush, 'The act of proclamations: a reinterpretation', *AJLH*, 27 (1983), 33–53; F. A. Youngs, *The Proclamations of the Tudor Queens* (Cambridge, 1976), p. 251.

40. V. J. Scattergood, *Politics and Poetry in the Fifteenth Century* (London, 1971), pp. 71–5; Ross, 'Rumour', pp. 22–4.

41. M. A. Shaaber, *Some Forerunners of the Newspaper in England, 1476–1622* (Philadelphia, PA, 1929), pp. 16–17, 39, 68, 139–40; STC² 9176; C. D. Ross, *Edward IV* (London, 1974), p. 292;' "The Spousells" of the Princess Mary', ed. J. Gairdner, in *The Camden Miscellany IX* (Camden Society new series 53, 1895). The second quotation is my translation from the Latin since the surviving copy of the English version is damaged at this point.

42. *The Gardyners Passetaunce*, ed. F. B. Williams (London, Roxburghe Club, 1985); *Tudor Royal Proclamations*, i, no. 65; S. H. Johnston, *A Study of the Career and Literary Publications of Richard Pynson* (University of Western Ontario PhD thesis, 1977), pp. 18–19, 87–9, 138–9, 141; J. Skelton, *The Complete English Poems*, ed. J. Scattergood (Harmondsworth, 1983), pp. 113–21, 359–72, 421–2;'A contemporary account of the battle of Floddon, 9th September 1513', ed. D. Laing, *Proceedings of the Society of Antiquaries of Scotland*, 7 (1870), 141–52; G. Walker, *John Skelton and the Politics of the 1520s* (Cambridge, 1988), pp. 45–7, 191–217; S. Anglo, *Spectacle, Pageantry and Early Tudor Policy* (Oxford, 1969), p. 263.

43. R. Rex, 'The English campaign against Luther in the 1520s', *TRHS*, 5th series 39 (1989), 85–106; Walker, *Skelton*, p. 218; Elton, *Policy and Police*, pp. 171–210; *The Divorce Tracts of Henry VIII*, ed. E. Surtz and V. Murphy (Angers, 1988); Haas, 'Henry VIII's *Glasse of Truthe*', pp. 355–62; Lockwood, 'Marsilius of Padua', pp. 89–119; *Humanist Scholarship and Public Order: Two Tracts against the Pilgrimage of Grace by Sir Richard Morison*, ed. D. S. Berkowitz (Washington, DC, 1984).

44. J. Loach, 'The Marian establishment and the printing press', *EHR*, 101 (1986), 135–48; D. M. Loades, 'The theory and practice of censorship in sixteenth-century England', in his *Politics, Censorship and the English Reformation* (London, 1991), pp. 96–108.

45. S. L. Jansen, *Political Protest and Prophecy under Henry VIII* (Woodbridge, 1991), pp. 1–61; *Lydgate's Fall of Princes*, ed. H. Bergen (4 vols, EETS, extra series 121–4, 1924–7), iv, p. 69; J. W. McKenna, 'Popular canonization as political propaganda: the cult of Archbishop Scrope', *Speculum*, 45 (1970), 609–16; McKenna, 'Piety and propaganda: the cult of Henry VI', in *Chaucer and Middle English Studies in honour of Rossell Hope Robbins*, ed. B. Rowland (London, 1974), pp. 73–6.

46. Elton, *Policy and Police*, pp. 210–16, 230–52; W. R. Jones, 'The English church and royal propaganda during the hundred years' war', *JBS*, 19 (1979), 18–30; A. K. McHardy, 'Liturgy and propaganda in the diocese of Lincoln during the hundred years war', in *Religion and National Identity*, ed. S. Mews (SCH 18, 1982), pp. 215–27; Thomson, *Early Tudor Church*, p. 74; *Registrum Ricardi Mayew, Episcopi Herfordensis A. D. MCMIV–MCXVI*, ed. A. T. Bannister (Canterbury and York Society 27, 1921), pp. 76–8; A. F. Pollard, *The Reign of Henry VII from Contemporary Sources* (3 vols, London, 1913), i, pp. 303–5.

47. Kingston-upon-Thames Borough Archives, KG2/2/1, p. 23; *The Accounts of the Chamberlains of Newcastle upon Tyne 1508–1511*, ed. C. M. Fraser (Society of Antiquaries of Newcastle upon Tyne Record Series 3, 1987), p. 193; Lincolnshire Archives Office, PAR St James Louth 7/2, fo. 42v; British Library, MS Egerton 2092, fos 357r, 437r.

48. *Spelman's Reports*, ii, p. *245*n; D. Cressy, *Bonfires and Bells: National Memory and the Protestant Calendar in Elizabethan and Stuart England* (London, 1989), pp. 50–66, 74, 117–20, 136–8; Hutton, 'Local impact', p. 119.

49. S. Anglo, *Images of Tudor Kingship* (London, 1992), pp. 6–8; S. Thurley, *The Royal Palaces of Tudor England* (New Haven, CT, and London, 1993); *The History of the King's Works*, iii, ed. H. M. Colvin (London, 1975), pp. 187–222, 311–15; G. Kipling, *The Triumph of Honour: Burgundian Origins of the Elizabethan Renaissance* (Leiden, 1977), pp. 3–8, 31–136; *Henry VIII: A European Court*, passim.

50. Armstrong, 'Inauguration ceremonies', pp. 70–2; Lloyd, Thurley, *Henry VIII*, pp. 28–40, 69.

51. McKenna, 'How God became an Englishman', p. 41; Challis, *Tudor Coinage*, pp. 49, 61, 212; C. Burns, 'Papal gifts and honours for the earlier Tudors', *Miscellanea Historiae Pontificiae*, 50 (1983), 175–97.

52. A. Goodman, *John of Gaunt: The Exercise of Princely Power in Fourteenth-Century Europe* (Harlow, 1992), p. 17; Anglo, *Images of Tudor Kingship*, pp. 28–73; H. Wayment, 'Stained glass in Henry's palaces', in *Henry VIII: A European Court*, pp. 29–31; M. Howard, *The Early Tudor Country House: Architecture and Politics 1490–1550* (London, 1987), p. 42; E. A. Danbury, 'The decoration and illumination of royal charters in England, 1250–1509: an introduction', in *England and her Neighbours, 1066–1453: Essays in Honour of Pierre Chaplais*, ed. M. C. E. Jones and M. G. A. Vale (London, 1989), pp. 175–7; PRO, E404/81/3, unnumbered warrant of 20 June 1494; Anglo, *Spectacle*, pp. 21–46; D. Carlson, 'King Arthur and court poems for the birth of Arthur Tudor in 1486', *Humanistica Lovaniensia*, 36 (1987), 147–83.

53. R. Osberg, 'The Jesse Tree in the 1432 London entry of Henry VI: messianic kingship and the rule of justice', *Journal of Medieval and Renaissance Studies*, 16 (1986), 213–32; McKenna, 'How God became an Englishman', pp. 31–6; Allmand, *Henry V*, pp. 409–12; Anglo, *Spectacle*, pp. 57–97; J. N. King, *Tudor Royal Iconography: Literature and Art in an age of Religious Crisis* (Princeton, NJ, 1989), pp. 19–101, 184–99, 216–21.

54. L. R. Mooney, 'Lydgate's "Kings of England" and another verse chronicle of the kings', *Viator*, 20 (1989), 255–89; A. Gransden, *Historical Writing in England ii: c.1307 to the Early Sixteenth Century* (London, 1982), pp. 231–3, 245, 479; A. Hanham, *Richard III and his Early Historians* (Oxford, 1975), pp. 103–17; C. Levin, *Propaganda in the English Reformation: Heroic and Villainous Images of King John* (Lewiston, NY, 1988), pp. 55–95, 106; S. J. Gunn, 'The French wars of Henry VIII', in *The Origins of War in Early Modern Europe*, ed. J. Black (Edinburgh, 1987), pp. 36–41; *Henry VIII: A European Court*, p. 95; S. J. Gunn, 'Chivalry and the politics of the early Tudor court', in *Chivalry in the Renaissance*, ed. S. Anglo (Woodbridge, 1990), pp. 110–11; Goodman, 'Henry VII and christian renewal', p. 122.

55. Gransden, *Historical Writing*, pp. 261–5, 429–43, 470–9; Johnston, *Richard Pynson*, p. 89; Starkey, 'England', pp. 157–8; McKenna, 'How God became an Englishman', p. 33.

56. Woolf, 'Power of the past', p. 34; Kipling, *Triumph of Honour*, pp. 68–71; Lloyd and Thurley, *Henry VIII*, pp. 44–56.

57. Anglo, *Images*, pp. 10–28, 98–130; P. Grierson, 'The origins of the English sovereign and the symbolism of the closed crown', *British Numismatic Journal*, 33 (1964), 131; *Henry VIII: A European Court*, pp. 84–5; Jones, *Tudor Commonwealth*, p. 141; Anglo, *Spectacle*, pp. 189, 247, 283–343.

58. Kipling, *Triumph of Honour*, pp. 123, 127, 130.

59. A. G. Dickens, 'The Tudor–Percy emblem in Royal MS. 18 D ii', in his *Reformation Studies* (London, 1982), pp. 41–6; *Henry VIII: A European Court*, p. 39.

60. Elton, *Reform and Renewal*, p. 115.

Conclusion

1. D. R. Starkey, 'Court and government', in *Revolution Reassessed: Revisions in the History of Tudor Government and Administration*, ed. C. Coleman and D. R. Starkey (Oxford, 1986), p. 49; G. R. Elton, *The Tudor Revolution in Government:*

Administrative Changes in the Reign of Henry VIII (Cambridge, 1953), pp. 276–82, 286–9.

2. S. T. Bindoff, *History of Parliament: The House of Commons, 1509–1558* (3 vols, London, 1982), iii, p. 72; F. G. Emmison, *Tudor Secretary: Sir William Petre at Court and at Home* (London, 1961), p. 182.

3. D. Hoak, *The King's Council in the reign of Edward VI* (Cambridge, 1976), pp. 160–1; *The Reports of Sir John Spelman*, ed. J. H. Baker (2 vols, SS 93–4, 1976–7), ii, p. *120*; G. W. Bernard, *The Power of the Early Tudor Nobility: A Study of the Fourth and Fifth Earls of Shrewsbury* (Brighton, 1985), p. 147; G. R. Elton, 'The early journals of the house of lords', in his *Studies in Tudor and Stuart Politics and Government* (4 vols, Cambridge, 1974–92), iii, pp. 58–92; W. C. Richardson, *History of the Court of Augmentations 1536–1554* (Baton Rouge, LA, 1961), p. 209.

4. F. Braudel, *The Mediterranean and the Mediterranean World in the age of Philip II* (2 vols, London, 1973), ii, p. 680; J. H. Burns, *Lordship, Kingship and Empire: The Idea of Monarchy, 1400–1525* (Oxford, 1992); M. G. A. Vale, *Charles VII* (London, 1974); J. N. Hillgarth, *The Spanish Kingdoms, 1250–1516* (2 vols, Oxford, 1976–8), vol. ii; A. Ryder, *The Kingdom of Naples under Alfonso the Magnanimous* (Oxford, 1976); H. J. Cohn, *The Government of the Rhine Palatinate in the Fifteenth Century* (London, 1965); R. Vaughan, *Charles the Bold* (London, 1973).

5. S. Haliczer, *The Comuneros of Castile: The Forging of a Revolution, 1475–1521* (Madison, WI, 1981); I. A. A. Thompson, *War and Government in Habsburg Spain 1560–1620* (London, 1976); A. Calabria, *The Cost of Empire: The Finances of the Kingdom of Naples in the time of Spanish Rule* (Cambridge, 1991); *Absolutism in Seventeenth Century Europe*, ed. J. Miller (Basingstoke, 1990); W. H. Beik, *Absolutism and Society in Seventeenth-Century France: State Power and Provincial Aristocracy in Languedoc* (Cambridge, 1985); S. Kettering, *Patrons, Brokers and Clients in Seventeenth-Century France* (New York, 1986); D. Parker, 'Sovereignty, absolutism and the function of the law in seventeenth-century France', *PP*, 122 (1989), 36–74; R. J. W. Evans, *The Making of the Habsburg Monarchy 1550–1700: An Interpretation* (Oxford, 1979). For English parallels, see V. Morgan, 'Some types of patronage, mainly in sixteenth- and seventeenth-century England', in *Klientelsysteme im Europa der frühen Neuzeit*, ed. A. Maczak (Munich, 1988), pp. 91–115.

6. P. K. O'Brien and P. A. Hunt, 'The rise of a fiscal state in England, 1485–1815', *HR*, 66 (1993), 129–76; M. Braddick, 'State formation and social change in early modern England: a problem stated and approaches suggested', *Social History*, 16 (1991), 1–17; P. Corrigan and D. Sayer, *The Great Arch: English State Formation as Cultural Revolution* (Oxford, 1985), pp. 114–65.

7. J. Harrington, *The Commonwealth of Oceana and a System of Politics*, ed. J. G. A. Pocock (Cambridge, 1992), pp. 54–5; S. G. Ellis, 'Crown, community and government in the English territories, 1450–1575', *History*, 71 (1986), 187–204.

8. P. Collinson, 'The monarchical republic of Queen Elizabeth I', *Bulletin of the John Rylands Library*, 69 (1986–7), 394–424.

9. S. B. Chrimes, *English Constitutional Ideas in the Fifteenth Century* (Cambridge, 1936), pp. 313–18; J. Fortescue, *De Laudibus Legum Angliae*, ed. S. B. Chrimes (Cambridge, 1942), pp. xc–xci, Appendix 2; S. Lockwood, 'Marsilius of Padua and the case for the royal ecclesiastical supremacy', *TRHS*, 6th series 1 (1991), 93–9.

10. *De Republica Anglorum by Sir Thomas Smith*, ed. M. Dewar (Cambridge, 1982), pp. 78–85, 96, 118; *A Relation, or rather a True Account, of the Island of England*, ed. C. A. Sneyd (Camden Society old series 37, 1847), p. 37.

BIBLIOGRAPHY

The detailed studies on which this book draws for particular points are best found in the notes, and the debate about the nature of early Tudor government can be traced through the notes to the introduction. This bibliography is intended as a guide to further reading.

The structures of later medieval government are usefully described in A. L. Brown, *The Governance of Late Medieval England 1272–1461* (London, 1989). Influential recent studies of the principles underlying their operation include C. Carpenter, *Locality and Polity: A Study of Warwickshire Landed Society, 1401–1499* (Cambridge, 1992), R. E. Horrox, *Richard III: A Study of Service* (Cambridge, 1989), E. Powell, *Kingship, Law and Society: Criminal Justice in the Reign of Henry V* (Oxford, 1989), and the essays in *Henry V: The Practice of Kingship*, ed. G. L. Harriss (Oxford, 1985).

Two different but complementary analyses of Tudor government can be found in *The Tudor Constitution: Documents and Commentary*, ed. G. R. Elton (2nd edn, Cambridge, 1982), and P. Williams, *The Tudor Regime* (Oxford, 1979). Many themes, especially concerning the council and financial administration, are illuminated by the essays in *Revolution Reassessed: Revisions in the History of Tudor Government and Administration*, ed. C. Coleman and D. R. Starkey (Oxford, 1986). The fullest general textbook on the period is J. A. Guy, *Tudor England* (Oxford, 1988), but G. R. Elton, *Tudor England* (3rd edn, London, 1991) and *Reform and Reformation: England 1509–1558* (London, 1977), and C. S. L. Davies, *Peace, Print and Protestantism, 1450–1558* (London, 1976) provide different and valuable points of view, and the last brings McFarlane's insights tellingly to bear on the early Tudor period. For Ireland see S. G. Ellis, *Tudor Ireland: Crown, Community and the Conflict of Cultures, 1470–1603* (Harlow, 1985), and for Wales G. Williams, *Recovery, Reorientation and Reformation: Wales, c.1415–1642* (Oxford, 1987). Useful surveys of contemporary developments on the continent include B. Guenée, *States and Rulers in Later Medieval Europe* (Oxford, 1985) and R. Bonney, *The European Dynastic States, 1494–1660* (Oxford, 1991).

Important studies of individual reigns and ministries include S. B. Chrimes, *Henry VII* (London, 1972), J. J. Scarisbrick, *Henry VIII* (London, 1968), P. J. Gwyn, *The King's Cardinal: The Rise and Fall of Thomas Wolsey* (London, 1990), *Cardinal Wolsey: Church, State and Art*, ed. S. J. Gunn and P. G. Lindley (Cambridge, 1991), M. L. Bush, *The Government Policy of Protector Somerset* (London, 1975) and D. M. Loades, *The Reign of Mary Tudor: Politics, Government and Religion in England, 1553–1558* (2nd edn, London, 1991). Many of the biographies cited in the notes are also instructive.

The issues raised in chapter 1 can be approached from a number of directions. Studies of individual counties – such as D. N. J. MacCulloch, *Suffolk and the Tudors: Politics and Religion in an English County 1500–1600* (Oxford, 1986) – and of the nobility as a group – such as H. Miller, *Henry VIII and the English Nobility* (Oxford, 1986) – must be placed alongside analyses of the careers of individual noblemen such as those in M. E. James, *Society, Politics and Culture: Studies in Early Modern England* (Cambridge, 1986) and *The Tudor Nobility*, ed. G. W. Bernard (Manchester, 1992). The court is

241

dealt with in rather different ways in *The English Court from the Wars of the Roses to the Civil War*, ed. D. R. Starkey (London, 1987), and D. M. Loades, *The Tudor Court* (London, 1986).

The best introduction to the legal system is *The Reports of Sir John Spelman*, ed. J. H. Baker (2 vols, SS 93–4, 1976–7), but two works on the legal profession also contain very helpful general material: E. W. Ives, *The Common Lawyers of Pre-Reformation England. Thomas Kebell: a Case Study* (Cambridge, 1983) and C. W. Brooks, *Pettyfoggers and Vipers of the Commonwealth: The 'Lower Branch' of the Legal Profession in Early Modern England* (Cambridge, 1986).

The only general survey of early Tudor finance remains F. C. Dietz, *English Government Finance 1485–1558* (Urbana, Ill., 1921), though many of the more recent studies cited in chapter 3 reveal its shortcomings. The historiography of the issues raised in chapter 4 is almost as diffuse, though there are good recent surveys of the Reformation: C. Haigh, *English Reformations: Religion, Politics, and Society under the Tudors* (Oxford, 1993); of parliament: M. A. R. Graves, *The Tudor Parliaments: Crown, Lords and Commons, 1485–1603* (London, 1985) and J. Loach, *Parliament under the Tudors* (Oxford, 1991); and of social policy: P. A. Slack, *Poverty and Policy in Tudor and Stuart England* (London, 1988).

INDEX

Places in England are given in their sixteenth-century counties. Dates after titles, included where helpful to avoid confusion, are those at which the individual concerned inherited or was granted the title. Incidental references to individual rulers have been omitted.

act in restraint of appeals (1533), 163, 188
actions on the case, 91–2
admiralty courts, 31, 75, 87
affinity, royal, 30–6, 115–16, 119, 203
Alciati, Andrea, 17
Alcock, John, bishop of Ely, 16, 105
alehouses, 94–5, 177
Alfonso the Magnanimous, king of Aragon and Naples, 208
almshouses, 180
altars, 166
alum, 120
ambassadors, 111, 196; *see also* diplomacy
Amboise, Cardinal Georges d', 171
amicable grant (1525), 138, 205
André, Bernard, 198
Angevin kings, 125, 209
Anglo-Saxon kings, 12
Antwerp, 120, 143–4, 160, 162
appeals of felony, 96–7
arbitration, 24, 25, 43, 46, 50, 84–5, 87, 90, 96, 100–1, 105, 107, 204
archery, 177
archives, 186, 207
Aristotle, 19
Armada, 195
arms and badges, royal, 172, 197, 200, 201; *see also* imperial crown, Tudor rose
Armstrong, Clement, 199
Arrival, 198
Arthur, King, 165, 197, 198–9
Arthur, prince of Wales, 23, 30, 56, 197, 199, 200
Ashby, George, 14, 110
assault, 74, 95
assignment, 148–9, 161
assizes, 74–5, 95, 96, 100, 102

attainders, 55, 57, 71
attorneys, 93
audiencias, 175
auditing, 43, 120, 146, 147, 149, 155–6
Audley, Thomas, Lord Audley (1538), 15, 20, 32, 78, 79, 86, 102, 104, 105, 106, 108, 128, 172, 174, 186
augmentations, court of, 5, 31, 32, 33, 75, 88, 116, 118–21, 148–50, 151, 152, 153, 154, 156, 157–9

Bacon, Sir Nicholas, 15, 20, 61, 78
Baker, Sir John, 88
Bale, John, 198
bankers, 143
bankruptcy, 104; in state finances, 160, 162
Barclay, Alexander, 191
barge, king's, 197
bastard feudalism, 3–4, 24, 46; *see also* liveries, maintenance, nobility, retaining
Battle, Sussex, 95
Bavaria, 167
Beauchamp, Richard, earl of Warwick, 27
Beaufort, Lady Margaret, 32, 40, 85, 126, 197
Beaumont, John, 106, 158
Becket, St Thomas, 170, 172, 198
Beckwith, Leonard, 32
Bedford, duke of, *see* Tudor
begging, 181
Belknap, Edward, 104
bells, bellmetal, 120; bell-ringing, 194–5
benefit of clergy, 170–1
benevolences, 137–9, 141, 142
Bergavenny, Lord, *see* Neville
Berkeley, Maurice, Lord Berkeley, 47

243

Index